Best Wildflower Hikes
Western Washington

Best Wildflower Hikes Western Washington

Year-Round Opportunities Including Mount Rainier
and Olympic National Parks and the North Cascades

Peter Stekel

GUILFORD, CONNECTICUT
HELENA, MONTANA

An imprint of Rowman & Littlefield
Falcon and FalconGuides are registered trademarks and Make Adventure Your Story is a trademark of Rowman & Littlefield.

Distributed by NATIONAL BOOK NETWORK

British Library Cataloguing-in-Publication Information Available

Library of Congress Cataloging-in-Publication Data Available
ISBN 978-1-4930-1868-0 (paperback)
ISBN 978-1-4930-1869-7 (e-book)

∞™ The paper used in this publication meets the minimum requirements of American National Standard for Information Sciences—Permanence of Paper for Printed Library Materials, ANSI/NISO Z39.48-1992.

The author and Rowman & Littlefield assume no liability for accidents happening to, or injuries sustained by, readers who engage in the activities described in this book.

To honor my friend, Rich Stowell, who first took me backpacking in the Sierra Nevada in 1965 and opened my eyes

Contents

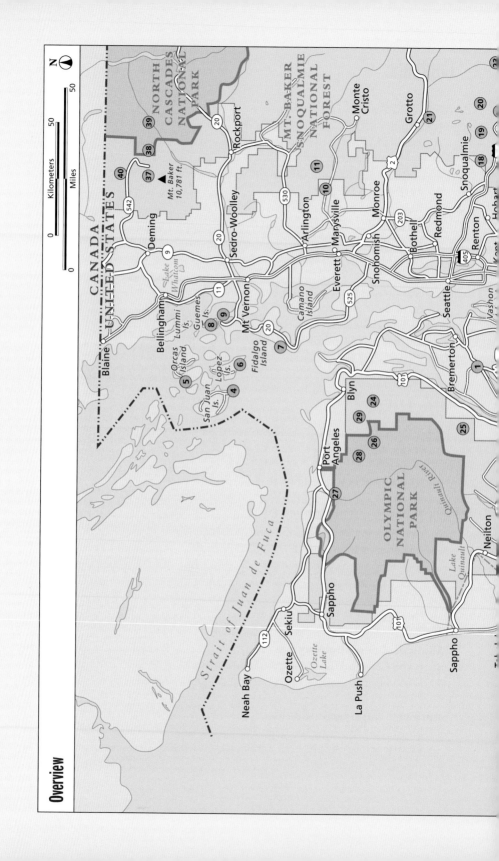
Overview

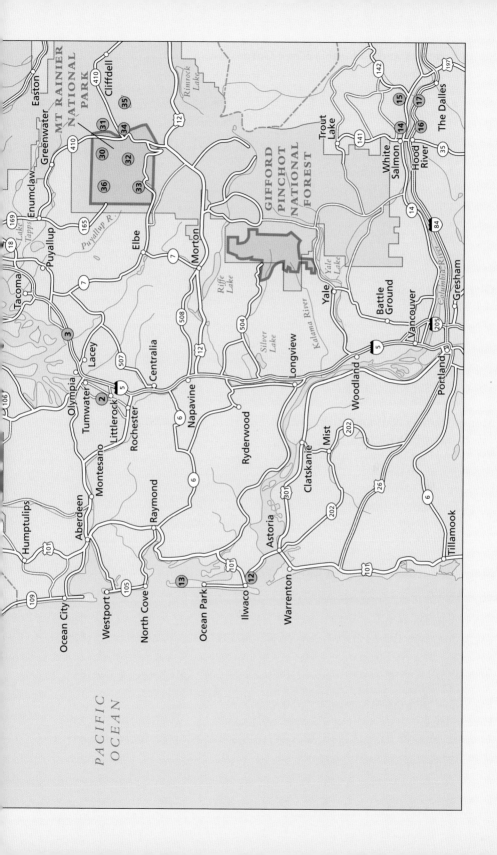

Acknowledgments

I am grateful to Dr. David Giblin at the Burke Museum and University of Washington Herbarium. He helped me choose not only the best hikes, but the best hikes in western Washington where the best displays and species diversity in wildflowers could be found. He was also there to help me with identification of the difficult species. Of course, any plants wrongly determined are my own responsibility, just as are any other errors in the text.

As to names of wildflowers: Please be kind. My UC Davis undergraduate botany degree was in 1975 and my graduate work at Humboldt State University was between 1976 and 1978. I tried *really* hard to update all the names I learned *so* long ago! If I missed a few, I apologize. Those *darn* splitters!

Thank you to my hiking companions while the field portion of this book was being researched: Peter Hesslein, Jane Hesslein, Sasha Kaufmann, Dawn Meekhof, Janet Cermak, Elizabeth Hurley, Alice Goldberg, and members of the Washington Native Plant Society 2015 Study Weekend at Mount Baker.

Thank you to Dave Flotree and Ellen Hauptmann for the use of their cottage on Lopez Island. Also to George Laird and Alina Dussort for the use of their home in Portland.

Here's a big shout out to Oboz Footwear for keeping me shod and Sherpa Adventure Gear for keeping me warm and dry. Also to Boo Turner at Footloose-Communications.com for making it happen. Thank you to Green Trails Maps for providing maps for this project so I wouldn't get lost.

To Dr. Paul Manner, Pete Hall, and physical therapists Gene Kopyt, Debbie Potter, and Carla Hofferber: Thanks for helping me walk again.

My editor, John Burbidge, helped shepherd this project through Falcon from beginning to end. What a guy! Thank you to Meredith Dias, senior production editor at Falcon, for her hard work.

Jennie Goldberg: Like everything else in my life, this book would not have happened but for you, your love, and your support.

Introduction

What is a "wildflower" anyway?

You needn't be a plant taxonomist (a botanist who studies, names, and classifies plants) to have an opinion of what constitutes a wildflower. A few things can probably be agreed upon by everybody. Wildflowers should grow wild and not in somebody's front yard garden. They should be showy (colorful), herbaceous (having no persistent aboveground woody stem), abundant (easy to find), widely distributed (common), and with simple structures (easy to identify). Some of our most popular wildflowers like Red columbine (*Aquilegia formosa*), Harsh paintbrush (*Castilleja hispida*), and Explorer's gentian (*Gentiana calycosa*) fit the bill.

On the other hand, once you start looking around, you discover that many wildflowers aren't necessarily showy, herbaceous, abundant, widely distributed, or with simple structures. For example, Fringecup (*Tellima grandiflora*) lacks showy flowers and is anything but grand. Oceanspray (*Holodiscus discolor*) is a shrub, and Madrone (*Arbutus menziesii*) a tree. Common butterwort (*Pinguicula vulgaris*) is not abundant. Floating water pennywort (*Hydrocotyl ranunculoides*) is not widely distributed in Washington. And grasses and grasslike plants! Because of their non-showy and non-simple structures, grasses and sedges are extremely difficult to identify. Amateurs and professionals alike find these wildflowers especially uninteresting. Actually, the common opinion is, "They all look alike." But that's judgment emanating from frustration.

A hiker gets excited by fields of wildflowers and can't help but tell everyone about it.

Perhaps you begin to see the wisdom in expanding the concept of "wildflower" in order to encompass a larger variety of plants. As any botanist will tell you, *all* plants are worthy of our study, contemplation, and appreciation. Appreciating wildflowers specifically, and plants in general, is a wide field of study that engages walkers, hikers, backpackers, horse packers, anglers, kayakers, and picnickers along every trail Washington has to offer and on nearly every day of the year. Even in the throes of deepest winter, though the showy blossoms are gone, there are still plants to see and cherish. On the ground can often be found the remains of what flowers become: fruits and seeds.

Plant and Flower Structure

Separating animals from plants is easy. Animals eat and plants are eaten. Plants provide their own food through the process of photosynthesis. Sunlight is the energy source allowing chloroplasts in the cells of leaves to chemically convert water and carbon dioxide into sugars and then into complex carbohydrates to build the internal structure of the plant body.

Large animals like mammals, birds, reptiles, and fishes have easily recognizable external structures. They possess such things as heads with eyes, ears, noses, and mouths. Fish have fins and birds have wings. Animals have bodies with arms, legs, tails, and either internal or external genitalia. Animals are also highly complex on the inside, with a skeletal structure and a number of organs like lungs and kidneys, a heart, liver, and all that other squishy, gooey stuff. As biologists like to joke, the difference between vertebrates and invertebrates is that when you step on them, one goes squish-crunch and the other goes crunch-squish.

Structurally, plants aren't nearly as complicated as animals. They have roots, a stem or trunk, branches, and leaves. Roots anchor plants to the ground and also absorb moisture and mineral nutrients from the soil. A plant's stem and branches transport water and nutrients throughout the plant and also serve to hold the leaves up to the sun. It is primarily in the leaves where photosynthesis and food production for the plant occurs.

The colorful and showy blossoms we find so interesting to display in our homes, or to photograph, are actually the reproductive organs of a group of plants called Angiosperms. They are also known more familiarly as the "flowering plants." Which begs the question, "Are there plants without flowers?" The answer would be a loud and resounding "Yes!"

The most common nonflowering plants seen in the Pacific Northwest are a group of Gymnosperms called conifers. These are the cone-bearing trees such as Douglas fir (*Pseudotsuga menziesii*), Western red cedar (*Thuja plicata*), and Mountain hemlock (*Tsuga mertensiana*). There are many Gymnosperms such as Ginkgos, Cycads, and South Africa's bizarre *Welwitschia* that are not conifers. Other nonflowering plants include ferns, horsetails, mosses, and all the algae and seaweeds.

Angiosperm flowers consist of distinct parts. There are exceptions but, generally speaking, the showy parts are the sepals and petals. Within the receptacle of sepals and petals are

Dodecatheon hendersonii, *Broadleaf shooting star*. DAVE FLOTREE

Physocarpus capitatus, *Nine-bark.*

the anthers or androecium (the male part of the flower where pollen is produced) and pistil or gynoecium (the female part where ovules are produced). Pollination by insects, other animals, or the wind leads to the fertilization of ovules, which leads to the production of fruits. Inside the fruit are seeds that germinate and allow the plant to make more plants.

The process of pollination works pretty much the same with Gymnosperms and conifers except that the wind does all the hard work. Insects or other vectors need not apply.

From here there's no need to go any further with the botany lesson; there are plenty of good books in stores and libraries for the budding botanist to read.

DON'T PICK THE FLOWERS!

It's tempting to pick a bouquet of trailside wildflowers and bring them home. Unlike the blooms you buy at the florist, nearly all wildflowers are fragile and will wilt away to nothingness long before you get home. Picking wildflowers then deprives those who follow you from enjoying the beauty you've experienced. Avoid the temptation and leave the flowers where you find them. Imagine the impact on a field of wildflowers along popular trails if even 25 percent of hikers picked bouquets!

There are other reasons to leave the flowers where they are. For pollinators like birds, butterflies, and other insects like ants and beetles, the pollen or nectar in flowers is a source of food. Weeks of hikers passing through an area, picking all the flowers, would have an adverse effect on the populations of these animals. Removing wildflowers from the wild can also negatively impact the survival of that species by not allowing it to set seeds and reproduce.

They might look pretty on your pack, but wildflowers wilt rapidly.

Geographic and Botanical Scope

Western Washington is that area west of the Cascade Mountains crest, east of the Pacific Ocean, south of British Columbia, and north of the Columbia River. According to the 2010 census, 77.8 percent or 5,229,486 of the state's 6,724,540 residents live in the nineteen counties comprising western Washington. Two million people live in King County, where Seattle is located, and a January 20, 2011, *Seattle Post-Intelligencer* article commented on their generosity: "People in King County contribute nearly 42 percent of the state's tax revenues, yet receive only 25 percent of the money spent from Washington's general fund."

The prominent physical features of western Washington are the Olympic Peninsula, Puget Sound, and the Cascade Mountains, with its string of volcanic peaks that stretch north–south along the mountain crest. From the south, the biggest volcanoes are Mount Adams (12,277 feet / 3,742 meters), Mount St. Helens (8,363 feet / 2,549 meters), Mount Rainier (14,411 feet / 4,392 meters), Glacier Peak (10,541 feet / 3,213 meters), and Mount Baker (10,781 feet / 3,286 meters). The highest point on the Olympic Peninsula is Mount Olympus (7,980 feet / 2,432 meters). Other important physical features of the region are the Columbia River, Straight of Juan de Fuca, San Juan Islands Archipelago, and the Pacific Ocean. This geographic diversity accounts for a diversity of habitats in western Washington, which in turn has led to lots of plant diversity.

Mount Rainier plays "peakaboo" with clouds.

Botanical Exploration of Western Washington

Most of the Pacific Northwest was first explored by fur trappers in the employ of the Northwest Company and Hudson's Bay Company. Primarily interested in beaver pelts, the trappers had little interest in the local flora except for how it could sustain them.

The first botanical explorer to our shores was the British physician and naturalist Archibald Menzies. He entered the Strait of Juan de Fuca on April 29, 1792, on HMS *Discovery* under the command of Captain George Vancouver. Menzies spent over a month collecting plants around the many arms of Puget Sound along the east coast of the Kitsap Peninsula.

It was while anchored off Restoration Point on Bainbridge Island that Captain Vancouver's expedition met the 6-year-old-child who would grow up to be Chief Sealth (Chief Seattle). Vancouver wrote that Sealth's village was "the most lowly and meanest of its kind. The best of the huts were poor and miserable," the people "busily engaged like swine, rooting up this beautiful meadow."

Between 1805 and 1806 came Meriwether Lewis and William Clark, who made botanical collections along the Columbia River. Neither possessed more than a rudimentary knowledge of science and botany but nevertheless made a credible contribution to our western flora. Also in 1806 the Russian Baron Georg Heinrich von Landsdorff, a member of the von Krusenstern Expedition, collected in Grays Harbor and along the Washington coast.

Botanical exploration in the Pacific Northwest leapt forward with the arrival in 1825 of David Douglas at the Hudson's Bay Company Fort Vancouver post on the Columbia River. Douglas worked for the Royal Horticultural Society of London. His goal was to collect flowers, seeds, and living plants of rare or striking beauty that could be cultivated back in England and sold for high prices to grace the great gardens established by that country's wealthy elites. Douglas penetrated far into the interior of eastern Washington, following the Columbia River northward. In western Washington he made it as far north as the region around the Chehalis River.

In his journal entries, Douglas composed rapturous descriptions of what was then called Oregon Territory. Of the hardships he faced, Douglas wrote, "I now know that such objects as I am in quest of are not obtained without a share of labor, anxiety of mind, and sometimes risk of personal safety." In the course of two years, Douglas traveled 7,032 miles on foot, horseback, and canoe and collected hundreds of species, many of them new to science. For his labor he was paid under £40. The sale of one species to wealthy landowners back in England, Red-flowering currant (*Ribes sanguineum*), more than covered the expense of Douglas's expedition.

David Douglas returned to western Washington in 1830 and built on his earlier explorations. Another collector that decade and many years into the future was Dr. William Fraser Tolmie. Dr. Tolmie was an employee of the Hudson's Bay Company, and his most notable botanical achievement was to collect plants on the lower slopes

HINTS ON HOW TO PHOTOGRAPH WILDFLOWERS

Taking photographs of wildflowers is nowhere near as difficult as it was during the film camera days. With digital cameras you can snap a close-up photo and instantly know if the exposure and composition are right and if the image is in focus—three things that were always a guessing game for amateur photographers in the "old days."

Even the least-expensive digital camera today has a macro setting. Look for it in your camera options. Macro settings allow you to get so close to a bloom that you can stare right down the flower's throat.

If you're serious about taking flower photos, you should invest in a tripod. Because, even with the anti-shake feature on digital cameras, the extreme close-up nature of macro photography precludes handheld still photography from being as perfect as when using a tripod. Your depth of field (i.e., the distance within your shot that will be in focus) is so narrow in macro photography that even the lightest shakiness on your point will produce a blurred image. Don't get one of those things that stand 6 feet tall! A mini tripod will do.

Another problem with depth of field involves automatic focus with digital cameras. In the film days when flower pictures were captured with a single-lens reflex camera with manual focus, photographers could frame their shot and focus on the floral part they found most interesting. Digital cameras tend to scan the entire zone available to the lens and focus on what the camera "thinks" is the most important feature in the viewfinder. This means that you will frequently want your camera to focus on one thing in the frame, but it focuses on another. This won't be a problem with more-expensive cameras, but the rest of us need to come up with an alternative solution.

If your camera has a "focus lock," it's easy. Holding your camera with one hand, put the finger of your other hand beside the flower you are photographing. Press the shutter slightly, to engage the focus lock. Likely the camera will focus on the most distinctive object in the finder—your finger. Now, remove your finger, and depress the shutter the rest of the way. This isn't a foolproof method because, sometimes, you can't fool the camera so easily. But it will work in most situations.

A few other hints: With macro photography, turn off your flash. Try to work in bright sunlight to ensure sharp, crisp images. Wait until any breezes die down so the image won't be blurred. Finally, practice! Take lots of pictures. Learn and develop your own techniques.

of Mount Rainier. In his position as a physician, he kept a medical garden at Fort Nisqually and is likely responsible for introducing Foxglove (*Digitalis purpurea*) to our area.

By the 1840s it was considered practical to include a scientific staff on voyages of discovery around the world. Accompanying the United States Exploring Expedition, under the command of Lieutenant Charles Wilkes, was the horticulturist William Dunlop Brackenridge. The expedition reached Cape Disappointment on the Columbia River on April 28, 1841, and Brackenridge went to work, collecting a plethora of herbaceous species, but was stymied by an impenetrable forest of huge trees from exploring the interior. A month later Brackenridge began a 1,000-mile overland journey from Fort Nisqually that took him north of Mount Rainier all the way to Fort Okanogan, with a return by mid-July.

In these days of highways and roads and well-defined trails, it's easy to forget the difficulties and dangers confronting the botanists who first explored our region during the nineteenth century. They had to make their way through a hostile landscape, sometimes guided, sometimes not. They crossed or canoed wild and raging rivers, on many occasions upsetting in rapids with loss of life and loss of equipment and botanical collections. For these pioneering plant hunters, searching high and low for posies was a venture into the unknown fraught with sacrifice, injury, and death. But the many risks they took also bore many rewards.

Weather and Climate

Let's face it. Despite all the negative press outsiders give us about our weather, people like living in the Pacific Northwest. We especially like western Washington. And it's all because we love the rain. Winter rain in the lowlands means snow in the mountains, and snow means skiing. Snow also means spring runoff in our rivers and creeks, and that makes whitewater kayakers and anglers happy. And, importantly for plant lovers, without rain we wouldn't have the spectacular diversity of species and abundance of wildflowers all over our region. Hikers who have lived in western Washington longer than one winter season don't let the thought of getting soggy get in the way of having a good time.

Topography in the Puget Sound Basin is an important determinant on local weather. This means that precipitation and cloud cover increase from west to east and, with elevation, all that rain turns to snow. The distribution of rainfall in the western part of the state is influenced by closeness to mountains and bodies of water. That's why places like North Bend (along I-90) with 60 inches of yearly rain and Monroe (along WA 2) with 47 inches of precipitation are wetter and cloudier than Seattle with its 37 inches of rain (measured at SeaTac Airport).

Based on weather data collected from 1981 to 2010 for the NOAA National Climatic Data Center (www.currentresults.com), here is the annual rainfall data for important places in western Washington: Friday Harbor in the San Juan Islands, 25 inches; Forks, 120 inches; Long Beach, 79 inches; Port Angeles, 25 inches; Bellingham,

North Head Lighthouse–Cape Disappointment.

36 inches; Bremerton, 56 inches; Everett, 38 inches; Olympia, 50 inches; Vancouver, 42 inches; Darlington, 81 inches; Paradise at Mount Rainier, 118 inches; and Mount Adams Ranger Station, 46 inches. The Hoh rain forest in Olympic National Park sees 140 to 170 inches (or 12 to 14 feet) of annual rainfall—most of it falling during the winter.

As to be expected, the rain shadow of the Cascades produces less rain in the eastern part of the state. Boundary Dam has the most annual precipitation (28 inches) and Kennewick and Yakima the least (8 inches).

As diverse as precipitation is across western Washington, rainfall can vary widely within a small geographic area. Data collected by volunteers participating in the nationwide Community Collaborative Rain, Hail & Snow Network shows that precipitation just within the Seattle area in calendar year 2014 varied between 44 and 83 inches. The tiny town of North Bend saw a variation between 89 and 103 inches. Olympia had a difference between 56 and 91 inches. Vancouver saw between 37 and 48 inches of variation.

Hikers are wise to pay attention to what is going on, weather-wise, not only around their home but in the area they plan to hike. Referring to the Washington State Department of Transportation website for road conditions is a good way to check on the weather. To get started, point your browser to www.wsdot.com/traffic. The latest weather conditions and forecasts for the Seattle area are available at www.wrh .noaa?.gov/sew and at www.accuweather.com. NOAA Weather Radio is available for conditions and forecasts. Radios that pick up only the NOAA broadcast can be purchased online or at consumer electronics stores. A smartphone app is also available.

In wintertime, be aware of a phenomenon called the "Puget Sound Convergence Zone" because it's responsible for some odd and locally heavy weather. Moisture coming in from the Pacific Ocean hits the Olympic Mountains and is diverted north and south. The southern flow moves through Chehalis Gap, where the Chehalis River helps fill the Pacific Ocean. The northern flow moves through the Strait of Juan de Fuca. Then the two flows encounter the barrier created in the east by the Cascade Mountains. The southern mass moves north, and the northern mass moves south through Puget Sound. When the two opposing currents collide (from Everett to Tacoma), the air rises, cools, and produces locally heavy rain or snow.

Everybody talks about the weather, but nobody does anything about it. Sure, be aware of the weather and be prepared for it, but don't let it keep you from going outside. Look at skiers! They don't let a little thing like a snowstorm keep them off the slopes. And hikers shouldn't let a little "liquid sunshine" keep them off the trails—as long as you are prepared to get wet. And as long as your vehicle is in tip-top mechanical condition with good tires with plenty of tread!

Because of western Washington's topography, the hiking season in the Pacific Northwest never ends. You'll always find some place to go that will be warmer or drier than somewhere else, even in winter. Those awful sweltering months of July and August (average high temperature of 75°F) may bring the evil yellow sky orb bearing down on you, creating the occasional heat wave driving temperatures into the barely survivable upper 80s or lower 90s. Expect to find the trails more crowded on such days, when the general population hits the trails in search of respite from the heat.

There is still real hiking and plant-hunting fun to be had when the "bad" weather arrives. Wet autumn hikes mean not having to share any huckleberries on the trail except with the usual tooth-and-claw forest dwellers. The fall colors are yours alone to enjoy. Just remember the Boy Scout motto to "Be Prepared" for the end of the day when you might be soaked to the bone. Carry, and wear, the best rain gear you can afford. Bring additional warm (and dry) clothes plus plenty of food and energy snacks. Wrap everything together inside a plastic garbage bag, shove the bag into your pack, and be on your way! Always leave a dry change of clothing behind in your car in case you do get caught in bad weather.

Trail Etiquette

Don't be rude. When passing fellow hikers, give them a wave and a hearty "Hello!" Stop and chat if you're both in need of a breather. Compare notes to what flowers you've seen. If the person you meet is zoning out to music and can't hear you, eye contact and a nod of the head go a long way in lieu of verbal exchange. The idea here is that we are not alone on this little blue orb circling the sun. Did you know we're rotating around the sun at 66,600 miles per hour? Let's slow down a bit and smell the wild roses! Human beings are a social species; let's show it when we meet each other

Wildflower Hikes by Months

Legend:
- ▨ Best month for hiking the hike
- ▧ Best month for seeing wildflowers on that hike

Hike #	Jan	Feb	Mar	Apr	May	Jun	Jul	Aug	Sep	Oct	Nov	Dec
1 hike												
1 flower												
2 hike												
2 flower												
3 hike												
3 flower												
4 hike												
4 flower												
5 hike												
5 flower												
6 hike												
6 flower												
7 hike												
7 flower												
8 hike												
8 flower												

Hike #	Jan	Feb	Mar	Apr	May	Jun	Jul	Aug	Sep	Oct	Nov	Dec
9 hike												
9 flower												
10 hike												
10 flower												
11 hike												
11 flower												
12 hike												
12 flower												
13 hike												
13 flower												
14 hike												
14 flower												
15 hike												
15 flower												
16 hike												
16 flower												
17 hike												
17 flower												

Hike #	Jan	Feb	Mar	Apr	May	Jun	Jul	Aug	Sep	Oct	Nov	Dec
18 hike					░	░	░	░	░			
18 flower						▓	▓	▓				
19 hike			░	░	░	░	░	░	░			
19 flower						▓	▓	▓	▓			
20 hike			░	░	░	░	░	░	░	░		
20 flower						▓	▓	▓				
21 hike					░	░	░	░	░			
21 flower						▓	▓	▓				
22 hike				░	░	░	░	░	░	░		
22 flower							▓	▓				
23 hike					░	░	░	░	░	░	░	
23 flower						▓	▓	▓	▓	▓		
24 hike				░	░	░	░	░				
24 flower							▓					
25 hike				░	░	░	░	░				
25 flower							▓					
26 hike						░	░	░				
26 flower						▓	▓	▓				

Hike #	Jan	Feb	Mar	Apr	May	Jun	Jul	Aug	Sep	Oct	Nov	Dec
27 hike												
27 flower												
28 hike												
28 flower												
29 hike												
29 flower												
30 hike												
30 flower												
31 hike												
31 flower												
32 hike												
32 flower												
33 hike												
33 flower												
34 hike												
34 flower												
35 hike												
35 flower												

Hike #	Jan	Feb	Mar	Apr	May	Jun	Jul	Aug	Sep	Oct	Nov	Dec
36 hike												
36 flower												
37 hike												
37 flower												
38 hike												
38 flower												
39 hike												
39 flower												
40 hike												
40 flower												

Check the reader board at trailheads to refresh your knowledge of rules and regulations.

on the trail. Don't you think it must look pretty silly when someone is walking up the trail and you are coming down, and you both avert your eyes as if this was some urban sidewalk?

It's considered polite to yield to uphill hikers, as it causes more stress and strain to start again from the resting position when faced by an acclivity. However, hikers resisting the force of gravity will graciously (even gratefully) take the initiative and stop, permitting speedy down-hillers to whiz past. This brief respite also allows for catching your breath, adjusting pack straps, snacking, and, in general, taking a load off. Especially at these times, a cheery greeting or an encouraging smile is always appreciated from passing hikers.

The trails we trod are designed and built to a high standard that will surprise everyone except highway engineers. Cutting switchbacks redirects water runoff during the rainy season and causes erosion that calls for expensive repairs not only in terms of dollars, but labor as well. It also hastens the destruction of that section of trail, which will then require the expenditure of limited resources to rebuild.

It's quite common now to see people hiking with earbuds firmly implanted in their craniums. Such a shame these good folk would rather listen to canned music than enjoy the sounds of nature. However, if you are one of those who must hike plugged into music, please keep the volume down. Your compatriots on the trail likely have different tastes in music and would prefer to listen to the sounds of silence or the cacophony of winter wrens or the gurgling of robins and hermit thrushes.

Some trails are very popular with runners. It's best if you make way for them. It's amazing how they seem to avoid tripping over tree roots, slipping on wet rock, sliding across puddles, and falling and breaking an ankle! If you are a trail runner who is catching up to somebody, please announce yourself. You'd be surprised how few people are aware of anyone being behind them. Think of it as ringing a bell or using your voice on a bike trail.

When you feel the need to rest, find a spot off the trail. Have a seat and keep your feet, legs, and hiking sticks out of the way so that other hikers don't trip over you or have to climb over your prostrate form. Remove your backpack if you like, and place it off the trail. If with your dog, ensure that Fido stays out of the way too. Your dog may be friendly but, hard to believe, there are those who don't like any kind of dog, especially while out hiking.

Should you happen to be a faster hiker than the people in front of you, whether this be going up or going down the trial, and you want to pass, announce your

WASHINGTON NATIVE PLANT SOCIETY

In 1976 a small coterie of native plant lovers were convened at the Pacific Science Center in Seattle by Dr. Art Kruckeberg, professor of botany at the University of Washington. Since that time the Washington Native Plant Society (WNPS) has grown to eleven chapters and over 1,800 members active in native plant study, conservation, and education.

A primary goal of WNPS has been the protection of Washington's rare plants. One example of this work has been the society's efforts to protect Olympic National Park's rare endemic species from depredations by Mountain goats (*Oreamnos americanus*) that were introduced to the park in the 1920s.

Another of the society's projects include a yearly study weekend. Members gather in especially botanically interesting places for three days of intensive educational workshops and hikes to view, and learn about, Washington's distinctive flora.

WNPS activities also include conservation of the state's native plant ecosystems, providing expert advice on gardening with native plants, field trips to study and explore Washington's flora, providing funding for floristic surveys and other research on the biology of native plants, as well as working to restore native plant habitat degraded by development or irresponsible behavior.

presence with a "Hello" or an "Excuse me." If someone asks you to pass, quickly but safely move aside so that others may get around you.

Hiking Poles

In days of old when knights were bold and danger stalked the wilds, people carried a stave while venturing across the countryside. This strong wooden stick probably initially evolved from iron rods carried as weapons during war and served travelers well for protection on the perambulations between farm and town or town and town.

By the mid-twentieth century, it was common to see hikers on the trail carrying a metal ski pole or a long lightweight pole fashioned from the stalk of the desert Century plant (*Agave americana*). The poles were especially helpful at stream or river crossings and assisting with traversing snowfields, and, in the era before carrying tents was a common occurrence, they provided a center pole for an emergency rain shelter using a poncho and some parachute cord.

Hiking poles help reduce the pounding on feet and knees, especially going downhill.

In the early 1970s came an explosion in popularity of hiking and backpacking over the then-preferred method of wilderness travel: horse packing. Tens of thousands of young people began hitting the trails for day trips and weekly excursions. As lightweight gear became popular and affordable, hikers began to make longer and longer trips, and cross-state and cross-continent excursions like the John Muir Trail, Pacific Crest Trail, Continental Divide Trail, and Appalachian Trail became popular with large numbers of people.

Sadly, the initial surge of hikers from the 1970s began to show signs of age. Not wishing to give up on the glorious sport of walking, these aging baby boomers turned to using ski poles in order to reduce the stress and strain on decrepit knees and hips. The outdoor recreation gear manufactures saw a good thing and began to build stout hiking poles to service this ever-growing population. And it came just in time! An explosion of hiking pole use ensued, and all of a sudden they were everywhere.

Today, everybody seems to use hiking poles and alongside every trail are the telltale divots made by sharp pole-points. The only question today seems to be, should you use one pole or two poles?

Man's Best Friend

Most trails in *Best Wildflower Hikes Western Washington* are open to leashed dogs, though national parks do not allow dogs on any wilderness trail. It's best to check any restrictions at reader boards placed at the trailhead.

All dogs on Forest Service trails must be kept on a 6-foot leash at all times. There is wisdom in this in addition to following the regulation. Long leashes present a trip-wire hazard to other hikers. When you leash and therefore control your dog, you eliminate the need to pull unleashed and the occasional fighting dogs apart. Keeping your dog under control is also a kindness extended to your fellow travelers who are walking without a pet. Remember, dogs are hunters; controlling your dog also keeps your pet from chasing or harassing wildlife.

Be kind to Rover and be kind to other hikers: Pick up after your pet. Know the trail situations that can be hazardous for a dog. People wear shoes; dogs don't. Trails contain sharp rocks that can tear a dog's feet. Keep all vaccinations up-to-date and provide flea and tick control. If your dog should become separated from you, make sure your pet has identification. Don't forget that dogs, like people, need to build up their endurance before attempting a long hike. When you stop to eat or drink, share your bounty with Fido.

What to Carry on Hikes

Discussing the "Ten Essentials" of what every hiker should carry in their pack during a hike has become an essential in all hiking and nature guides. It's a good subject. Deciding on what is or isn't essential can be entertaining because one person's essential is another's not so essential.

Bird-watchers, wildflower hunters, anglers, photographers, and hikers view what is essential through different eyes. What one brings, the other would leave behind. Birders never leave home without binoculars and a bird book. Flower lovers can't botanize without a hand lens, field guide, or flora. Anglers can't angle without a pole. Photographers can't photograph without their camera. Don't forget extra batteries and memory cards for your digital camera!

As far as essential gear to carry, day hikers require less than backpackers. Shorter, simpler trails require a shorter list of essentials. A Mima Mounds walk (hike 2) requires significantly less of everything than an Ebey's Landing hike (hike 7), which in turn demands less than a serious daylong excursion to Spray Park (hike 36) in Mount Rainier National Park. If you're going on an overnight backpacking trip, you'll find there are many more than ten essentials.

What to bring? A compass and topographic map are usually listed as primary essentials. But if you don't know how to use them, what good are they? After all, there's more to using these tools than finding north, and if you don't know where you are, a map and compass aren't going to help much. But a GPS will.

So, what about GPS (Global Positioning System)? Can't you simply use GPS like Hansel and Gretel used bread crumbs and let it guide you to and fro? Yes, mostly. The biggest thing working against a GPS are its technological weaknesses. These include interference, issues with accuracy, need for batteries, and keeping the device out of water.

The most essential of essentials is to use your head. You can eliminate most problems encountered in the outdoors with proper planning. This means being prepared for weather, being familiar with the route, and knowing the time needed to complete your hike in plenty of daylight. Staying

Taking a GPS, along with map and compass, helps hikers stay found and not get lost.

found is better than trying to find your way home when lost. You are responsible for your own actions, decisions, and behavior.

Consider the following list of essentials as a guide. Use your own judgment to add, delete, modify, adapt, and expand the list based on the situation, where you're going, your experience, and what you can afford to buy. Keep in mind that you can never have too much in the way of emergency or survival equipment. There may come a time when you, or some less-prepared person, may need it.

At the least, bring a liter of water (more on hot days), and drink it. It does you no good if your water bottle spends the entire day inside your pack. If your urine is not clear, frequent, and copious, you're not drinking enough. Bring food, *real* food. For snacking, energy bars are a good idea, but there is no substitute for real food. Never consider your day on the trail as part of a weight loss plan. If you are hiking with a dog, be kind. Carry food and water for your pet as well.

Have some sort of navigation device (see above) with you. This is always preferable to hiking blind. As you dig deeper into this book you will discover that *Best Wildflower Hikes Western Washington* contains trail descriptions and colorful area maps. Consider this information not as a navigation guide, but as the barest of hints for where trails and significant features are located. The map itself is of such a general nature that it should be considered solely as a guide for planning your trip and not as a navigational aid.

First-Aid Kit

Some sort of first-aid kit is good to carry, but this introduces its own set of essentials. Prone to blisters? Then carry a lot of Band-Aids, moleskin and/or molefoam, plus antiseptic. If you regularly take medication, carry that day's dose and an extra dose as well in case you're late in getting home. Asthmatics, carry your inhaler. Allergic to bees and wasps? Bring your EpiPen and antihistamines, although you know that EpiPens should be considered a last resort. Consult your physician or allergist about a regimen of desensitizing shots. Begin with the Northwest Asthma & Allergy Center (www.nwasthma.com). They have offices all over Washington.

Consider these other first-aid kit items: gauze pads (many purposes and functions); waterproof tape; scissors (for cutting gauze pads, tape, or bandages); Band-Aids (many sizes and shapes); antibacterial ointment (check expiration date); pencil and paper (for recording health data in case of serious injuries); fire starter; and oral thermometer. Over-the-counter medications to forestall the negative effects of hiking (stiff muscles and sore joints) are helpful. So is a pocketknife (leave the Bowie knife at home). Bring toilet paper and extra plastic bags for waste. Carry a whistle, spare batteries for your GPS unit, matches and/or lighter, and a small flashlight or headlamp (check the batteries and carry extras in your first-aid kit). This list is by no means exhaustive. Add or delete items according to what personal experience has taught you.

Apparel

Many hikes in this book are in deep forest, but just as many are not. Outsiders like to believe the sun never shines in the Pacific Northwest, but we know the truth. Therefore, carry sunglasses, sunscreen, and a cap (with a bill). You might start the day in the sun but the weather can always turn inclement, so have a hat (to keep your head warm), gloves (to keep your paws warm), wool or pile sweater (to keep the rest of you warm), rain jacket (doubles as a windbreaker), extra dry socks (keep them in a sealable plastic bag), and a clean shirt for the drive home (left behind in your car). Put your first-aid kit into a stuff sack to keep it separate from your lunch and your emergency or comfort gear, stuff it all into a backpack, and hit the trail!

The essentials of what to wear when hiking are as varied, subject to discussion, and personal as there are people in the world. Some people prefer shorts; others long pants. If you do wear shorts, carry wind pants (non-waterproof nylon shell) in case the temperature drops. On top, you can wear a T-shirt or a long-sleeved sport shirt (to protect sun-sensitive bodies). Cotton is preferred for hot days because of its superior sweat-absorption characteristics, though there are plenty of high-tech fabrics that are advertised as being just as good or better. Sports bras provide support and comfort for women.

Single or double walking sticks help with steep or uneven stretches of trail. They also serve to steady you on snow, talus, or stream crossings. Some manufacturers produce camera mounts for hiking poles so they can double as a mono-pod for serious photographers.

Blister Prevention

Blisters are caused either by ill-fitting footwear or the skin of your foot rubbing against the interior of your boot. This rubbing happens because your socks are loose or wet (from sweat or from a poor job of crossing a creek) and moving independently of your foot inside the shoe. Rubbing can also occur because your boots don't fit well. Blisters, those tiny and not-so-tiny bubbles of water on your feet and between your toes, can defeat even the hardiest hiker and turn a nice walk into misery. What to do?

Obviously, get a pair of boots that fit. Not so obviously is how. Fortunately, there are dozens of boot manufacturers and plenty of places to buy what you need. If one store's lineup has nothing that fits your feet, try another place. Keep at it until you find the "perfect fit."

Assuming your feet have been measured correctly for size and width, when you first try on a pair of boots, they should "fit like a glove," as the old cliché goes. If the boots are not immediately comfortable, they will certainly *not* be comfortable after a few hours or a day on the trail. It doesn't matter how cool the boots look or how dazzling the shoelaces are, put them back on the shelf and try something else. Lace up the boots firmly but not so tight they feel like they're cutting off circulation. Push your foot forward into the boot until your toes touch the end. There ought to be enough space at the back of the boot to force your forefinger down to the heel.

Once you've found that comfortable pair of boots, take them for a fifteen- or twenty-minute spin around the store. Don't be in a hurry! Climb some stairs. Stand around. Do some yoga. Are the boots *still* comfortable or do they begin to bind in a place or two? Are they starting to feel unnecessarily heavy? Don't be in a hurry! The time you spend in the store trying those puppies on will reap days, weeks, and months of benefits once you're on the trail. Dedicate as much time as you can to finding that "perfect fit." You'll find that foot joy on the trail is directly proportional to the time you take in the store to find the right boot.

Some hikers also insist on replacing the thin shoe inserts that come with their new boots with some sort of orthotic. A good place to start with getting your own footbeds is Custom Boot Service (www.CustomBootService.com) in Seattle.

Cell Phones

Are cell phones essential or nonessential? That all depends on how you plan on using them. As an emergency device, cell phones can be helpful—as long as you are in an area with coverage! Some cell phone carriers have coverage in areas where other carriers do not. However, a lot of the hikes in this book do not have cell phone coverage *at all* along the trail or at the trailhead no matter who your carrier is. Therefore, if you feel you can't leave your cell phone behind or are concerned about somebody breaking into your car and stealing it (that's reasonable), by all means, bring it with you. But, be aware that you may not be able to rely upon it as an emergency device.

Forgetting for the moment that phone coverage could be limited or nonexistent, how essential is a cell phone for nonemergency purposes? If you've downloaded the e-book version of *Best Wildflower Hikes Western Washington*, you'll be able to carry the entire book in a nice little package. That's a good thing. But few things are more annoying to the rest of us than hearing someone deep in a telephone conversation while hiking. Somehow, it feels even worse than experiencing the same thing on the bus! So, if you have a cell phone, go ahead and carry it with you, but please turn it off and save the battery just in case you really do need it for the drive home.

Other Sources for Trails

Some people say there is no longer a need for hiking guides because everything in the world you need to know can be found on the web. This presupposes that everything in the world worth knowing began in the mid-1990s when the Internet began revolutionizing data manipulation and information storage and transfer.

That being said, there is a lot of stuff on the web. A search engine response for the simple phrase "Washington wildflowers" garners 786,000 hits. "Washington wildflower hikes" gets 91,000 hits. And "Washington day hikes" receives 5.5 million hits!

One thing about a book: When you look something up, you get one hit.

Books make it easier to find a place to hike because they provide a discrete number of possibilities. There is no need to wade through thousands of search results to come up with a hike you want to do. In essence, the book's author has done all that hard work for you. For people new to western Washington or new to hiking, who haven't a clue where anything is or how to search properly for a hiking spot, books are clearly an advantage.

This isn't to say that the web doesn't offer a plethora of options for finding hikes. A good online source is the Washington Trails Association (www.wta.org). Their trip descriptions date back many years. Contributions aren't monitored or edited and run the gamut in usefulness. Trails.com (www.trails.com) has many hike descriptions for the state as well. For wildflower walkers the weakness of online sources is their focus on trails and not on anything you would see along the way, like plants.

Restrictions and Regulations

Fires are prohibited above 4,000 feet on the west side of the Cascades and above 5,000 feet on the east side in the Mount Baker–Snoqualmie National Forest. Other forest areas may have fire restrictions due to high use and/or no fuel. Check for specific regulations pertaining to the area you plan to visit. Fires are highly restricted in city or county parks to supplied barbecue grates in picnic areas. No fires are allowed on any Washington State Department of Natural Resources land covered in this book.

Ah, wilderness! Take nothing but pictures and leave nothing but footprints.

Motorized and mechanized equipment are not allowed in any national forest or national park wilderness area. This includes bicycles, carts, wagons, chain saws, hang gliders, off-road vehicles and other wheeled vehicles, and landing aircraft. You cannot air drop or pick up supplies, materials, or people. There is an overnight limit of twelve for a group, in any combination of people and pack and saddle animals. Groups exceeding twelve must divide into physically and logistically separate parties and maintain a minimum distance of 1 mile.

Camping with pack and saddle animals is allowed only at designated sites in the national forests and is prohibited in many other areas. Pack and saddle animals are not allowed within 200 feet of lakes except to get a drink or pass on a trail. Forage is poor throughout the region.

Permits

The number and kinds of permit fees, passes, and exemptions required to use our public lands will make your head spin. Trailheads normally have a reader board (conveniently located next to the toilet) that explains which permit or permutation of permits are needed to park and play. Pay close attention or it could cost you some of your hard-earned cash. These fees are constantly changing (read: increasing), so it's not prudent to list exact fee amounts here. Best to check land agency websites for the most current information before heading out.

Cars parked at trailheads in Washington's national forests will need to display a Northwest Forest Pass. There is a hefty fine for not using this pass—an expense that has continued to increase every few years. Enforcement varies by season, location, popularity, use, and closeness to paved roads and towns, and may seem sporadic to hikers who go out multiple times each month. Don't be fooled. In the past, the Forest Service has spent as much as 50 percent of monies collected for the Northwest Forest

Don't forget to stop, rest, and appreciate the scenery.

Pass for enforcement and prosecution of scofflaws. They're serious about collecting and holding on to that other 50 percent, so consider yourself warned. It's some small consolation to having to pay to use our public lands that the Northwest Forest Pass is also valid in all Oregon national forests. Buy the pass at most outdoor retailer stores.

Nearly every trailhead into national forest wilderness also asks that you self-register (for free permits) for day-use and overnight trips and dangle the permit from your packs.

Muddying the permit waters on Forest Service lands is that they will also accept other Federal Access passes in lieu of a Northwest Forest Pass. For people 62 or older, consider purchasing an Interagency Senior Pass. It's valid for the rest of your life, and you can use it on all federal public lands, nationwide. If under 62, the same *annual* pass (now called an Interagency Annual Pass) can be purchased. There are some advantages to being old! Mount St. Helens National Volcanic Monument, which is a unit of the USDA Forest Service, has its own pass. Read more about all these different passes, such as the free Interagency Annual Military Pass and the free Interagency Access Pass (for the disabled), as well as requirements and possible exemptions, at www.fs.usda .gov/detail/r6/passes-permits/recreation/?cid=stelprdb5352358.

When entering a national park, you will encounter another fee structure. Either pay the single entry fee or purchase an annual pass for a specific national park. You can also use the Federal Access pass mentioned above.

The State of Washington requires a Discover Pass to use state park, Washington Department of Fish and Wildlife (WDFW), or Department of Natural Resources (DNR) lands. The pass is a vehicle parking pass, so if you park on private property and then walk onto state park, WDFW, or DNR land, the pass is not necessary.

Should you be caught using state lands without a Discover Pass, you'll get a hefty ticket. This penalty is reduced later if you can demonstrate to the court that you purchased a Discover Pass within fifteen days after the notice of violation. The pass can be used with two vehicles; there is space on the pass to write each vehicle's license plate number or phrase.

Purchase your Discover Pass either when renewing vehicle registration or at many outdoor store retailers, other retailers, or online. Be aware that retailers add a "transaction fee" to the purchase cost. There are plenty of user exemptions to the Discover Pass. At some sites a handicap placard is allowed. Study the fine print at www.discoverpass.wa.gov/faq/#buying.

A Washington Department of Fish and Wildlife Vehicle Assess Pass can sometimes be used at certain sites requiring a Discover Pass. Check the reader board postings at trailheads to be sure. WDFW Vehicle Access Passes are available for free when you get a hunting or fishing license. Read all about it at https://fishhunt.dfw.wa.gov.

The reason given for needing all these permits is "budgetary." This is where some of the tax-cutting/reduce-government-spending chickens have come home to roost. With the exception of gaining access to national parks (but not national monument or historic or battlefield sites), it was only a generation ago when the public did not have to pay to use their public lands.

▶ Bear hunting starts in early August. Deer season opens mid-October across much of the state. Elk season opens at the end of October. If you hear shooting, stop. Raise your voice to let hunters know you're near. While moving through the landscape, wear bright clothing. Talk while you walk to alert hunters of your presence. Or, turn around and find another place to walk.

Some of the aggravation in having to buy the Northwest Forest Pass is the lack of physical improvement seen on many trails. If not for volunteers from the Washington Trails Association, the Mountaineers, and other groups that perform vital trail repair and construction, there would be no improvements visible at all. It appears that Northwest Forest Pass monies are either eaten up by administration, enforcement and adjudication, or the paving of trailhead parking lots and construction of vault toilets.

Nevertheless, the Forest Service maintains that "the majority—80-95 percent—of proceeds from recreation fees goes right back into maintaining and improving the trails, land and facilities you use most." They also say, "Most of this work is not, and should not be, noticeable." That is peculiar. It strikes one as an odd way to tout your accomplishments to a doubting public. Read more about how the Forest Service implements the

Northwest Forest Pass in our region at www.fs.usda.gov/detailfull/r6/passes-permits/recreation/?cid=fsbdev2_026999&width=full.

As with many changes wrought by the anti-tax climate in our country, we have come to acquiesce to the presence of user fees to cover the cost of what used to be free government services. However, in some areas it is still possible to park some distance away from the trailhead and escape the requirement to pay. If you are a registered guest at a Forest Service campground and there is a trailhead adjacent, you need not have a Northwest Forest Pass as long as your car remains in your campsite.

Are you tired of all these fees? Then, do something about it! If people using public lands don't make their voices heard and express their desires, disagreeable decisions will continue to be made in our names. You may feel that a hiking guide is an odd place to lobby for public lands administrative change. Since we live in a democracy, it is our duty to participate in the decisions of our government and not let those decisions be made by people we disagree with or whom we feel do not have our best interests at heart.

Diversity of habitat gives the Columbia Gorge stupendous wildflower displays.

How to Use This Book

A Trail Finder and regional map begins the hiking section, allowing you to visually spot all the trails mentioned in the text of *Best Wildflower Hikes Western Washington* and choose a route based upon special preferences. Each trail is numbered 1 through 40 and is grouped numerically into nine regions, reflecting the complex and interesting geography of Washington. Each region is introduced by an overview on features the author found interesting or edifying.

Aiding with quick decision-making, each hike begins with a summary of what makes it special. Next come the hike "specs," including where the hike starts, hike distance and type of hike, approximate hiking time, difficulty rating, trail surface, best hiking season, best time to see wildflowers, other trail users, status on dogs, what agency manages the land, towns closest to the trailhead, information about fuel and other services available in the area, which kind of pass is necessary to park and/or hike, useful topographic maps, and whom to contact for updated trail information. Also included are driving directions to the trailhead with GPS coordinates, and any special conditions such as availability of toilet and potable water at the trailhead or special hazards you might encounter along the way.

The types of maps recommended for hikes in this book are mostly either USGS topographical maps, GreenTrails topographic maps, or maps from the *DeLorme*

Club moss grows in wet, or damp, and cool areas.

Washington Gazetteer. The 7.5 minute USGS maps are the most detailed because of their large scale. However, the smaller scale GreenTrails maps more accurately show trails and also include many social features like historical structures and waytrails. DeLorme maps are the largest scale of all and are mostly suitable for giving you an overview of huge sections of Washington. Trails Illustrated topographic maps are great resources for national parks or recreation areas because they show the entire park or area on one sheet.

The difficulty rating and required time to hike each trail is purposely open-ended. There is no way in the world any author can remotely understand the level of fitness or need for adventure of people he has never met. To help readers with this book's subjective judgments of difficulty and time, it might help to know that during the entire field season for *Best Wildflower Hikes Western Washington*, the sexagenarian author was recovering from hip replacement surgery. In previous years, a younger and more fit author could have made all the hikes in this book in less time and would have considered them all at least one level of difficulty easier!

"Finding the trailhead" provides directions to where the hike begins from the closest significant location that readers can find on a highway map. For the San Juan Islands and Whidbey Island, directions begin at the ferry terminal on each individual island.

In the "Plants You Might See" section, you'll find a partial list of wildflowers and other significant, distinctive, or profuse plants you could see along the trail. To assist the range of flower lovers hiking the trails, the plants are listed in the standard botanical way by both their Latin binomial (genus+species), or "botanical," name and common (i.e., vernacular) name along with the family the species belongs to.

All the field work for *Best Wildflower Hikes Western Washington* was performed between April and August 2015, following one of the driest winters and longest, hottest spring and summers in recent years. We all suffered the heat, but wildflowers suffered even greater. Plants that should have been in bloom throughout August had already set seed at the end of July. In retrospect, this was not the best year for research of this kind. But! There will be wet years in the future along with dry years. We cannot plan our hiking and botanizing on what we *want* the season to be, only on what it is.

With the size of Washington's flora and our geographic/orographic variation, it's impossible to list every wildflower you might possibly see. Also, the time of year

Even after the flowers are gone there is plenty to appreciate with Fireweed.

plants are in flower (i.e., phenology) will affect what you encounter. Something visible one month most likely won't be visible the month before or the month after. For this reason, the date the author hiked the trail is given so you'll know what he saw when writing up trail descriptions. Species lists created by the Washington Native Plant Society and other sources help fill in the blanks of wildflowers you might come across at different times of year. To see the WNPS species lists, visit www.wnps.org/plant_lists/exploring_native_plants.html.

"The Hike" presents this author's impressions of the trail and highlights of what predominant wildflower species existed at the time the trail was hiked. When giving directions on the trail, it is assumed the reader is following the same course as the author. However, for times when this is not the case, turns are not only described as left, right, or straight but by referencing the compass.

It's impossible to cover everything viewable on the trail, and who would want that anyway? Taking a hike is not just about exercise or getting outside. It's also about exploring a place and learning about it on your own. The hike description is meant as a guide.

Suggested times of when to visit each trail are also given. Most of the lowland hikes can be done 365 days a year. Snow precludes hiking in the higher elevations, though snowshoes and skis can take you to some places to enjoy the trees. "Spring" is a hard-to-define concept when discussing wildflower season in Washington because, as the lowlands dry out towards calendar-summer, the high-country snow is melting away and an entirely different spring begins. On the positive side, this means it is possible to actually start spring in March or April and follow it all the way into the mountains as late as September or October.

"Miles and Directions" includes specific mileages from the trailhead to significant waypoints, trail junctions, etc.

With "Other Nearby Hiking Options," you have suggested hike extensions or interesting detours. When it appears, "Hike Information" provides miscellaneous local resources or anything else that didn't fit elsewhere in the trail description.

Scattered throughout the text are numerous "sidebars" and "tidbits" that provide educational information about Washington's wildflowers and occasionally historical or cultural information.

Appendixes at the end of this guide give data on clubs and organizations that advocate for trails and Washington's plants, and suggest further reading for those who wish to expand their knowledge of wildflowers, botany, and Washington history. Contact information for all the governmental agencies mentioned in *Best Wildflower Hikes Western Washington* is also provided.

Mileage and Maps for This Book

Mileage for the forty hikes in this book was first determined by paying attention to trail signs. Where trail signs indicated distance, it was noted and compared to Green Trails Maps distances (when available) and then cross-referenced to a Garmin 76CSx

THE "USUAL SUSPECTS"

When it comes to trees, you can't go anywhere in western Washington without seeing the "usual suspects." These trees are ubiquitous and most are found on every hike in this book. Rather than repeat the common name, botanic name, and family name for these trees in each of the forty hike descriptions, they are given here. Only the common name will be given in the text. You can always refer back here at any time to refresh your memory as to the botanic name.

Bigleaf maple, *Acer macrophyllum*, Aceraceae

Douglas fir, *Pseudotsuga menziesii*, Pinaceae

Grand fir, *Abies grandis*, Pinaceae

Lodgepole, or Beach, or Shore pine, *Pinus contorta*, Pinaceae

Mountain hemlock, *Tsuga mertensiana*, Pinaceae

Noble fir, *Abies procera*, Pinaceae

Pacific silver fir, *Abies amabilis*, Pinaceae

Red alder, *Alnus rubra*, Betulaceae

Subalpine fir, *Abies lasiocarpa*, Pinaceae

Western hemlock, *Tsuga heterophylla*, Pinaceae

Western red cedar, *Thuja plicata*, Cupressaceae

Western white pine, *Pinus monticola*, Pinaceae

Mountain hemlock is common at higher elevations.

Western hemlock is common at lower elevations.

Subalpine fir produces both male and female cones.

Unlike pine cones which dangle down, fir cones are erect.

using two-minute tracking intervals stored in an ACTIVE LOG. The Positional Format was hddd mm.mmmm with a Datum of WGS84. The receiver was set to WAAS/EGNOS, Distance/Speed was Statute, Elevation was recorded in Feet, Temperature in Degrees Fahrenheit, and Atmospheric Pressure in Millibars. Waypoints were recorded for parking lots, trailheads, toilets, prominent or interesting features, and wherever trail junctions occurred. Since atmospheric pressure can impact the performance of a GPS, especially in determining elevation, before every hike both the altimeter and compass on the Garmin 76CSx were left on for at least one hour before the hike and then recalibrated at the trailhead.

At the end of every day's hike, all mapping data were exported to version 4.4.6 of Garmin's proprietary BaseCamp software and saved as a GPX file. From there, the GPX file was imported into GPSVisualizer (www.gpsvisualizer.com), free mapping software made available by its developer, Adam Schneider. The software is simple to use, with a high degree of flexibility. The output can be in the form of Google Maps, KML files for Google Earth, JPEG maps, SVG drawings, elevation profiles, or plain-text tables. The maps generated by GPSVisualizer were saved in Adobe PDF format and marked up in Adobe Acrobat 8.0 to include all waypoints and other important labels such as highways, points of interest, and geographic features. These maps were then provided to the FalconPress cartographer who created the maps printed in this book.

Any day is a fine day for hiking and seeing wildflowers, clouds or not.

Trail Finder

Best Wildflower Hikes with Amazing Views

  4. Finlayson Ridge, American Camp, San Juan Island
  5. Turtleback Mountain Preserve, Orcas Island
  6. Iceberg Point, Lopez Island
  12. North Head Lighthouse, Cape Disappointment State Park
  14. Dog Mountain
  15. Hamilton Mountain
  20. Kendall Katwalk
  21. Tonga Ridge
  23. Ingalls Lake
  25. Mount Ellinor
  26. Elk Mountain–Badger Valley Loop
  28. Hurricane Hill
  30. Berkeley Park Camp
  31. Grand Park
  32. Panorama Point
  35. Naches Loop
  36. Spray Park
  37. Artist Ridge
  38. Bagley Lakes Loop
  39. Galena Chain Lakes
  40. Yellow Aster Butte Fern Garden

Best Wildflower Hikes for Beach and Coastal Lovers

  1. Theler Wetlands
  3. Nisqually National Wildlife Refuge
  4. Finlayson Ridge, American Camp, San Juan Island
  6. Iceberg Point, Lopez Island
  7. Ebey's Landing Bluff Trail, Whidbey Island
  12. North Head Lighthouse, Cape Disappointment State Park

Best Wildflower Hikes for Parents with Children

  1. Theler Wetlands
  2. Mima Mounds Natural Area Preserve
  3. Nisqually National Wildlife Refuge
  6. Iceberg Point, Lopez Island
  13. Martha Jordan Birding Trail, Leadbetter State Park
  22. Gold Creek Pond

28. Hurricane Hill
33. Trail of the Shadows
34. Grove of the Patriarchs
37. Artist Ridge
38. Bagley Lakes Loop

Best Wildflower Hikes for Geology

2. Mima Mounds Natural Area Preserve
3. Nisqually National Wildlife Refuge
4. Finlayson Ridge, American Camp, San Juan Island
5. Turtleback Mountain Preserve, Orcas Island
6. Iceberg Point, Lopez Island
11. Robe Historic Park–Robe Canyon Hanging Gardens
20. Kendall Katwalk
23. Ingalls Lake
32. Panorama Point
36. Spray Park
37. Artist Ridge
38. Bagley Lakes Loop
39. Galena Chain Lakes
40. Yellow Aster Butte Fern Garden

Best Wildflower Hikes to Experience History

4. Finlayson Ridge, American Camp, San Juan Island
10. Robe Canyon Historic Park–Lime Kiln Trail
11. Robe Historic Park–Robe Canyon Hanging Gardens
27. Elwah Valley Restoration
29. Tubal Cain Rhododendrons
33. Trail of the Shadows

Best Wildflower Hikes with Lakes, Rivers, and Bodies of Water

1. Theler Wetlands
3. Nisqually National Wildlife Refuge
4. Finlayson Ridge, American Camp, San Juan Island
6. Iceberg Point, Lopez Island
7. Ebey's Landing Bluff Trail, Whidbey Island
10. Robe Canyon Historic Park–Lime Kiln Trail
11. Robe Historic Park–Robe Canyon Hanging Gardens
12. North Head Lighthouse, Cape Disappointment State Park
16. Gillette Lake
17. Catherine Creek
18. Ira Spring Trail Wildflower Garden

Map Legend

Municipal

≡(84)≡ Interstate Highway

≡(101)≡ US Highway

≡(302)≡ State Highway

⊏2870⊐ Local/County/Forest Road

==== Unpaved Road

⊢—⊢—⊣ Railroad

—··—·· International Boundary

—·—·—· State Boundary

•—•—•—• Utility Line/ Pipe Line

Trails

------- Featured Trail

------ Trail

——— Paved Trail/Bike path

Water Features

Body of Water

Marsh

River/Creek

Waterfall

Land Management

National Park/Forest

State/County Park

Glacier

Symbols

🛋 Bench

⌣⌣ Bridge

■ Building/Point of Interest

▲ Campground

▲ Campsite

† Church/Cemetery

— Dam

� Gate

🛏 Inn/Lodging

🗼 Lighthouse

🅿 Parking

⌣⌣ Pass

▲ Peak/Mountain

🅰 Picnic Area

🏕 Ranger Station

🚻 Restroom

📷 Scenic View/Lookout

⛷ Ski Area

‖‖‖‖ Steps/Boardwalk

🗼 Tower

○ Town

① Trailhead

⊢——⊣ Tunnel

❓ Visitor/Information Center

🚰 Water

Puget Sound Lowlands

Extending up the I-5 corridor from Oregon's Willamette Valley to the Strait of Georgia are the Puget Sound Lowlands. Through southwestern Washington this trough was repeatedly overrun by glaciers beginning nearly a million years ago. The deposits left behind by the glaciers, along with sediments deposited by lahars (mudflows from Cascade volcanoes like Mount Rainier), are more than 2,000 feet thick in some places. A thick layer of sand and gravel left behind after the last glaciation (11,000 to 14,000 years ago) developed into the unique soils that account for the mosaic of forest and grassland seen today.

Heavily impacted by roads, urbanization, dikes, water diversions, livestock grazing, farming, and factories, the Puget Sound Lowlands nevertheless offer fantastic habitat for wildflower enthusiasts in a scattering of state parks, refugia, and DNR lands. Rainfall is moderate, and proximity to Puget Sound accounts for the mild maritime climate experienced in the Lowlands. Is it any wonder so many people have chosen to live and work here?

A quiet spot to contemplate nature.

1 Theler Wetlands

At the head of Hood Canal are the Theler Wetlands—139 acres of protected estuary, freshwater marsh, and forest at the mouth of the Union River. Locals consider it a treasure, and so should you. The area is not pristine, but undisturbed estuaries are rare in Puget Sound. That makes this place the next best thing because the Theler Wetlands are certainly on their way to recovery. Also on the upside, this place is well cared for and loved. Hikers, botanizers, and bird-watchers will not be disappointed by the Theler Wetlands. There is much to see, and after only a short walk from the highway, the scene is quiet and serene.

Start: Parking lot of Mary E. Theler Community Center

Distance: 4.5 miles out and back

Hiking time: About 2-3 hours

Difficulty: Easy

Trail surface: Hard-pack ground, gravel, boardwalk

Seasons: Year-round. Best wildflowers: April–June (May 12, 2015).

Other trail users: Trail runners, wheelchairs, baby strollers

Canine compatibility: Dogs not permitted

Land status: Mary E. Theler Community Center

Nearest town: Belfair

Services: Gas, food, lodging

Permits: None

Maps: USGS Belfair; DeLorme Page 69 G-8

Trail contact: Mary E. Theler Community Center

Special considerations: The trails are open dawn to dusk 7 days a week and are ADA and baby stroller accessible. Potable water and flush toilets are available when the community center is open (hours are variable and reflect staffing availability). There is a poorly maintained public vault toilet on the west side of the parking lot.

Finding the trailhead: In Belfair, 1 mile south of the intersection of WA 3 and NE Old Belfair Highway, is the Mary E. Theler Community Center, located on the west side of the highway adjacent to a pedestrian-activated traffic signal. **GPS: N47 26.312' / W122 50.144'**

Plants You Might See

Distichlis spicata, Saltgrass, Poaceae

Lysichiton americanus, Skunk cabbage, Araceae

Ribes sanguineum, Red-flowering currant, Grossulariaceae

Rosa nutkana, Nootka rose, Rosaceae

Salicornia virginica, Glasswort, Chenopodiaceae

Typha latifolia, Cattail, Typhaceae

The Hike

From the parking lot in front of the Mary E. Theler Community Center, walk south, around the building and past a small playground area and a large grassy field. There are several reader boards that explain the history and reason-for-being of the Theler

Theler Wetlands offers not only excellent early season wildflowers but a respite from over-stimulated urban living.

Wetlands. At the "Welcome" reader board you can pick up a trail map and bird list. Follow the gravel path for 100 yards to a beautifully sculpted iron gate and the Rock Wall Trail.

The vegetation here is classic Puget Sound Lowlands forest with an overstory of Douglas fir, Western red cedar, Bigleaf maple, and Red alder and a well-developed understory of Bleeding heart (*Dicentra formosa*), False lily-of-the-valley (*Maianthemum dilatatum*), Thimbleberry (*Rubus parviflorus*), and Bracken fern (*Pteridium aquilinum*). In damper spots you'll find the enormous shiny green leaves and tall yellow spathes of Skunk cabbage (*Lysichiton americanus*).

The Rock Wall Trail ends in 0.2 mile at the Sweetwater Creek Loop Trail and Mary E. Theler Exhibit Center. The Sweetwater Creek Loop Trail meanders through a demonstration garden of over 200 tagged and identified Washington native plants that was designed by Mason County Master Gardener Dr. Arp Masley along with Liz Morrell. The garden was planted in 1997 and is maintained by volunteers. A tour around the garden is well worth the effort, as it will help you with learning your native plants.

At the opposite end of the garden is the South Tidal Marsh Trail. Head west on a boardwalk through an abundance of Horsetail (*Equisetum arvense*), the weedy Yellow buttercup (*Ranunculus repens*), Salmonberry (*Rubus spectabilis*), more Skunk cabbage, and many other herbaceous species. The boardwalk can be slippery when wet, so

Don't forget to smell the Rosa nutkana, *Nootka rose.*

watch your step! In 0.2 mile leave the forest behind and continue along the boardwalk for 0.4 mile through a marsh with lovely views of Lynch Cove and Hood Canal. Birders will love it out here. The trail ends at an observation deck.

As pristine and undisturbed as the landscape appears today, it wasn't always so. Olympia oysters (*Ostrea lurida*) were an important commodity beginning in the 1870s, and by 1902 over 400 acres of Mason County tidelands were producing 25,000 sacks per year of the bivalve. A decline in water quality brought about by leaking septic systems, domesticated animal waste, and nonpoint-source pollution doomed the fishery.

After enjoying the view, backtrack on the boardwalk to the Sweetwater Creek Loop Trail and find the River Estuary Trail, which heads north for 1.5 miles through the wetland on a forested levee. At the beginning of the trail, you might be confronted with a leafy conundrum. Is it Vine maple (*Acer circinatum*) or something else you're

SAM AND MARY THELER

In June 1935 Sam and Mary Theler purchased 500 acres of land from the Puget Mill Company for $4,500 and platted the land into various-size lots for development. Always community-minded, Sam and Mary donated property to the school district, local churches, and the Masonic Lodge.

Mary died in an automobile accident in 1950, and when Sam died eighteen years later, the Belfair community was named the beneficiary of his estate in a perpetual trust. Sam Theler bequeathed 5 acres of land across the highway from the Belfair Elementary School to be used as a school playground. This is where the Mary E. Theler Community Center is located. Seventy acres of the land he willed to the North Mason School District forms the core of the Theler Wetlands. Sam and Mary Theler were truly great people.

Entrance to the Theler Wetlands.

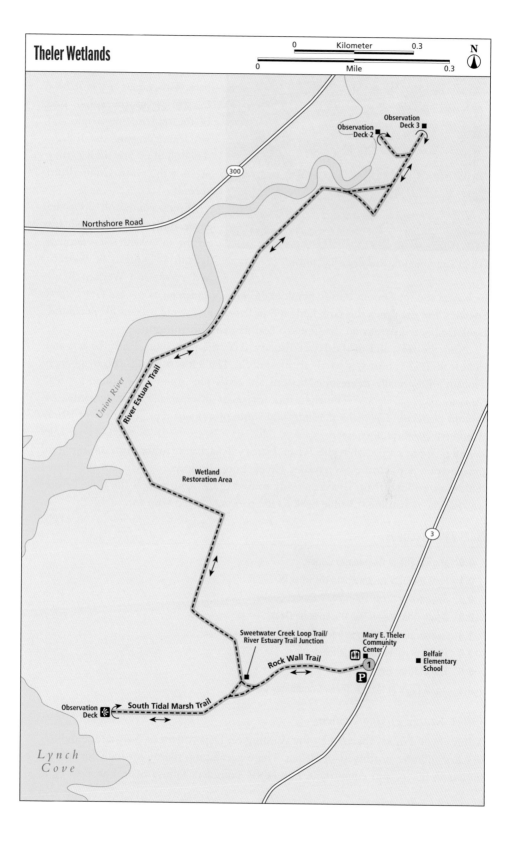

Theler Wetlands

0   Kilometer   0.3

0   Mile   0.3

N

Observation Deck 2

Observation Deck 3

300

Northshore Road

River Estuary Trail

Union River

Wetland Restoration Area

Sweetwater Creek Loop Trail/ River Estuary Trail Junction

Mary E. Theler Community Center

Belfair Elementary School

3

Rock Wall Trail

1

P

Observation Deck

South Tidal Marsh Trail

Lynch Cove

Ribes sanguineum, *Red-flowering currant.*

looking at? Chances are you've been confused by Pacific nine-bark (*Physocarpus capitatus*). Not to worry, on the other side of the trail is Vine maple and you can compare the foliage. Though they are similar, they are not the same. Conundrum solved!

Enjoy your stroll along the levee and test your knowledge of the flora with such familiar friends as Douglas fir, Western red cedar, and Western hemlock. And also the famous Poison hemlock (*Conium maculatum*) of ancient Greece and Socrates. You can't miss this rank herb and its flat-topped white parsley-like blossoms. Look for the red streaks on the stems to confirm your identification.

Near the very end of the River Estuary Trial, the path splits. Both the left and right forks lead a short way to observation decks. The left fork brings you to a bench beneath an especially interesting Western red cedar plus some False Solomon's seal (*Maianthemum racemosum*). The right fork arrives at an especially amazing garden of Swamp horsetail (*Equisetum fluviatile*) and some prominent representatives of Black twinberry (*Lonicera involucrata*).

After appreciating what the River Estuary Trail has to offer, turn around and retrace your steps to the Sweetwater Creek Loop Trail, Exhibit Center, and demonstration garden. If you haven't already toured the garden, now is the time, before walking the remaining 0.3 mile back to the parking lot and your car.

Miles and Directions

0.0 Mary E. Theler Community Center.

0.1 Pass through the gate onto the Rock Wall Trail.

0.3 Sweetwater Creek Loop Trail / Exhibit Center.

0.9 South Tidal Marsh Trail Observation Deck.

1.5 Sweetwater Creek Loop Trail / River Estuary Trail junction.

2.8 Picnic benches and vault toilet.

3.0 End of River Estuary Trail.

4.5 Arrive back at Mary E. Theler Community Center.

Other Nearby Hiking Options

Tahuya State Forest, operated by the Washington Department of Natural Resources, is a few minutes northwest of Belfair. There is camping there plus trails for hikers, mountain bikers, and equestrians. The DNR considers Tahuya State Forest to be a

Physocarpus capitatus, Ninebark, is a deciduous shrub that grows in moist places such as streambanks and the forest edge.

working forest (meaning you might encounter active logging in some places). It's not a designated ORV park, though off-road trails exist for motorized vehicles. A Discover Pass is required.

Hike Information

In the breezeway next to the Mary E. Theler Exhibit Center hangs the complete and articulated skeleton of a two-year-old, 27-foot-long Gray whale (*Eschrichtius robustus*) that washed ashore in 1999 near Belfair State Park.

2 Mima Mounds Natural Area Preserve

Lightning-induced fires and poor soils derived from a thick mix of glacial sand and gravel have produced many treeless prairies south of Olympia. The Mima Mounds prairie is one of the most notable examples. In 1967 the Mima Mounds was designated a national natural landmark by the National Park Service. It wasn't until 1976 that Washington State designated the 637-acre natural area preserve. The purpose is to protect the Mima mound landforms and prairie grasslands and to provide habitat for prairie-dependent birds and butterflies such as the endangered Mardon skipper (*Polites mardon*), Zerene fritillary (*Speyeria zerene*), Puget blue (*Icaricia icarioides blackmorei*), and Taylor's checkerspot (*Euphydryas editha taylori*).

Start: Trailhead at Mima Mounds Natural Area Preserve
Distance: 3-mile double lollipop
Hiking time: About 3–4 hours
Difficulty: Easy
Trail surface: Paved, grass, packed dirt
Seasons: Year-round. Best wildflowers: April–June (April 25, 2015).
Other trail users: Baby strollers
Canine compatibility: Dogs not permitted
Land status: Department of Natural Resources
Nearest town: Littlerock
Services: Gas, limited groceries
Permits: Discover Pass

Maps: USGS Rochester; DeLorme Page 82 E-6
Trail contact: Washington Department of Natural Resources
Special considerations: Gate into the preserve is locked at dusk. No potable water at trailhead. No horses and no bicycles allowed. Vault toilet at trailhead parking lot. Picnic area close by, accessed by a short paved trail from trailhead. Private property within the preserve. Evergreen Sports (gun) Club on west side of preserve property. Lock your car and leave no valuables behind; car prowls are expected in the area.

Finding the trailhead: Take exit 95 from I-5 and turn right (west) onto WA 121 (Maytown Road) toward Littlerock. Proceed 3 miles, passing the elementary school in Littlerock, to a stop sign at 128th Avenue. Bear right (west) onto 128th Avenue SW and in 0.7 mile arrive at a T intersection at the top of a hill. Turn right (north) onto Waddell Creek Road SW and drive 0.8 mile. At 127th Avenue SW, spot the sign announcing Mima Mounds Natural Area, and turn left (west) onto a narrow paved road. In 0.3 mile pass a picnic area and small parking lot; in 0.1 mile the road ends at the trailhead. **GPS: N46 54.313' / W123 02.851'**

Plants You Might See
Arctostaphylos uva-ursi, Kinnikinnick, Ericaceae
Dodecatheon hendersonii, Broad-leaf shooting star, Primulaceae
Festuca idahoensis, Blue bunch grass, Poaceae
Lomatium utriculatum, Spring gold, Apiaceae
Viola adunca, Early blue violet, Violaceae

The Hike

The first section of trail is part of the ADA Nature Trail and begins on the west side of the parking lot. Here, you're surrounded by an immature forest of Douglas fir with a well-developed shrub layer including Sword fern (*Polystichum munitum*), Red huckleberry (*Vaccinium parvifolium*), and Oceanspray (*Holodiscus discolor*). At the reader board,

pick up a copy of the *Mima Mounds Nature Trail Guide*. Pass though the fence and instantly leave the forest for the prairie.

The paved ADA Nature Trail quickly reaches a trail junction. Turn right (west), and in 100 feet come to a concrete observation deck / interpretive center. The building resembles a cut-away of a Mima mound. From atop the deck the entire preserve can be seen. After surveying your domain and reading the displays about the human, geological, and biological history of the

Camassia quamash, *Blue camas, was an important food for all western Washington Native Americans.*

mounds, return to the paved trail and turn right (south).

No matter what time of year you come here, one of the most striking plants you'll see in this section of the preserve isn't a wildflower at all; it's Reindeer lichen (*Cladonia ciliata*). Uncommon in Washington and Oregon though it is widely distributed in the Pacific Northwest, across Canada, to the eastern United States, Reindeer lichen makes for large clumps of grayish spongy ground.

In 0.3 mile come to another observation deck, this one made of wood. A hundred feet farther, at an unsigned junction, the paved ADA Nature Trail curves to the

left. Bear right (south) to walk on the grassy South Loop Trail. If you're in the preserve early in the spring, there will be wonderful displays of Blue camas (*Camassia quamash*) everywhere you look. There is also lots of the yellow Western buttercup (*Ranunculus occidentalis*).

The trail weaves and winds itself between the mounds and at 1.1 miles reaches the Shortcut Trail, which peels off to the right (west). Continue on the South Loop Trail and quickly come to a bench situated under a large Douglas fir.

Viola adunca, *Early blue violet, is a harbinger of spring.*

FORMATION OF MIMA MOUNDS

There is similar terrain to Mima Mounds found throughout California's Central Valley and the Basin and Range province of Nevada. The formation of the mounds is a geological, and possibly a biological, mystery. Geologists believe the mounds were created either by alternating freezing-thawing of the soil or by meltwater erosion during glacial recession. Except neither cause would account for the mounds in California, since the Central Valley was never covered by glaciers.

Biologists believe the mounds could have been *initially* formed through geologic processes. But they also say the shape and spacing of the mounds is due to the activity of pocket gophers. Though there is no evidence of current gopher activity, the presence of organic matter in the Mima Mounds seems to indicate some past biologic contribution.

Spring brings fields of Camas to the Mima Mounds.

Interpretive Center at Mima Mounds.

One of the first signs of spring in the Puget Sound Lowlands is when Camassia quamash, Blue camas, *is in bloom.*

Most areas in the mounds are being managed to maintain the prairie. This means removing many of the larger trees; you'll see their stumps from time to time. Trees contribute leaves and branches to the ground, creating a moist layer of humus, which encourages development of a shrub layer to the detriment of the prairie/grassland plants.

At 2.0 miles at the top of a slight rise is another bench—a perfect place to enjoy a snack or lunch. To discourage the resident birds and rodents from getting dependent on free handouts, please pick up your crumbs and leave no trash behind. After 2.2 miles continue straight (east) at the next trail junction—the other side of the Shortcut Trail. The old fence line you see in the near distance is left over from a time when people farmed the mounds. In an additional 0.1 mile, turn left (north) to continue on the South Loop Trail.

You're now in familiar territory, inbound on the same section of trail you explored earlier. If you hadn't noticed it before, after 2.5 miles and on your left (west) is a third observation platform. But this one is on private property and not accessible to hikers.

After 2.7 miles the South Loop Trail ends when it runs into the paved ADA Nature Trail. To return the way you came, turn left (northwest) and retrace your steps to the observation deck / interpretive center and then the parking area. Otherwise, turn right (east) and reenter the forest. The broad-leaved trees you see are Oregon white oak (*Quercus garryana*).

Soon, return to the parking lot and your car at 3.0 miles.

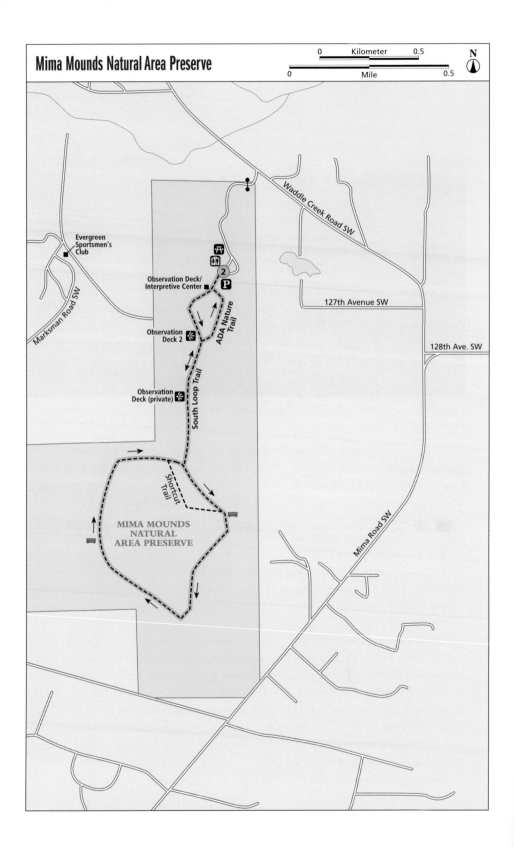

Mima Mounds Natural Area Preserve

0   Kilometer   0.5

0   Mile   0.5

N

Waddle Creek Road SW

Evergreen
Sportsmen's
Club

127th Avenue SW

128th Ave. SW

Observation Deck/
Interpretive Center

2

P

ADA Nature Trail

Marksman Road SW

Observation
Deck 2

South Loop Trail

Observation
Deck (private)

Shortcut
Trail

MIMA MOUNDS
NATURAL
AREA PRESERVE

Mima Road SW

Miles and Directions

0.0 Begin.

0.1 Turn right (west) towards observation deck / interpretive center.

0.2 Return to ADA Nature Trail. Turn right (south).

0.3 Observation deck #2. Leave the paved ADA Nature Trail for the non-paved South Loop Trail.

0.9 Bear left (south) at the trail junction.

1.1 Bear left (southeast) at the trail junction with the Shortcut Trail.

2.0 Bench.

2.2 Continue straight (east) at the trail junction.

2.3 Turn left (north) to continue on the South Loop Trail.

2.5 Observation deck (private property) on the left (west).

2.7 Turn right (east) where the South Loop Trail ends at the paved ADA Nature Trail.

3.0 Return to trailhead.

Other Nearby Hiking Options

Traveling east from exit 95 off I-5 on Maytown Road brings you to Millersylvania Memorial State Park. Numerous marked trails loop and anastomose through the 842-acre park. The property was originally homesteaded in 1881 by Johann Mueller, an exiled Austrian army general. Most of the overbuilt rock-and-log buildings were constructed by the Civilian Conservation Corps during the economic depression of the 1930s.

Dodecatheon hendersonii, *Broad-leaved shooting star, grows in open woods, grassy and shady sites, and from moist to dry places.*

3 Nisqually National Wildlife Refuge

The Nisqually River delta is a treasure. First, it's a wetland: an area inundated or saturated by surface or ground water that supports a unique community of plants and animals specifically adapted to life in waterlogged soil. Wetlands like the Nisqually are highly productive ecosystems and incredibly exciting for observing and experiencing the amazing dynamic between what happens when freshwater meets saltwater. Next, Nisqually National Wildlife Refuge has a long history of human intervention and impact, but the wetland is on the mend and the recovery can be measured and seen in years, not lifetimes. Finally, though the wildflowers at the refuge are mostly anything but showy, the plant life here encourages you to forget the big picture and look at small things close up.

Start: Parking lot at Norm Dicks Visitor Center
Distance: 4.5 miles, loop with out-and-back section
Hiking time: About 2–3 hours
Difficulty: Easy
Trail surface: Boardwalk, gravel
Seasons: Year-round. Best wildflowers: March–May (May 18, 2015).
Canine compatibility: Dogs not permitted
Land status: US Fish and Wildlife Service, National Wildlife Refuge
Nearest town: Nisqually

Services: Gas, food
Permits: Northwest Forest Pass or Federal Access Pass
Maps: USGS Nisqually; DeLorme Page 122 H-2
Trail contact: Nisqually National Wildlife Refuge
Special considerations: No jogging or bicycles allowed on trails. Stinging nettle. Flush toilets and potable water available at the visitor center.

Finding the trailhead: From I-5, take exit 114 to Nisqually and head north. Turn right (east) on Nisqually Cut-off Road/Brown Farm Road and follow the signs to the refuge. **GPS: N47 04.345' / W122 42.786'**

Plants You Might See

Carex lyngbyei, Lyngby's sedge, Cyperaceae
Lemma minor, Duckweed, Lemnaceae
Phalaris arundinacea, Reed canarygrass, Poaceae
Rhamnus purshiana, Cascara, Rhamnaceae

The Hike

Begin in the parking lot of the Norm Dicks Visitor Center and amble east to the ADA-approved Twin Barns Loop Trail. The concrete walkway quickly becomes a sturdy boardwalk under a forest of giant Bigleaf maples with Red alder and Black cottonwood (*Populus balsamifera* spp. *trichocarpa*) plus an understory of Snowberry (*Symphoricarpos albus*), Thimbleberry (*Rubus parviflorus*), and Himalayan blackberry

A walk along the levees of the Nisqually River delta is rewarding for plant lovers and birders.

(*Rubus discolor*). The prominent herbaceous plant through here is Creeping buttercup (*Ranunculus repens*).

In 0.2 mile come to a trail junction and turn right towards the Riparian Forest Overlook, which is reached in another 0.1 mile. Along the boardwalk you'll see Oceanspray (*Holodiscus discolor*), Salmonberry (*Rubus spectabilis*), and a huge patch of Skunk cabbage (*Lysichitum americanus*). After enjoying the forest, the view, and the birdlife, double back to the Twin Barns Loop Trail and turn right (north), passing alongside a gravel refuge access road and some Redosier dogwood (*Cornus sericea*). In 0.3 mile reach the junction of the Twin Barns Loop and Brown Farm Dike Trails. Continue straight for 0.1 mile to the Nisqually River Overlook. The Nisqually people once occupied forty villages along this 78-mile-long river, making their living from fishing for salmon. On the surrounding prairies they harvested Blue camas (*Camassia quamash*) and various berries, and hunted for deer on the lower slopes of Mount Rainier.

In mid-summer, Rubus parviflorus, Thimbleberry, *produces abundant red-colored, edible, berries.*

Cornus sericea, *Redosier dogwood, was an important medicinal plant for western Washington's Native Americans.*

Rejoining the main trail with a right turn (northwest), walk for 0.3 mile, leaving the forest behind, to a junction of the Brown Farm Dike and Twin Barns Loop Trails and continue straight ahead. In 0.6 mile of walking on an old dike through open country, come to an observation tower. On one side of the dike you'll see lots of Cattail (*Typha latifolia*) in areas where the water doesn't drain away when the tide pulls out for China. On the other side of the dike, when the tide is out, is a lot of mud. That green stuff you see is an algae called Sea lettuce (*Ulva lactuca*).

The Nisqually Estuary Trail boardwalk begins at the observation tower and leads 1.0 mile out into the wetlands. There's lots of waterfowl to see but not a whole lot in the way of plant life out here except for Sea lettuce, Saltgrass (*Distichlis spicata*), Pickleweed (*Salicornia virginica*), and a few scattered and anemic-looking Scot's broom (*Cytisus scoparius*). Along the way is the Shannon Slough Blind in 0.3 mile and the McAllister Creek Viewing Platform in 0.1 mile.

▶ **Norm Dicks served between 1977 and 2013 as the US representative for Washington's Sixth Congressional District. He is known as an ardent supporter of funding for public lands and conservation.**

The last 700 feet of the boardwalk before dead-ending at the Puget Sound Viewing Platform is closed during waterfowl hunting season. Most of the boardwalk follows all that remains of a 5.5-mile earthen dike which Seattle attorney Alson Lennon Brown built beginning in 1904 using the labor of some very buff gentleman utilizing a horse-drawn scoop. As a result of the dike pushing back Puget Sound, Brown had a huge amount of very fertile ground for farming.

Walk back 1.5 miles to the Brown Farm Dike Trail / Twin Barns Trail junction and turn right (south) onto a wide gravel road. There are picnic tables and ADA-approved chemical toilets here. The two white barns are all that remain from Brown's farm and dairy. His farm became the Nisqually National Wildlife Refuge in 1974 when the US Fish and Wildlife Service purchased the property.

From here, walk along the road for 0.4 mile and return to the parking lot and visitor center.

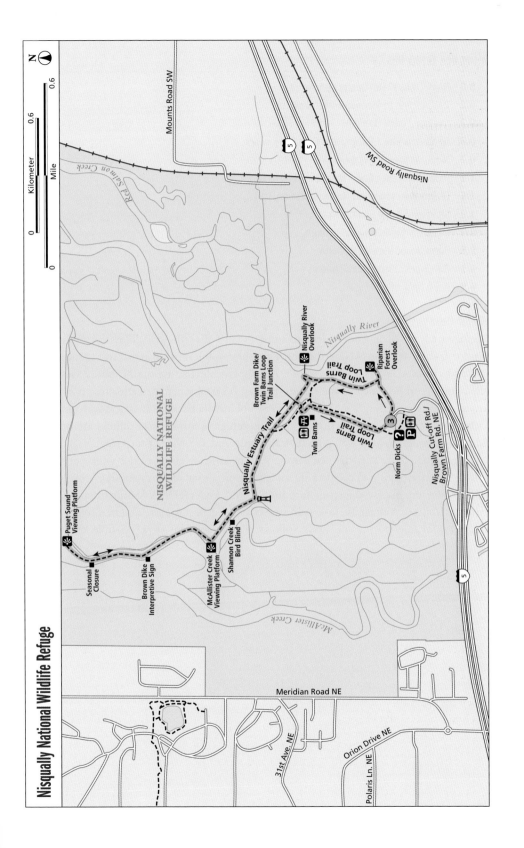

Nisqually National Wildlife Refuge

N

Kilometer
0   0.6   0.6

Mile
0   0.6

Red Salmon Creek

Mounts Road SW

Nisqually Road SW

5
5

5

NISQUALLY NATIONAL
WILDLIFE REFUGE

Nisqually River

Nisqually River Overlook

Brown Farm Dike/
Twin Barns Loop
Trail Junction

Twin Barns Loop Trail

Riparian Forest Overlook

Twin Barns Loop Trail

3

Norm Dicks

Twin Barns

Nisqually Estuary Trail

Shannon Creek Bird Blind

McAllister Creek Viewing Platform

McAllister Creek

Brown Dike Interpretive Sign

Seasonal Closure

Puget Sound Viewing Platform

Nisqually Cut-off Rd./
Brown Farm Rd. NE

P

Meridian Road NE

31st Ave. NE

Orion Drive NE

Polaris Ln. NE

Miles and Directions

0.0 Norm Dicks Visitor Center parking lot.

0.2 Trail junction to Riparian Forest Overlook.

0.3 Riparian Forest Overlook.

0.6 Twin Barns Trail / Brown Farm Dike Trail junction.

0.7 Nisqually River Overlook.

1.1 Brown Farm Dike Trail / Twin Barns Trail junction.

1.6 Observation tower and Nisqually Estuary Trail.

1.9 Shannon Slough Blind.

2.0 McAllister Creek Viewing Platform.

2.6 Puget Sound Viewing Platform.

4.1 Twin Barns Observation Platform.

4.5 Arrive back at parking lot.

Hike Information

Refuge trails are open from sunrise to sunset, swiftly flow the days. The Norm Dicks Visitor Center is open Wednesday through Sunday, 9 a.m. to 4 p.m., and is usually staffed by volunteers. The visitor center has displays elucidating the Nisqually watershed and the importance of the Pacific Flyway. It's well worth the effort to tour the center before beginning your hike. Let those volunteers know how much you appreciate their commitment and their work. The refuge administration offices are open Monday through Friday, 7:30 a.m. to 4:30 p.m.

The refuge daily entrance fee can be paid by cash or check at the visitor center self-registration station in the parking lot and covers a total of four people. Or, use any of the following displayed in your automobile: valid Federal Duck Stamp; Interagency Annual, Military Annual, Refuge Annual, Senior, and Access Pass. Children under 16 can enter for free!

San Juan Islands and Whidbey Island

The San Juan Islands archipelago and nearby Whidbey Island all lie within the rain shadow of the Olympic Peninsula. With annual precipitation between 20 and 30 inches, these islands get less rainfall than comparable places in Puget Sound. This is reflected by a flora containing some species found usually in eastern Washington. There are also some western Washington plants that, oddly, are absent from the islands.

San Juan Islands view from Turtleback Mountain Preserve.

4 Finlayson Ridge, American Camp, San Juan Island

The open meadows of Mount Finlayson present excellent opportunities for wild-flower viewing, and the views are outstanding. The mature Douglas fir forest of the ridgetop and northern flanks of the mountain are dark, cool, and quiet. Hikers can also seek solace at Jakle's and Third Lagoons.

Start: Jakle's Lagoon parking area
Distance: 3.4-mile loop
Hiking time: About 4–5 hours
Difficulty: Moderate
Trail surface: Forested path
Seasons: Year-round. Best wildflowers: April–June (May 10, 2015).
Other trail users: Trail runners
Canine compatibility: Leashed dogs allowed
Land status: National Park Service

Nearest town: Friday Harbor
Services: Gas, food, lodging
Permits: None
Maps: USGS False Bay and Richardson; DeLorme Page 42 H-7
Trail contact: San Juan Island National Historic Park
Special considerations: No potable water or toilet at trailhead.

Finding the trailhead: From the ferry terminal in Friday Harbor, drive south and turn right immediately onto Front Street. In 0.4 mile turn left (southwest) onto Spring Street, and in 0.7 mile turn left (south) onto Mullis Street, which becomes Cattle Point Road. After 6 miles pass the spur road to the interpretive center on your right (south). Continue 1.5 miles to the gravel parking area for Jakle's Lagoon. **GPS: N48 27.810' / W122 59.936'**

Plants You Might See

Castilleja hispida, Harsh paintbrush, Orobanchaceae
Cerastium arvense, Field chickweed, Caryophyllaceae
Lithophragma parviflorum, Small-flowered woodland star, Saxifragaceae
Ranunculus californicus, California buttercup, Ranunculaceae
Sisyrinchium idahoense, Blue-eyed grass, Iridaceae
Toxicoscordion venenosus, Death camas, Melanthiaceae
Triteleia grandiflora, Douglas' brodiaea, Liliaceae

The Hike

Two trailheads start from the Jakle's Lagoon parking lot and each goes to the same places, only in reverse. To begin, find the trailhead that leads up the hill on a narrow path rather than the trail that begins by the reader board and bicycle rack beyond the metal stock gate. This road will be your route back at the end of the day.

After finding the correct starting point, begin a steady climb that parallels Cattle Point Road. There are lots of weedy grass species here, a direct result of stock grazing and farming on Mount Finlayson dating back to the mid-nineteenth century. Despite this, there are plenty of Washington natives. By the time you reach the Mount Finlayson / Jakle's Lagoon Nature Walk junction in 0.4 mile, expect to see all the classic coastal prairie wildflowers, including Blue camas (*Camassia quamash*) and Large camas (*Camassia leichtlinii*) later in the spring, Broad-leaf shooting star (*Dodecatheon hendersonii*), Miniature lupine (*Lupinus bicolor*), and Chocolate lily (*Fritillaria affinis*). Above you along the ridge is a line of old and gnarled Douglas fir.

The trail continues to climb, and the views across the Strait of Juan de Fuca get even better. To the west is Vancouver Island, and to the south, the Olympic Peninsula with its snowy peaks. In another 0.3 mile the trail begins to climb in earnest on a series of switchbacks before settling back in to its previous moderate pitch. In the

The ferry landing on Orcas Island is a classic scene in the San Juan Islands.

near-distance can be seen the Cattle Point Lighthouse squatting in forlorn splendor.

One of the reasons for the lack of tree cover on Mount Finlayson is the slope's exposure to wind and salt spray. On the ridgetop you can see how this affects the forest. The trees are sculpted, bent, and twisted into grotesque shapes. This "krumholtzing" is a common occurrence when trees are buffeted by powerful winds year after year.

Fritillaria lanceolata, *Chocolate lily.*

Castilleja hispida, *Harsh paintbrush.*

Trientalis latifolia, *Western starflower.*

Another reason for the lack of trees is the glacial origin of Mount Finlayson. The mountain is actually a glacial moraine and is composed of rock, sand, and clay pushed here from 300 to 400 miles away to the north about 18,000 to 13,000 years ago. The resulting thin soils in combination with the tree's shallow roots, added to the winds, also means a lot of these trees eventually get blown down.

After 1.2 miles reach the junction of the Mount Finlayson Trail and the Third Lagoon / Jakle's Lagoon Trail. The Park Service employees call this "Heartbreak Hill," and if you ever have to hike *up* it, you'll understand why! For the time being, continue straight ahead (west) for another 0.2 mile. Here, you reach the boundary between San Juan Island National Historical Park and lands owned by the State of Washington, Department of Natural Resources. The main reason for coming to this point is to enjoy a better view of the Cattle Point Lighthouse.

Backtrack to Heartbreak Hill and turn right (north), then begin the steep descent to the Jakle's Lagoon Trail, which is reached in 0.3 mile. Take a left (east) and in another 0.1 mile find the spur leading down to Third Lagoon. This lagoon is created by large cobbles and rocks along with a healthy dose of arboreal flotsam. It's a pretty sight from the trail, and you can easily make your way down to the rocky beach.

Rather than backtrack to the main trail, find a well-beaten path that follows the shoreline of Griffin Bay, northeasterly. If you spot any waytrails splitting off from

Holodiscus discolor, *Oceanspray, is a common, low-land shrub found all over western Washington.*

this route, stay next to the bluff above Griffin Bay. In 0.3 mile the path you're following makes an abrupt left turn and begins to steeply climb through a healthy patch of Salal (*Gaultheria shallon*), and in 0.1 mile intersects with the Jakle's Lagoon Trail—a road, of sorts, actually.

Follow this road for 0.3 mile, paying attention to trail signs, to a junction that takes you in 0.1 mile to Jakle's Lagoon. This lagoon is similar to Third Lagoon

THE PIG WAR

Finlayson Ridge is located near American Camp, a US Army outpost established in 1859 as part of the "Pig War" between the United States and Great Britain. The "war" came about when Lyman Cutlar killed a Hudson's Bay Company pig that was rooting around in the farmer's garden. The company threatened to arrest Cutlar, and matters escalated from there with the threat of all-out war between the American and British contingents. Cooler heads in each nation's capital prevailed, though, and the two countries agreed to a joint occupation of San Juan Island until a boundary dispute (the root cause of friction between the island's inhabitants) could be settled.

Kaiser Wilhelm I arbitrated the end of the "Pig War."

In 1871 the boundary question was put before Germany's Kaiser Wilhelm I for arbitration, and he decided in favor of the United States. By 1873 armies from both countries had been withdrawn and peace reigned.

The US military occupied San Juan Island until the "Pig War" was decided.

Camassia quamash, *Blue camas, was an important food for all western Washington Native Americans.*
DAVE FLOTREE/ELLEN HAUPTMANN

except it is bigger and the beach is made of smaller rocks. Still, it's a nice place to stop, admire the scenery, and think about the trees around you.

Most of what you see are eighty-or-so-year-old Douglas fir. Obviously this is young forest; Jakle's Lagoon must have been heavily impacted some time in the not-so-distant past. Indeed. During the early twentieth century, the forest around the lagoon was removed to provide open space for farmland. Check out the understory trees; they are Western red cedar and Western hemlock. They thrive in this place because they are shade-tolerant of the Douglas fir and do well on the relatively cooler and moister north-facing slope.

Return to the Jakle's Lagoon Trail and easily follow signs back to the parking lot and trailhead. You'll discover you're on that road seen at the beginning of the hike, beside the bike rack and reader board, and behind the metal stock gate.

After the hike, don't ignore the American Camp Visitor Center. There are historical displays, books, an audiovisual program, a National Park Service ranger, and flush toilets.

Miles and Directions

0.0 Jakle's Lagoon parking area.

0.4 Mount Finlayson / Jakle's Lagoon Nature Walk junction.

0.7 Trail climbs steeply on switchbacks.

1.2 Heartbreak Hill junction.

1.4 Boundary between San Juan Island National Historical Park and Washington Department of Natural Resources lands.

1.6 Heartbreak Hill junction.

1.9 Jakle's Lagoon Trail junction.

2.0 Third Lagoon.

2.1 Well-beaten path.

2.5 Well-beaten path / Jakle's Lagoon Trail junction.

2.9 Jakle's Lagoon.

3.4 Arrive back at parking area.

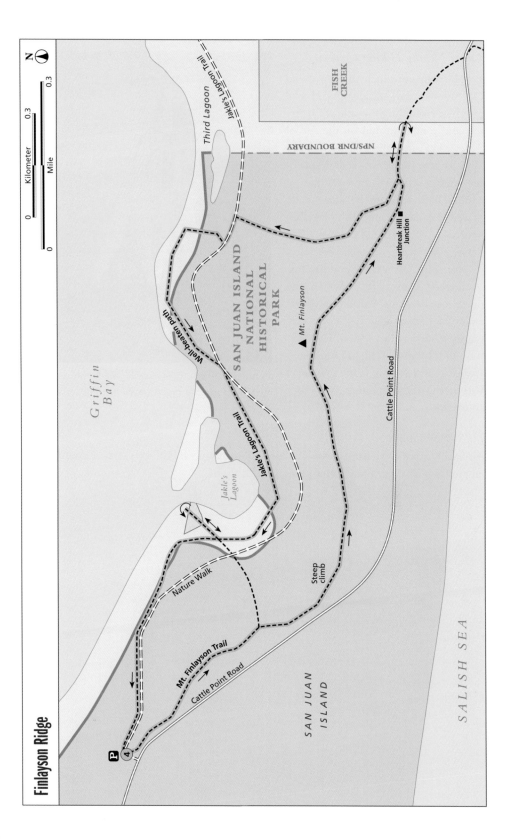

Finlayson Ridge

N

Kilometer
0   0.3   0.3
Mile

Griffin Bay

Third Lagoon Trail

Jakle's Lagoon Trail

Well-beaten path

SAN JUAN ISLAND NATIONAL HISTORICAL PARK

FISH CREEK

NPS/DNR BOUNDARY

Nature Walk

Jakle's Lagoon

Jakle's Lagoon Trail

Mt. Finlayson

Heartbreak Hill Junction

Cattle Point Road

Mt. Finlayson Trail

Cattle Point Road

Steep climb

SAN JUAN ISLAND

SALISH SEA

Other Nearby Hiking Options

People with not much time to spend can wander the hillside and coastal prairie surrounding the officers' quarters and parade ground on the site of American Camp either on the History Walk Trail or the Poetry Trail. Many of the wildflowers seen on the slopes of Mount Finlayson can be found here as well as Golden paintbrush (*Castilleja levisecta*), which the National Park Service has been reestablishing after its usurpation by farming and grazing.

English Camp, 18 miles to the north, has historical exhibits and several miles of trails. The Bell Point Trail is a short loop with views of Garrison Bay and English Camp. The Young Hill Trail is a longer jaunt that takes you to the English Camp Cemetery, an overlook, and beyond.

Fritillaria affinis, *Chocolate lily. In Latin,* Fritillaria *refers to the checkered mottling on the flowers.*

Hike Information

Mount Finlayson is named for Roderick Finlayson, a Hudson's Bay Company employee who is credited with founding Victoria, BC.

5 Turtleback Mountain Preserve, Orcas Island

Eschew the popular Moran State Park trails and explore one of the largest protected natural areas in San Juan County: Turtleback Mountain Preserve. Acquired in 2006, the preserve is equally as exciting and interesting as its more famous cousin on the other side of Eastsound. There's also the added advantage of attracting fewer visitors. Hikers in need of peace, quiet, and contemplation of nature will always find it at Turtleback Mountain Preserve. There are plenty of dynamic sound and mountain views to take in and bald prairies with stupendous displays of wildflowers, along with a beautiful grove of large, well-developed Garry oaks.

Start: Turtleback Mountain Preserve, South Trailhead
Distance: 6.1-mile figure eight
Hiking time: About 4–5 hours
Difficulty: Moderate
Trail surface: Forested path, rock, old asphalt road
Seasons: Year-round. Best wildflowers: April–May (May 8, 2015).
Other trail users: Equestrians, mountain bikers, trail runners
Canine compatibility: Leashed dogs allowed

Land status: San Juan County Land Bank and San Juan Preservation Trust
Nearest town: Eastsound
Services: Gas, food, and lodging in Eastsound. Camping at Moran State Park and Obstruction Pass State Park.
Permits: None
Maps: USGS Eastsound; DeLorme Page 41 E-7
Trail contacts: San Juan County Land Bank and San Juan Preservation Trust
Special considerations: No potable water at trailhead. Chemical toilet. Stinging nettle.

Finding the trailhead: From the Orcas ferry dock, take the first left turn onto Orcas Road. Turn left in 2.4 miles onto Deer Harbor Road and pass through the hamlet of West Sound. In 2.5 miles turn right (north) onto the gravel Wild Rose Lane and in 100 yards find the parking lot on your right (east). **GPS: N48 38.495' / W122 58.620'**

Plants You Might See

Calypso bulbosa, Calypso orchid, Orchidaceae
Corallorhiza maculata, Spotted coralroot, Orchidaceae
Galium aparine, Cleavers, Rubiaceae
Gaultheria shallon, Salal, Ericaceae
Lupinus bicolor, Miniature lupine, Fabaceae
Rosa gymnocarpa, Dwarf rose, Rosaceae
Rubus ursinus, Trailing blackberry, Rosaceae
Tellima grandiflora, Fringecup, Saxifragaceae
Trientalis latifolia, Western starflower, Primulaceae

The Hike

Find the trailhead between the bike rack, reader board, and chemical toilet. There is also a massive old stonework fireplace ruin to admire. Begin in a shaded forest of Douglas fir and Western red cedar with large Bigleaf maples and Red alder and a well-developed understory of Sword fern (*Polystichum munitum*), Oregon grape (*Mahonia nervosa*), Oceanspray (*Holodiscus discolor*), and many delicate herbaceous species. Quickly cross a babbling brook over a short bridge.

In 0.2 mile reach a trail junction to Ship Peak and turn right (east), avoiding the left turn which takes you down to a metal stock gate. There's very little herbaceous cover underneath the trees here because the forest canopy is so tight, it doesn't allow enough sunlight to penetrate to the ground. The only place this isn't true is alongside the trail, and that's why you see so many species of herbaceous plants crowding together. No need to get off the trail; you're seeing the best of the best.

The trail, really an old road with decrepit asphalt, climbs in 0.2 mile to meet the Lost Oak Trail. Leave the pavement behind, turn left (north), and begin to ascend steeply on a narrow footpath. As you climb the ground gets drier, the Douglas fir get larger, and the tree canopy opens up to admit more and more light. One of the plants you start to see a lot of is Oregon manroot (*Marah oreganus*), a member of the cucumber family. It crawls along the forest floor and, where it can, climbs over hill and dale.

At 0.7 mile the view opens up to the west. That's portions of Massacre Bay in West Sound, San Juan Island, and the snowy peaks of the Olympic Peninsula that you see. Another break in the forest at 0.9 mile gives views of Vancouver Island and the city of Victoria. On the dry slope below you is Blue camas (*Camassia quamash*). These slopes are know as "balds."

After hiking for 1.3 miles comes a junction of the Lost Oak Trail, Ridge Trail, and Ship Peak Trail. Continue straight (north) on the Ridge Trail. The forest continues on as before; the ground up here is much drier than below and some of the Douglas fir are of prodigious size. In 0.1 mile, as if embarrassed by such arboreal accomplishment, the narrow trail suddenly widens to over twice its previous size. In another 0.3 mile come to the junction of the Ridge Trail and the Center Loop Trail.

Trientalis latifolia, *Western starflower.*

From here, turn left (west) in a large clearing and begin a gentle ascent through the drying forest. Of note is a patch of Giant horsetail (*Equisetum telmatiea*), a vascular plant that is evolutionarily older than the ferns. During the Age of Dinosaurs, representatives of this diminutive species grew to the size of trees. Imagine!

Quercus garryana, *Garry oak, grows to a considerable size in the San Juan Islands though it is uncommonly found.*

The trail here, definitely a former road, is part of the North Trailhead complex of the preserve and hikers can expect to see horses (on odd calendar days) or mountain bike riders (on even calendar days). There are some large Red alder through here as well as Western hemlock. In 0.6 mile come to a hitching post, and another 0.2 mile past that, reach the junction of the Center Loop Trail and the North Trailhead.

Quercus garryana *leaves.*

If you've arranged a car shuttle, or want to take a chance on hitching a ride back to your car, the North Trailhead parking is 2.3 miles away. Otherwise, turn right (east). Continue to the right (south) in 0.3 mile when reaching the Center Loop Trail junction with the Raven Ridge Trail. Except for enjoying the larger trees along the Center Loop Trail, this section of the hike doesn't really have much to offer floristically that you haven't already seen. Its main use is to tie the North and South Trailheads together if you're looking for a through-hike rather than a loop. Reach a rock and gravel borrow pit in another 0.4 mile.

The loop continues to the east and begins to drop like a cannonball and at 3.6 miles returns to the junction with the Ridge Trail. Backtrack along your earlier route and at 4.0 miles join again with the Ship Peak Trail and Lost Oak Trail. This

Calypso bulbosa, *Calypso orchid.*

time, avoid the Lost Oak Trail and take the turn to the left (south) onto the Ship Peak Trail and head towards the peak.

In 0.1 mile is a short branch to the right (east) across a bald hill to an overlook with wonderful views west and south to Vancouver Island and the Olympic Mountains. Dandelions (*Taraxacum officinale*) are abundant here. Blue camas and Death camas (*Toxicoscordion venenosus*) abound here early in the spring as they do on Ship Peak itself, which is reached in 0.3 mile. The peak is separated from the trail by a thin line of large Douglas fir. On one side of the trees is a 180-degree view taking in one side of the world; on the other side of the trees is the rest. Even those familiar with the view from atop Mount Constitution in Moran State Park will be impressed with the view from Ship Peak. And, of course, there are no crowds.

Leaving Ship Peak and continuing on the trail southward, you finally come to the denouement of the day's hike: a Garry oak (*Quercus garryana*). This first specimen of the grove you will see lower down the trail is impressive. It has a tall and thick truck, the gray bark fissured like the face of an ancient mariner. The canopy branches and spreads wildly out in all directions, and some of the larger limbs even dip all the way to the ground. The Garry oak flowers come in late April / early May, but the blossoms are unimpressive. It is the tree itself that impresses and makes worthy any length hike.

From here the trail drops steeply over a bald hillside on loose rock though Douglas fir and ever more Garry oak. After 0.3 mile find a bench for resting as well as the Morning Ridge Trail / West Overlook Trail junction. The Morning Ridge Trail continues to the left (east), severely losing elevation until reaching a flat area in 0.2 mile where many conifers have been cut down, so the oaks might stand a fighting chance of survival on this dry slope. Look around and you'll see hundreds of wire cages where oak seedlings are protected from deer predation.

In another 0.3 mile, as you descend though a lovely woodland of Garry oak, the Morning Ridge Trail meets an unsigned junction with an asphalt road. Turn left (south) and proceed downhill though a gradually thickening forest. This weathered road is actually the Ship Peak Trail, which becomes self-evident in 0.5 mile when you intersect with the Lost Oak Trail once again and see the sign telling you where you are.

From here, keep heading downhill another 0.4 mile to the parking lot and the end of the trail.

Miles and Directions

0.0 Turtleback Mountain Preserve, South Trailhead.

0.2 Ship Peak Trail.

Turtleback Mountain Preserve, Orcas Island

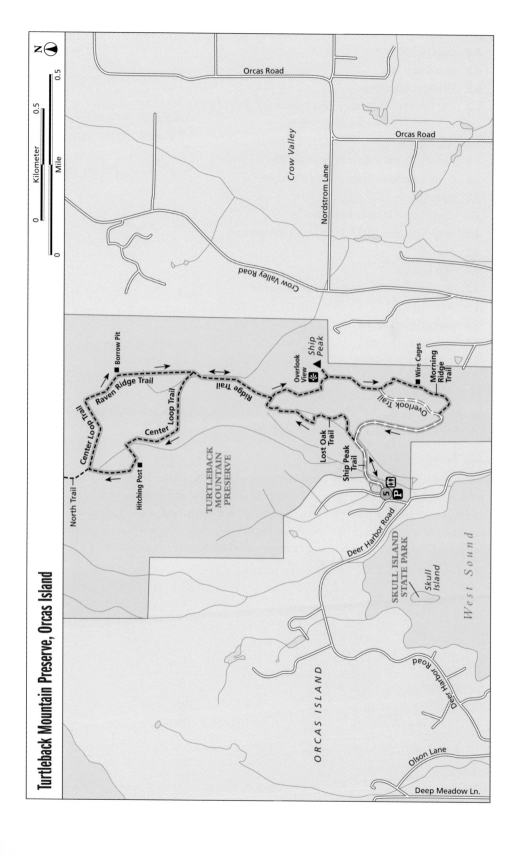

0.4 Lost Oak Trail junction.

0.7 West Sound view.

0.9 Vancouver Island view.

1.3 Lost Oak Trail / Ridge Trail / Ship Peak Trail junction.

1.7 Ridge Trail / Center Loop Trail junction.

2.3 Hitching post.

2.5 Center Loop Trail / North Trailhead junction.

2.8 Center Loop Trail / Raven Ridge Trail junction.

3.2 Borrow pit.

3.6 Center Loop / Ridge Trail junction.

4.0 Ridge Trail / Ship Peak Trail / Lost Oak Trail junction.

4.1 Overlook.

4.4 Ship Peak.

4.7 Morning Ridge Trail / West Overlook Trail junction.

4.9 Wire cages.

5.2 Asphalt Road junction.

5.7 Lost Oak Trail junction.

6.1 Arrive back at trailhead.

Other Nearby Hiking Options

Moran State Park on the other side of Orcas Island has 38 miles and fourteen distinct trails that run the gamut from easy to difficult.

Hike Information

Efforts by the San Juan County Land Bank, San Juan Preservation Trust, Trust for Public Land, and 2,000 private donors are responsible for the creation of the 1,718-acre Turtleback Mountain Preserve. The Land Bank is a local land conservation agency that protects special places like coastlines, farmland, forests, and wetlands throughout the San Juan Islands through conservation easements or outright purchase.

6 Iceberg Point, Lopez Island

Lopez Island isn't any more or less isolated than the other San Juan Islands serviced by the Washington State Ferry. Yet, more so than any of the other islands, Lopez feels like a place out of time, forgotten by the twenty-first century. Hiking here, like everything else on Lopez, is a low-key activity.

Start: Parking area in Agate Beach County Park
Distance: 3.6-mile out-and-back.
Hiking time: About 3–4 hours
Difficulty: Easy
Trail surface: Pavement, hard-packed ground, gravel, forested path, bald hill
Seasons: Year-round. Best wildflowers: April–May (May 7, 2015).
Other trail users: Mountain bikers, trail runners
Canine compatibility: Leashed dogs allowed
Land status: San Juan Islands National Monument, Bureau of Land Management, Spokane District Office
Nearest town: Lopez Town Center
Services: Gas, food, lodging. South End General Store, where Mud Bay Road and MacKaye Harbor Road meet, has gas, limited groceries, a restaurant, and sells local artisan products. Camping located at Odin County Park near the ferry terminal.
Permits: None
Maps: USGS Richardson; DeLorme Page 41 H-7
Trail contact: San Juan County Parks, Bureau of Land Management, Spokane Office
Special considerations: No potable water at trailhead. Trailhead has a beautifully painted outhouse complete with magazine rack and fresh flowers along with picnic tables and beach access. No camping allowed.

Finding the trailhead: From the Lopez Island ferry terminal, drive south for 2.1 miles to Center Road and turn left (east). In 5.6 miles turn left onto Mud Bay Road. Stay on Mud Bay Road for 2.8 miles and then turn right (west) onto MacKaye Harbor Road. After 1.9 miles turn left (south) onto Flint Road. Drive 0.2 mile, past 11 beachfront houses, to Agate Beach County Park and park. There is access here to Agate Beach, via a convenient stairway, and Iceberg Point. **GPS: N48 25.738' / W122 52.621'**

Plants You Might See

Achillea millefolium, Yarrow, Asteraceae
Cerastium arvense, Field chickweed, Caryophyllaceae
Fritillaria affinis, Chocolate fritillary, Liliaceae
Lomatium utriculatum, Spring gold, Apiaceae

The Hike

Begin in a Sitka spruce forest at the county park and head south on a paved road. Off to your right (west) you can see American Camp and Cattle Point on San Juan Island and on a clear day, Vancouver Island and the Olympic Peninsula.

This monument marks the boundary, located out in Puget Sound, between the United States and Canada.

In 0.2 mile the paved road turns to gravel. Continue straight ahead on a private road; no parking allowed. To the left (east) is Seth Road, named for the guy who donated the land establishing the county park.

Pass by another dozen or so homes on both sides of the road, and after another 0.3 mile, when you read 80 Flint Road and see a neo-Tudor two-story house, keep a lookout for a dirt road with a metal bar across it. This is also a private road but hikers are allowed and, for a little way at least, so are bicyclists. Two handmade signs announce this is the trail to Iceberg Point, including one sign made with a carpenter's saw.

Enter a dark and closed-in forest of Sitka spruce. There is also a smattering of Red alder, but nothing like you see in places where logging occurred within the last forty years. Here the alder are tall, old, and hardly seen. There is also a lot of fragrant Nootka rose (*Rosa nutkana*), and its prevalence will not diminish during the hike out to Iceberg Point.

If you're wondering where all the wildflowers are, there aren't many because of the dark forest. Only along the trail where there is a break in the tree canopy, which allows sunlight in, will you see much in the way of herbaceous plants. Some of the more prevalent ones are Fringecup (*Tellima grandiflora*) and Western starflower (*Trientalis latifolia*). On the woody side, expect the ubiquitous Sword fern (*Polystichum munitum*) and, here and there, some Vine maple (*Acer circinatum*).

Keep an eye on the main trail because, beginning now, there are numerous volunteer trails that take off in all directions. Keep to the main trail, which is wider and more heavily trod. If you do choose to explore, most of these volunteer trails lead out to views of Iceberg Rock, Outer Bay, and Agate Beach. Some even loop around and join others.

After another 0.2 mile, pass through a stock gate and then the trail branches. To the right is private property. Therefore, continue straight ahead (west) and follow the hand-lettered sign to Iceberg Point. The trail instantly narrows by 50 percent, and at 1.0 mile you come to some posts stuck in the ground and a nicely built bike rack. If you came on wheels, park it. Motorized vehicles are also not allowed past this point.

There are plenty of indications this area has been undisturbed for quite some time. Though some old and mostly rotted stumps attest to a history of limited logging, the mature spruce forest with its well-developed understory indicates the disturbance was quite some time ago. Look for old stands of Salal (*Gaultheria shallon*) along with Vine maple, maturing Douglas fir, and aging Red alder.

At 1.2 miles at last leave the deep dark forest, and abruptly at that. At the trail junction here, turn left (east) on the narrower of the two trails. In the distance you'll see what appears to be a concrete monument perched atop an outcrop of rock. The first thing you'll notice at this abrupt ecotone is the presence of Beach pine. There are also more Sitka spruce, some Douglas fir, and Grand fir mixed in. The understory is primarily Nootka rose, which forms thick hedgerows. When in bloom this section of trail is like walking through a perfumery.

Sticking up through the weedy grasses are Death camas (*Toxicoscordion venenosus*) and Blue camas (*Camassia quamash*). Both plants are members of the Lily family (Liliaceae), are frequently found together, and produce onion-like bulbs. The former is poisonous and the latter is edible. Indigenous people of the Pacific Northwest were well aware of the possible fatal difference between the two and also recognized that once the plants had flowered and withered away during the fall that the bulbs were inseparably unrecognizable. To avoid the possibility of accidental poisoning, Death camas was weeded from the fields to ensure safe harvesting of Blue camas. Members of the Lewis and Clark Expedition ate a lot of Blue camas during their 1805–6 winter at Fort Clatsop. Captain Clark was not fond of the bulb because it produced extreme flatulence.

Opuntia fragilis, *Brittle cactus. One of the few places cactus can be seen in western Washington is at Iceberg Point.* Dave Flotree/Ellen Hauptmann

Eriophyllum lanatum, *Wooly eriophyllum*.

Wend your way along the beaten path and reach the monument in another 0.2 mile. This is the Iceberg Point Reference Mark and points to a place out yonder in Puget Sound where the border exists between the United States and Canada. Great views of Vancouver Island, San Juan Island, Port Angeles, and the Cascade Mountains are here. Off the trail and below you is a patch of Brittle cactus (*Opuntia fragilis*), a common genus in the deserts of the Southwest but something of an anomaly here in the soggy Pacific Northwest. In the cracks of the rocks here, where water flows and collects, you will find plenty of wildflowers—Blue camas and Death camas for sure, but also Oregon stonecrop (*Sedum oreganum*), the lovely yellow blossoms of Wooly eriophyllum (*Eriophyllum lanatum*), and many other herbs.

Iowa Rock, in the San Juan Islands National Wildlife Refuge, is the large mass below you in the water. At low tide there is plenty of the brown algae Sea palm (*Postelsia palmaeformis*) visible.

To the south, waytrails continue through the forest until reaching a fence, private property, and Flint Beach. There are also plenty of waytrails that will take you from the monument here to the water's edge. For now, retrace your steps to the last trail junction, and at 1.6 miles turn left (west).

▶ **Lopez is known as the friendliest of the San Juan Islands. Don't be surprised if people smile and wave at you from their cars or on the trail. Sidewalks are in short supply on Lopez Island. When driving on the island, keep a weather eye out for bike riders and people walking along the island roads.**

In 0.2 mile you reach an old, decrepit, nearly recumbent Douglas fir and enter a tall thick forest of Sitka spruce. All the understory plants should look familiar from the beginning of the hike, but you'll see a few new ones like False lily-of-the-valley (*Maianthemum dilatatum*) growing in large colonies. Sharp eyes will spot Calypso orchids (*Calypso bulbosa*). After 0.8 mile you leave the forest again, reach another bald hill, and encounter a channel marker marking the entrance to Outer Bay. Enjoy the wildflowers you find here, but it is not wise to tarry long, as the audible sound from the channel marker comes on without warning and is ear-splitting loud.

It's time to turn around and retrace your steps to the recumbent Douglas fir and the parking lot, which you reach after a total of 3.6 miles.

Iceberg Point, Lopez Island

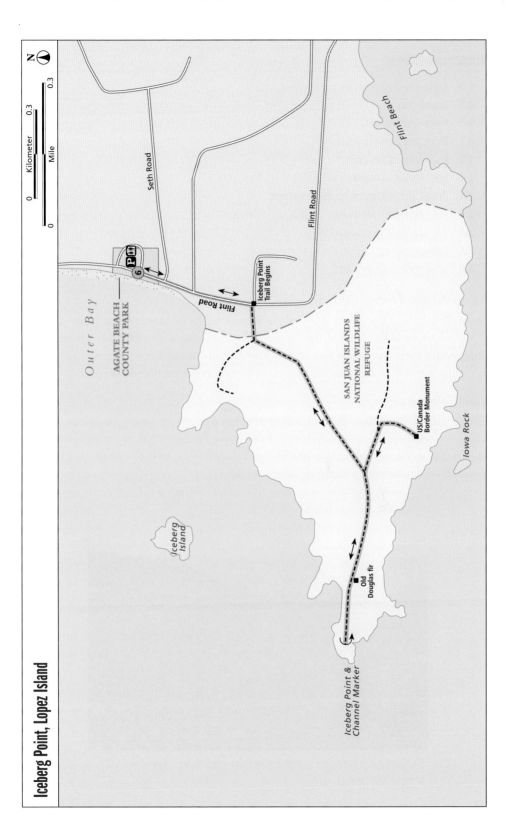

0.0   Agate Beach County Park parking area.

0.2   Gravel road.

0.5   Trail to Iceberg Point.

0.7   Stock gate / trail branches.

1.0   No bikes past this point.

1.2   Trail junction to monument.

1.4   United States–Canada border monument.

1.6   Trail junction to monument.

1.8   Trail junction / old Douglas fir.

2.6   Channel marker.

3.6   Arrive back at parking area.

Other Nearby Hiking Options

Point Coville and Chadwick Hill, in the Bureau of Land Management's San Juan National Monument, provide hiking through quiet forests to views of Admiralty Inlet. Shark Reef Sanctuary, part of San Juan County Parks, has a short trail to the water. Lopez Hill (www.lopezhill.org) is the highest point on the island.

Hike Information

At the parking area, Agate Beach County Park has a short trail underlain with wood chips. It wanders for a quick loop trip into the forest. Find the trail's beginning beside the outhouse. There's also a drop box to make donations as well as a Mutt Mitt dispenser to help you with picking up after your dog.

The bald hills and prairies of the San Juan Islands are stupendous with spring wildflowers.

7 Ebey's Landing Bluff Trail, Whidbey Island

Within the Ebey's Landing National Historic Reserve's 17,500 acres are a wealth of habitats that account for a wide variety of wildflowers. It's a stunning landscape here—rich in natural and human history. From the bluffs above Puget Sound, hikers and wildflower enthusiasts can see Gray whales migrating to and from the Bering Sea. The snowy caps of the Olympic Mountains are a constant spring and summer companion. The reserve also lies beneath the Pacific Flyway, and this equates to fantastic birding for migratory shorebirds and waterfowl.

Start: Parking lot for Ebey's Landing State Park
Distance: 3.5-mile loop
Hiking time: About 3–4 hours
Difficulty: Moderate
Trail surface: Sandy/rocky beach, hard-packed ground, gravel
Seasons: Year-round. Best wildflowers: April–August (May 16, 2015).
Other trail users: Trail runners
Canine compatibility: Leashed dogs allowed
Land status: National Park Service, Washington State Parks, Island County, The Nature Conservancy, and Town of Coupeville
Nearest town: Coupeville

Services: Gas, food, lodging. Camping at Fort Ebey State Park, Fort Casey State Park, and Island County's Rhododendron Park.
Permit: Discover Pass
Maps: USGS Coupeville; DeLorme Page 55 D-8
Trail contact: Ebey's Landing National Historic Reserve, National Park Service
Special considerations: The trail along the bluff has a precipitous drop-off that will make agoraphobics, acrophobics, and parents with small children quiver with concern for their safety. Unisex vault toilet located at trailhead. No potable water at trailhead.

Finding the trailhead: Approach Ebey's Landing either from the north, via Mount Vernon and Fidalgo Island, or from the Mukilteo-Clinton Ferry in the south. Follow WA 20 towards Coupeville for either route and turn south at Ebey Road. When the two-lane country road bends to the left (east), continue straight. This is a dangerous intersection, especially when farm vehicles are using the road, so keep a sharp lookout! Ebey Road continues all the way to the shoreline. Some maps show the road changing names to Ebey's Landing Road. Where the two-lane makes a sharp left to become Hill Road, turn right into a small gravel parking lot. **GPS: N48 11.549' / W122 42.509'**

Plants You Might See

Abronia latifolia, Yellow sand verbena, Nyctaginaceae
Achillea millefolium, Yarrow, Asteraceae
Fritillaria lanceolata, Chocolate lily, Liliaceae
Grindelia integrifolia, Gumweed, Asteraceae
Heterotheca villosa, Hairy false goldenaster, Asteraceae
Maianthemum dilatatum, False lily-of-the-valley, Liliaceae
Symphoricarpos albus, Snowberry, Caprifoliaceae

From the parking lot, head west to find the Bluff Trail past the vault toilet and a couple of weathered picnic benches. For the history of Ebey's Landing, stop at several reader boards.

In 100 feet of walking, come to a set of wooden stairs that climb the bluff above you and Admiralty Inlet. For the next 1.5 miles, the view to the south and west gets better and better. By the way, that's Marrowstone Island across the water and the Olympic Mountains you see.

The plant life on the prairie atop the bluff is a hodgepodge of natives and introduced species. On the weedy side, home gardeners will recognize Common mustard (*Brassica campestris*), Shepherd's purse (*Capsella bursa-pastoris*), Poison hemlock (*Conium maculatum*), Scot's broom (*Cytisus scoparius*), Orchard grass (*Dactylis glomerata*), Filaree (*Erodium cicutarium*), Pineapple weed (*Matricaria matricarioides*), Oysterplant (*Tragopogon dubius*), Salsify (*T. porrifolius*), and Stinging nettle (*Urtica dioica*).

Among the native herbs you'll discover along the trail are Fiddleneck (*Amsinckia intermedia*), Field chickweed (*Cerastium arvense*), Blue camas (*Camassia quamash*), Wooly eriophyllum (*Eriophyllum lanatum*), Spring gold (*Lomatium utriculatum*), Miniature lupine (*Lupinus bicolor*), Sleepy catchfly (*Silene scouleri*), and Death camas (*Toxicoscordion venenosus*).

Hiking along the bluff above Puget Sound at Ebey's Landing.

BOTANICAL NAMES

There are lots of books to help with identifying wildflowers.

What's in a name anyway? We get so hung up on identifying a particular plant, we forget there is more to the flower than its label. As Juliet tells Romeo in Shakespeare's play, "That which we call a rose by any other name would smell as sweet." The name can be a starting point, but the essence of understanding and appreciation requires more than a simple designation that "this is this."

From the beginning of written records, plant names have been passed down from one generation to the next. Anthropologists have discovered that where a written language doesn't exist, a strong oral tradition accomplishes the same thing. It seems we have always recognized the importance of knowing which plants can be eaten or used for clothing, construction, and medicine—and which plants to stay away from.

Plant taxonomists are botanists who use names not only to identify a plant, but to establish the relationship of one plant to another. A "species" is the basic recognition that a large number of individuals possess similar physical and genetic characterizations. One species that shows similarities to another species, but which has significant differences, can be placed into a "genus." Several genera that are closely related are placed into a "family." Most botanical-type people can identify plant families on sight, and many can also recognize plants all the way to genus and species.

Never let it be said that naming things has gotten any easier since the days of Adam. Being designed to show relationships between species, botanical (aka "Latin" or "scientific") names are also supposed to be conservative. That is, a botanical name should be as close to immutable as fallible human beings can make it. If only this was so! Taxonomists who find ways to divide one species from another like finely split hairs are called "splitters." Those who feel the other way around, that hairs must be grouped together, are called "lumpers." This helps account for the conundrum of changing botanical names.

Explore the distictive flora at Perrigo's Lagoon.

Reaching the top of the stairs, the route continues northwest and at 0.5 mile from the trailhead comes to a fence line. This is the boundary between Ebey's Landing State Park and the Nature Conservancy's Robert Y. Pratt Preserve. Pratt died in 1999 and in his will donated the 147 acres of land that constitute the Bluff Trail. A further 407-acre parcel was purchased after the Nature Conservancy organized Whidbey Island residents and other donors in a fund-raising campaign, which also saw significant federal money contributed.

From the property line a 1-mile round-trip trail takes off to the right (northeast) to the NPS visitor contact station and the historic Jacob Ebey House, Davis Blockhouse, and Sunnyside Cemetery. However, the Bluff Trail continues straight ahead (northwest) and begins to climb. There's plenty of Nootka rose (*Rosa nutkana*) here, and the Douglas fir forest, just ever so close to the spine of the bluff, stays slightly downhill on the lee side. Those trees exposed to the wind and salt spray have been grotesquely twisted and mangled. In the understory of the forest are Salal (*Gaultheria shallon*), Oceanspray (*Holodiscus discolor*), and Tall Oregon grape (*Mahonia aquifolium*). There are several side trails along the way that will take you to the forest for a look-see.

After 1.1 miles on the bluff, descend to the beach through tall grass with thick patches of the weedy Horehound (*Marrubium vulgare*). Reach the beach and Perrigo's Lagoon in 0.3 mile. Popping out in, around, and above the logs and driftwood is American dunegrass (*Leymus mollis*) and Black knotweed (*Polygonum paronychia*), plus

Gaultheria shallon, *Salal.*

Achillea millefolium, *Yarrow, is one of the most common wildflowers found in western Washington.*

Ebey's Landing Bluff Trail, Whidbey Island

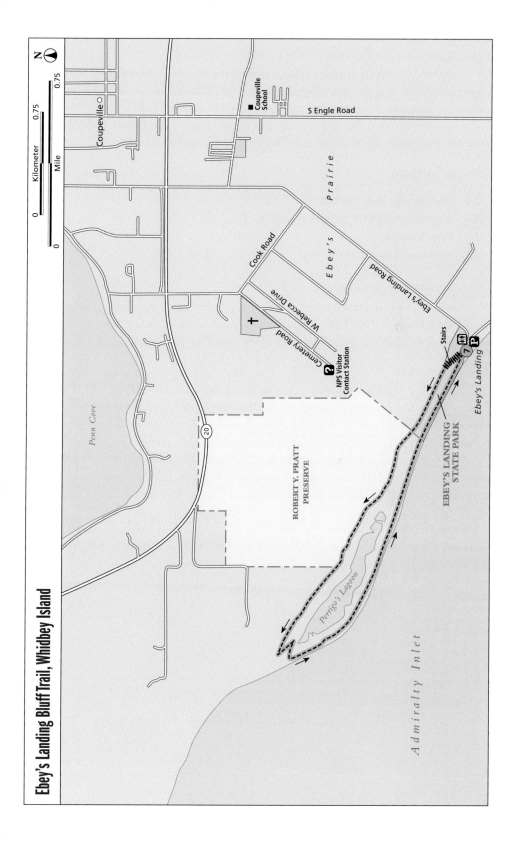

a native and a weedy Searocket (*Cakile edentula* and *C. maritima*). Check the lagoon for Pickleweed (*Salicornia perennis*), which survives the saline environment by sequestering salt within its stems and reduced leaves. If you're here after a storm, expect to see Torrey's surfgrass (*Phyllospadix torreyi*), washed up on the beach. It's a marine flowering plant that grows in about five to ten feet of cold Puget Sound water. From here, walk 1.6 miles along the beach to close the loop and return to your car.

Miles and Directions

- **0.0** Ebey's Landing State Park parking lot.
- **0.5** State park / Robert Y. Pratt Preserve boundary.
- **1.9** Perrigo's Lagoon.
- **3.5** Arrive back at parking lot.

Other Nearby Hiking Options

It's possible to walk along the beach at low tide on the Pacific Northwest National Scenic Trail between Fort Casey State Park, through Ebey's Landing State Park, to Fort Ebey State Park and on to Deception Pass State Park.

Hike Information

Ebey's Landing National Historic Reserve is the first unit of its kind within the National Park System. It is managed by the Trust Board of Ebey's Landing National Historic Reserve, a unit of local government created between the National Park Service, Washington State, Island County, town governments, and the residents of the Central Whidbey Island community. Much of the land within the reserve is in private ownership, with the NPS purchasing development rights to key sites while working cooperatively with Washington State Parks, Island County, and the Town of Coupeville for the ongoing protection of the historic rural landscape.

Island Transit provides free, but slow, bus service Monday through Friday on Whidbey Island. No service on weekends. For schedules visit their website at www .islandtransit.org.

8 Mount Erie-Sugarloaf Traverse, Whidbey Island

The City of Anacortes Parks and Recreation Department has nearly 2,800 acres of forest, wetlands, lakes, and meadows within its Community Forest Lands. Despite extensive logging that took place in the past, there's still old-growth forest to see. The land has been dedicated solely to recreation since 1991. What makes the Community Forest Lands so interesting is its mosaic of lakes, bogs and wetlands, low mountains, and rocky cliffs. Sugarloaf is a preferred hiking destination because it is inaccessible to cars. On the other hand, you can drive to the summit of Mount Erie, which has the best views. And that's why this hike begins there.

Start: Mount Erie parking lot
Distance: 4-mile lollipop and loop
Hiking time: About 3–4 hours
Difficulty: Easy to moderate
Trail surface: Forested path, rocky, asphalt road
Seasons: Year-round. Best wildflowers: March–June (May 23, 2015).
Other trail users: Rock climbers, bicyclists, and equestrians. Two-wheeled motorcycles are allowed in limited areas (check signs at trailheads and along trails).
Canine compatibility: Leashed dogs allowed
Land status: City of Anacortes

Nearest town: Anacortes
Services: Gas, food, lodging
Permits: None
Maps: Green Trails #41S Deception Pass; Anacortes Community Forest Lands maps; USGS Deception Pass and Anacortes South; DeLorme Page 41 H-10
Trail contacts: City of Anacortes; Friends of the Forest
Special considerations: Always carry a map. The maze of trails here makes it easy to get confused and lost. No potable water at trailhead. Chemical toilet at trailhead.

Finding the trailhead: From I-5 in Burlington, head west on WA 20 for 14 miles to Sharpes Corner and Campbell Lake Road and turn left (south). In another 2.8 miles turn right (north) on Heart Lake Road. In 1.5 miles turn right onto Mount Erie Road (signed) and continue 1.6 miles up the hill until reaching the summit of Mount Erie. Parking is limited. **GPS: N48 27.247' / W122 37.559'**

Plants You Might See

Claytonia perfoliata, Miner's lettuce, Montiaceae
Corallorhiza maculata, Spotted coralroot orchid, Orchidaceae
Heuchera micrantha, Small-flowered alumroot, Saxifragaceae
Lunula parviflora, Small-flowered woodrush, Juncaceae
Polystichum munitum, Sword fern, Polypodiaceae
Sambucus racemosa, Red elderberry, Adoxaceae
Tellima grandiflora, Fringecup, Saxifragaceae
Trientalis latifolia, Western starflower, Primulaceae

The Hike

The hikers-only Trail 216 begins opposite the microwave station and is marked by a small sign nailed to a convenient tree. Leaving the parking area, you immediately begin to lose elevation, plunging on a rocky, root-strewn trail through a lush and maturing second-growth Douglas fir, Western hemlock, and Western red cedar forest. The understory is thick with Salal (*Gaultheria shallon*), along with Thimbleberry (*Rubus parviflorus*), Nootka rose (*Rosa nutkana*), and the usual herbaceous associates of Douglas fir. In 0.1 mile come to a junction, turning right (northeast) and ignoring the waytrail on the left.

▶ Sugarloaf (1,044 feet) is Fidalgo Island's second-highest peak. Mount Erie (1,273 feet), 0.6 mile to the south, is the highest. On the summit of Mount Erie is a bronze statue by Philip McCracken called *Mountain Guardian.*

After 0.3 mile the trail almost succeeds in kissing Mount Erie Road but like a spurned lover, turns to the right and continues its downhill course. In 0.6 mile reach a wooden post gate, quickly followed by a junction with Trail 26 and Trail 207. Bear right (north) onto Trail 207 towards Whistle Lake. Don't be surprised if you see the occasional mountain biker or equestrian along here: This is a shared trail.

There are a lot of weedy species alongside this section of trail. First is Herb Robert (*Geranium robertianum*); its other common name is "Stinky Bob." The little

The Mount Erie–Sugarloaf Traverse trail is steep and root-strewn in places.

plant has a rank odor when its leaves are crushed. Other common weedy species through this section of forest are Stinging nettle (*Urtica dioica*) and Creeping buttercup (*Ranunculus repens*). The latter is easy to confuse with the decidedly non-weedy Large-leaved avens (*Geum macrophyllum*) also found here. Their leaves are somewhat similar, but avens flowers more closely resemble a yellow strawberry than the buttercup.

Claytonia sibirica, Candy flower. DAVE FLOTREE/ELLEN HAUPTMANN

Like Trail 216, Trail 207 loses elevation and in 0.2 mile reaches a junction with Trail 230. Motorcycles are allowed on Trail 230, but we're only on this uphill stretch for 0.3 mile until reaching another junction, this time with Trail 226. Turn left (west) and quickly come to, and pass, a junction with Trail 225. The forest is so thick and dark that it's startling to encounter the few breaks in the tree canopy where light streams in. Here you'll find Bigleaf maple, Red alder, and ferns galore.

The ascent of Sugarloaf begins in earnest, climbing steeply to a junction with the hikers–only Trail 238 in 0.3 mile. Turn left (west) and with 0.1 mile to go, reach the summit of Sugarloaf with its bald hill west face. On this dryer slope can be found woody species like Beach pine, Kinnikinnick (*Arctostaphylos uva-ursi*), Pacific madrone (*Arbutus menziesii*), and Oregon grape (*Mahonia nervosa*) along with herbs such as Blue camas (*Camassia quamash*) and Death camas (*Toxicoscordion venenosus*).

The trail goes over the top of Sugarloaf, descends, makes a 0.2-mile loop around the west face of the mountain, and meets Trail 228. Turn left (southwest) onto this hikers–only trail and see if you can spot the large patch of Twinflower (*Linnaea borealis*). This creeping semi-woody low shrub produces tiny white pendulous blooms with a pleasing aroma. The drier sections of Trail 228 are also home to Wooly eriophyllum (*Eriophyllum lanatum*), Harsh penstemon (*Castilleja hispida*), and Larkspur (*Delphinium menziesii*).

Arctostaphylos uva-ursi, Kinnikinnick. DAVE FLOTREE/ELLEN HAUPTMANN

In 0.2 mile there is a junction with the hikers-only Trail 215; turn left (south). Switchback steeply downhill, playing hide-and-seek with increasingly smaller and smaller dry meadows. After 0.3 mile come upon Mount Erie Road and turn left (southeast). Walk up the road 0.1 mile, passing

Mt. Erie–Sugarloaf Traverse, Whidbey Island

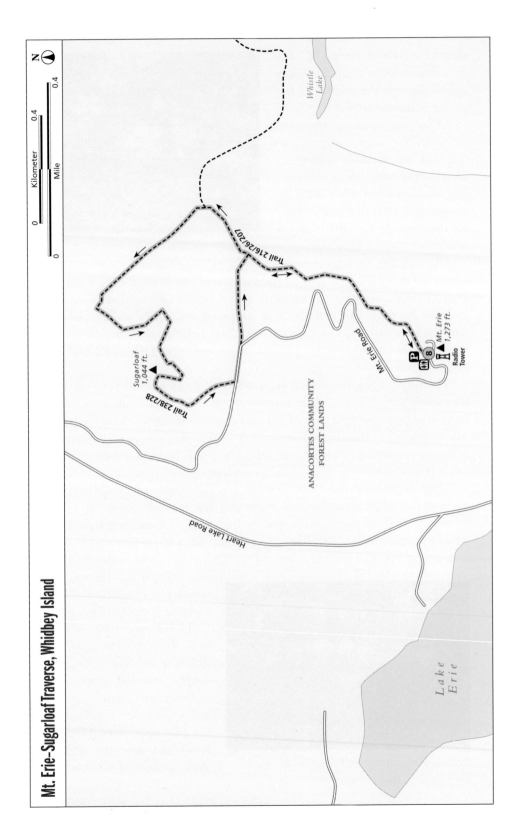

N

Kilometer
0   0.4   0.4

Mile
0   0.4

Whistle
Lake

Trail 216/26/207

Trail 238/228

Sugarloaf
1,044 ft.

ANACORTES COMMUNITY
FOREST LANDS

Mt. Erie Road

Heart Lake Road

P

8

Mt. Erie
1,273 ft.

Radio
Tower

Lake
Erie

a large patch of Skunk cabbage (*Lysichiton americanus*) to Trail 26 and turn left (east). You're likely to see horses here, or at least evidence they've been on the trail recently. Follow Trail 26 for 0.3 mile, where it makes a junction with Trail 216 and Trail 207. This should look familiar; you passed this way once before, early in the hike.

Turn right (south) onto Trail 216 and begin the painfully steep ascent to the summit of Mount Erie. It's only another mile, but it can feel much longer. When you reach the top, take a little extra time to wander around the summit to visit all the scenic viewpoints and enjoy the vistas. On a sunny day, Mount Baker looks close enough to touch. There are some bronze plaques scattered here and there, memorializing children who got too close to the edge of Mount Erie and fell to their deaths.

Miles and Directions

0.0 Trailhead on summit of Mount Erie.
0.1 Trail 216 / waytrail junction.
0.4 Trail 216 / Mount Erie Road junction.
1.0 Trail 216 / Trail 26 / Trail 207 junction.
1.2 Trail 207 / Trail 230 junction.
1.5 Trail 230 / Trail 226 junction.
1.8 Trail 226 / Trail 238 junction.
1.9 Sugarloaf summit.
2.1 Trail 238 / Trail 228 junction.
2.3 Trail 228 / Trail 215 junction.
2.6 Trail 215 / Mount Erie Road junction.
2.7 Mount Erie Road / Trail 26 junction.
3.0 Trail 26 / Trail 216 / Trail 207 junction.
4.0 Arrive back at trailhead.

Other Nearby Hiking Options

Deception Pass State Park, with campgrounds, saltwater access, and many miles of forest and beach trails, is a few miles to the south.

Hike Information

There are 50 miles of multiple-use trails in the Anacortes Community Forest Lands. The set of three Anacortes Community Forest Lands maps, published by the City of Anacortes, can be purchased at the nearby Lake Erie Grocery (junction of Heart Lake Road and Rosario Road).

Friends of the Forest is a nonprofit citizens' organization dedicated to the preservation of the Anacortes Community Forest Lands through education, outreach, and stewardship; PO Box 2213, Anacortes, WA 98221; http://friendsoftheacfl.org.

9 Goose Rock, Whidbey Island

At 484 feet, Goose Rock, in Deception Pass State Park, is the highest point on Whidbey Island. And Deception Pass is also considered Washington's most popular state park. Is it any wonder? The park offers three campgrounds, the Cornet Bay Retreat Center, and 3 miles of bike trails, 6 miles of horse trails, and 38 miles of hiking trails with 77,000 feet of saltwater shoreline. There are three sizable lakes, sand dunes, and dynamite views of Puget Sound. For plant lovers there is an old-growth forest and rhododendrons. All on 4,134 acres. The only thing marring this perfect place are the intermittent and unannounced flyovers by US Navy jets from nearby Whidbey Island Naval Air Station.

Start: West Beach parking lot at Cranberry Lake

Distance: 6.1-mile double loop

Hiking time: About 4–5 hours

Difficulty: Easy to moderate

Trail surface: Sand dune, forested path, asphalt, roadway

Seasons: Year-round. Best wildflowers: March–June (May 23, 2015).

Other trail users: Trail runners

Canine compatibility: Leashed dogs allowed

Land status: Washington State Parks

Nearest towns: Burlington (north) and Coupeville (south)

Services: Gas, food, lodging. Camping available within the park (reservations recommended). Restaurant, gas, and limited services at Seabolt's Smokehouse near park entrance.

Permit: Discover Pass

Maps: Green Trails #41S Deception Pass; USGS Deception Pass; DeLorme Page 55 A-9

Trail contacts: Washington State Parks, Deception Pass State Park; Deception Pass Park Foundation

Special considerations: Flush toilets, potable water, and picnic tables located at trailhead, North Beach, and Cranberry Lake at the park entrance. There is a fine for unleashed pets. Park hours are 6:30 a.m. to dusk, April through September; 8:00 a.m. to dusk, October through March.

Finding the trailhead: From the south, drive 20 miles on WA 20 from Coupeville to Deception Pass Road. Turn left (west) at the traffic signal. From the north, follow WA 20 from Burlington, crossing Fidalgo Island. After crossing the Deception Pass bridge, drive 1 mile and turn right (west) at the traffic signal on Deception Pass Road. Drive west for 0.9 mile, passing the park's campgrounds, to the trailhead for West Beach. **GPS: N48 23.971' / W122 39.844'**

Plants You Might See

Castilleja hispida, Harsh paintbrush, Orobanchaceae

Holodiscus discolor, Oceanspray, Rosaceae

Lithophragma parviflorum, Woodland star, Saxifragaceae

Maianthemum dilatatum, False lily-of-the-valley, Liliaceae

Orobanche uniflora, Naked broomrape, Orobanchaceae

Piperia elegans, Elegant rein-orchid, Orchidaceae

Rosa nutkana, Nootka rose, Rosaceae

Sambucus racemosa, Red elderberry, Adoxaceae

Sisyrinchium angustifolium, Blue-eyed grass, Iridaceae

Tellima grandiflora, Fringecup, Saxifragaceae

The Hike

Begin on the south side of the humongous West Beach parking area and pick up the trail beside the reader board and bicycle rack. Head out towards the food concession building and flush toilets on the right side of the asphalt Sand Dune Trail beside Cranberry Lake. Growing here are Yellow sand verbena (*Abronia latifolia*) and Beach morning glory (*Convolvulus soldanella*). Both plants have a big taproot that anchors them quite nicely in the shifting sand. Along the trail is the lovely blue-and-white Seashore lupine (*Lupinus littoralis*).

Rhododendron macrophyllum, *Pacific rhododendron.*

At the head of this 1.2-mile loop trail is a short path that leads through the dunes to West Beach. The predominant plants here are American dune grass (*Leymus mollis*) and a sedge (*Carex macrocephala*), both of which stabilize the sand dunes. You'll also see Searocket (*Cakile edentula*) and the deep-blue blossoms of Beach pea (*Lathyrus japonicus*) in and amongst the driftwood.

After enjoying this underappreciated community of sand dune plants, return through the forest along the other side of the loop. The forest contains Douglas fir,

Gaultheria shallon, *Salal.*

Sitka spruce, Beach pine, and shrubs like Salal (*Gaultheria shallon*) and Kinnikinnick (*Arctostaphylos uva-ursi*). There's also a smattering of Rocky Mountain juniper (*Juniperus scopulorum*) in there, uncommon along the coast. The long, stringy stuff hanging from the trees and shrubs is Methuselah's beard (*Usnea longissima*), a lichen that

Castilleja hispida, *Harsh paintbrush*.

thrives in this moist environment. Closer to Cranberry Lake you'll see Hooker's willow (*Salix hookeriana*) and Red alder.

Returning to the parking lot, head northward 0.2 mile and pick up the North Beach Trail for the main part of this wildflower hike. In 0.1 mile reach the campground amphitheater, pass through the parking lot, and pick up the trail again, which remains in the forest above gravelly and cobbled North Beach. There are some enormous Douglas fir along this stretch of trail along with Sitka spruce, Red alder, Western red cedar, and Western hemlock.

In 0.5 mile come to a group picnic site with a large shelter. The trail goes through another parking lot here (toilets and water available) and continues on the other side to two new trails. Take the one signed "Bridge .2 / Goose Rock .4" and begin a moderately steep and exposed forested climb protected by a wooden guardrail.

Growing in the bare rock you can expect to find Yarrow (*Achillea millefolium*), the canary-yellow blooms of Broad-leaved stonecrop (*Sedum spathulifolium*), and

Abronia latifolia, *Sand verbena*.

Thimbleberry (*Rubus parviflorus*). After 0.3 mile of climbing, there is a parking lot above you on the right (south) and the trail passes under the Deception Pass bridge (WA 20). Immediately find a sign with the disconcerting announcement that Goose Rock is *still* 0.4 mile away! Nevertheless, turn right (south) to follow this route. The trail climbs, sometimes steeply, and in 0.2 mile reaches a trail junction after first passing the James D. Endres Memorial Bench. Turn left (east) onto the NW Goose Rock Summit Trail. A hundred yards past that comes another trail junction, this time with a well-defined waytrail. Keep going straight ahead to remain on route.

The last 0.2 mile to the summit is steep. Goose Rock is a bald hill scraped clean by glaciers 11,000 years ago. Even after all this time, not enough soil has developed to support much else but herbaceous plants like Blue camas (*Camassia quamash*), Wooly eriophyllum (*Eriophyllum lanatum*), Self-heal (*Prunella vulgaris*), a carpet of moss, and some weedy grasses. On the edge of forest that includes Douglas fir and Beach pine is the red-barked Pacific madrone (*Arbutus menziesii*) and Kinnikinnick.

Continue straight across the summit and the trail begins to switchback steeply down. The plants on this side of Goose Rock reflect its southern exposure. The forest is thinner, there isn't as much Methuselah's beard hanging from the trees, and there are several dry

Rhododendron macrophyllum.

meadows and rocky outcrops. Towards the bottom of the hill, the forest regains its previous moister character. At 0.5 mile below the summit, enter a beautiful grove of Pacific rhododendron (*Rhododendron macrophyllum*), our state flower. You'll find the heaviest concentration of blooms alongside the trail where there is more light.

In another 0.3 mile reach a junction of the Summit Trail and the Goose Rock Perimeter Trail. Turn right (south) and in another 0.1 mile continue straight, onto the Lower Forest Trail. In 0.2 mile come to the restricted-access Cornet Bay Youth Camp (shown on maps as the Cornet Bay Retreat Center). The trail, now called the Discovery Trail, continues downhill for another 0.3 mile and reaches the Quarry Pond Campground. Walk 0.2 mile through the campground to Cornet Bay Road and follow this another 0.2 mile to the traffic signal at WA 20.

Once safely across the highway, walk alongside the park entrance road, past the picnic area and welcome center. The road curves to the left, and after 0.3 mile find the Cranberry Lake Trail. In another 0.3 mile cross the park road and find the trail, now called the West Beach Trail, on the other side. Follow this for 0.9 mile, always within shouting distance of the campground, to trail's end at the West Beach parking lot and trailhead.

Miles and Directions

0.0 West Beach parking lot and trailhead.

0.6 End of Sand Dune Loop Trail.

1.2 Return to parking lot.

1.4 Trailhead for North Beach Trail.

1.5 Campground amphitheater.

2.0 Group picnic site and shelter / North Beach parking lot.

2.1 Goose Rock trailhead.

2.4 Pass under Deception Pass bridge (WA 20).

2.6 NW Goose Rock Summit Trail junction.

Goose Rock, Whidbey Island

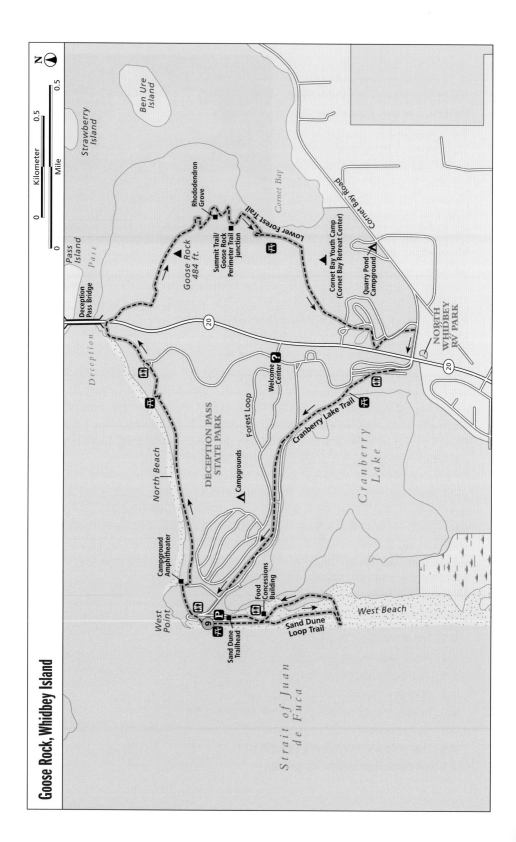

N

Kilometer
0   0.5

0   0.5
Mile

Strawberry Island

Ben Ure Island

Pass Island

Pass

Deception Pass Bridge

Deception

Rhododendron Grove

Goose Rock 484 ft.

Summit Trail/ Goose Rock Perimeter Trail junction

Cornet Bay

Lower Forest Trail

Cornet Bay Youth Camp (Cornet Bay Retreat Center)

Quarry Pond Campground

Cornet Bay Road

NORTH WHIDBEY RV PARK

20

Welcome Center

Forest Loop

DECEPTION PASS STATE PARK

Campgrounds

North Beach

Cranberry Lake Trail

Cranberry Lake

20

Campground Amphitheater

West Point

Sand Dune Trailhead

P

9

Food Concessions Building

West Beach

Sand Dune Loop Trail

Strait of Juan de Fuca

2.8 Goose Rock summit.

3.3 Rhododendron grove.

3.6 Summit Trail / Goose Rock Perimeter Trail junction.

3.7 Lower Forest Trail junction.

3.9 Cornet Bay Youth Camp (Cornet Bay Retreat Center).

4.2 Quarry Pond Campground.

4.6 WA 20 / traffic signal.

4.9 Cranberry Lake Trail.

5.2 Cross Park Road. Trail becomes West Beach Trail.

6.1 Arrive back at trailhead and parking lot.

Other Nearby Hiking Options

There are also trails at nearby Hoypus Point Natural Forest Area on Whidbey Island. Across Deception Pass are hiking trails on Fidalgo Island, in the north unit of the park, around Bowman Bay and Lighthouse Point.

Hike Information

The Deception Pass Park Foundation is a 501(c)(3) nonprofit corporation formed in 2005 to address the disparity between the lack of money available to the park from the State of Washington and the funding backlog of education projects and resource protection. In the intervening years they have built bridges (literally and figuratively), started a junior ranger program to educate the next generation of Deception Pass Park lovers, and supplied interpretive signs and displays. Their periodical publication is called *The Current*. For more information visit www.deceptionpassfoundation.org/about.

Mountain Loop Highway

The South Fork of the Stillaguamish River has always drawn people for its beauty and for its challenges. Loggers and miners fought the land, not only to extract its resources, but to get those resources to market through the river's narrow Robe Canyon. Early attempts at building a railroad met with abject failure and millions of dollars washed away by winter floods and the raging whitewater river.

Over the years the Stillaguamish has defied mankind to conquer it. At times the river has been beaten, but it always comes back bigger and stronger. Even today the Mountain Loop Highway through the South Fork of the Stillaguamish River is closed every winter by snow.

The beautiful Stillaguamish River at lower flows.

10 Robe Canyon Historic Park–Lime Kiln Trail

Part of the Lime Kiln Trail follows the old Everett–Monte Cristo Railroad (built 1892–93 and abandoned 1933), which was used to haul timber from the forests upstream, copper ore from the Wayside Mine, and silver and gold from the town of Monte Cristo. In 1936 the tracks were pulled up and sold to companies in Japan for scrap. At trail's end you wind up at a rock-and-mortar lime kiln. It was built circa 1900 to provide anhydrous lime, from a nearby limestone quarry, which was used as a whitening agent at the Lowell paper mill. The lime was also used as a flux agent, helping in the process of melting ore for smelters in Everett.

Start: Robe Canyon Historic Park
Distance: 7.0 miles out and back
Hiking time: About 4 hours
Difficulty: Easy
Trail surface: Forested path, historic railroad grade
Seasons: Spring, summer, and fall. Best wildflowers: April–May (May 3, 2015).
Other trail users: Trail runners, equestrians
Canine compatibility: Leashed dogs allowed
Land status: Snohomish County Parks; private property
Nearest towns: Granite Falls and Lake Stevens

Services: Gas in Granite Falls; gas, food, lodging in Lake Stevens
Permits: None
Maps: Green Trails #109 Granite Falls; USGS Granite Falls; USDAFS Mount Baker-Snoqualmie National Forest; DeLorme Page 57 E-7
Trail contact: Snohomish County Department of Parks and Recreation
Special considerations: No toilet at trailhead. No potable water at trailhead or on trail. Stinging nettle and Devil's club. Stillaguamish River is cold and swift with dangerous rapids and is not suitable for swimming.

Finding the trailhead: From the town of Granite Falls on WA 92, turn right onto S. Alder Avenue. Turn left at a T intersection onto E. Pioneer Street (becomes Menzel Lake Road). In about 1 mile turn left onto Waite Mill Road. Follow this for a short distance and, after passing a school bus turnaround, bear left at the Y and follow a short gravel road uphill to the trailhead and parking lot for Robe Canyon Historic Park. **GPS: N48 04.640' / W121 55.932'**

Plants You Might See

Claytonia sibirica, Candy flower, Montiaceae
Lysichitum americanus, Skunk cabbage, Araceae
Rubus spectabilis, Salmonberry, Rosaceae
Sambucus racemosa, Red elderberry, Adoxaceae
Trillium ovatum, Trillium, Liliaceae

The Hike

At the reader board beside the trailhead, study up on the history of the Everett–Monte Cristo Railroad. Begin the hike in a nice Douglas fir and Western hemlock

A hiker crosses the creek amidst springtime flowers.

forest with a healthy understory of Sword fern (*Polystichum munitum*). Judging by the occasional tree stumps viewed through the thick second-growth, this used to be a forest of giants. No longer. On the other hand, the Bigleaf maples are of truly impressive size.

After 0.2 mile the trail enters private property for the next 0.8 mile. Please stay on the trail. Red alder is common along this stretch of trail and so is Hazelnut (*Corylus cornuta*). In every wet spot it seems are the bright yellow flowers and shiny green leaves of Western buttercup (*Ranunculus occidentalis*).

Dicentra formosa, *Bleeding heart.*

In 0.7 mile come to a trail junction and turn right (east). The left fork is blocked off. Expect to start seeing loads of Thimbleberry (*Rubus parviflorus*).

At 1.0 mile the trail splits; turn left (east) here, following the sign to Robe Canyon Park and Lime Kiln. At 1.2 miles enter Robe Canyon Historic Park and at 1.4 miles cross over Hubbard Creek on a substantial bridge. Quickly come to another trail junction and turn left (west) where a sign informs you that only hikers may proceed past this point. Horses must turn around.

The trail now begins to drop steeply and the understory of Sword fern and Hazelnut, which has been absent for nearly a mile, returns. Far below can be heard the roar of the South Fork Stillagua-mish River. Seeps along the uphill side of the trail are perfect for find-

Historic artifacts left over from the Lime Kiln.

ing Bleeding heart (*Dicentra formosa*) and Fringecup (*Tellima grandiflora*). If solely judging by its name, the latter wildflower disappoints. In the spring, both species remain common blooms all the rest of the way.

After 1.9 miles comes a sidehill bridge over a portion of the hillside that has slid away. There is also a nice view of the river down below, wide and placid in this one spot. Kayakers affectionately call the river the "Stilly" and prize it for its challeng-ing—some say, dangerous—whitewater. Nowhere along this stretch of river is it safe to swim, as the water is swift, cold, and dangerous. You are now traversing the old Monte Cristo Railroad grade.

In short order, cross a log bridge (with convenient handrail) and then another sidehill bridge. Keep your eyes open and you may see Lady fern (*Adiantum pedatum*). There are huge Bigleaf maples here too, and they're all covered from ground to canopy with moss and epiphytic ferns.

Reach Cutoff Junction in 2.5 miles. Don't be disappointed because there is no cutoff trail here. It appears to be a place-name, but the meaning is not clear. After hiking 3.0 miles is the Lime Kiln, a bulky stone and brick structure (note the lack of mortar between the stones) standing about 25 feet tall and covered with epiphytic ferns.

From here the trail continues in a fairly level 0.8-mile loop to the river with a short side trail dropping steeply to the water. This is an ideal place for a picnic lunch beside the Stilly. Keep in mind that just below and around the corner there is an impressive river-wide rapid. It is wise to ignore the large, deep, inviting pool at your feet and remain on dry land. From here, turn around and retrace your route to the trailhead and parking lot.

Miles and Directions

0.0   Robe Canyon Historic Park trailhead and parking lot.

0.2   Enter private property.

0.7   Trail junction.

Robe Canyon Historic Park–Lime Kiln

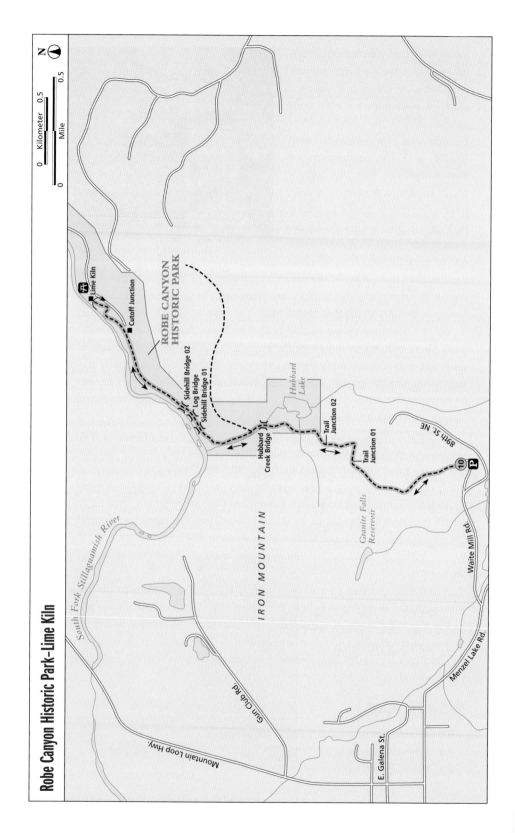

0.8 Leave private property.

1.0 Robe Canyon Park and Lime Kiln sign.

1.9 Sidehill bridge.

2.5 Cutoff Junction.

3.0 Lime Kiln.

3.5 South Fork Stillaguamish River.

7.0 Arrive back at trailhead and parking lot.

Other Nearby Hiking Options

At the picnic spot below the Lime Kiln there used to be a railroad bridge spanning the South Fork Stillaguamish River. Had it not washed away years ago, it could have connected the two sections of Robe Canyon Historic Park. See hike 11.

Hike Information

Robe Canyon Historic Park was established in 1995 when Snohomish County purchased 160 acres encompassing the original town site of Robe at the head of the South Fork Stillaguamish's Robe Canyon. Additions in 1997 and 2001 to the park increased its size to the current 970 acres on both sides of the river. The trails through these two sections were built, and are maintained, by volunteers.

Sharp and rusted artifacts from the area's logging and railroad days lie hidden alongside the trail in the vegetation. Wildflower hunters should exhibit extreme caution in where they step or place their hands. Previous hikers have gathered up some of the larger and more interesting pieces and have placed them on display at the kiln and alongside the trail. Please leave them for others to enjoy. Snohomish County prosecutes people who remove historic artifacts.

The Lime Kiln Trail provides wildflower lovers access to a portion of the historic Everett–Monte Cristo Railroad—abandoned since 1933.

Back in the day, some men with a lot of money believed they could thumb their noses at nature and build a railroad through Robe Canyon. They called it the Monte Cristo Railroad, after the upriver gold-mining town. There was a town here as well and they called it Robe, after one of the area's early settlers. After a few years of seeing their investment get washed away by the South Fork Stillaguamish River or covered with rock and fallen trees due to landslides, the money men gave up.

Over a hundred years after the fact, these men's folly has given hikers and wild-flower lovers access to a wonderful canyon with vertical rock walls and hanging gardens. Many parts of the trail are narrow or washed away, so care is warranted.

Start: OLD ROBE CANYON sign on south side of WA 92, the Mountain Loop Highway
Distance: 3.0 miles out and back
Hiking time: About 2-3 hours
Difficulty: Strenuous
Trail surface: Forested path, old railroad bed, rocky
Seasons: Spring, summer, and fall. Best wild-flowers: March-June (May 26, 2015).
Other trail users: None
Canine compatibility: Leashed dogs allowed
Land status: Snohomish County of Depart-ment of Parks and Recreation
Nearest town: Granite Falls

Services: Gas, food, lodging
Permits: None
Maps: Green Trails #109; USGS Granite Falls; USDAFS Mount Baker-Snoqualmie National Forest; DeLorme Page 96 D-2
Trail contact: Snohomish County Department of Parks and Recreation
Special considerations: Loose and slippery rock, exposure, cliffs, trail washouts, and sections of trail missing. No potable water or toilet at trailhead. Stinging nettle alongside the trail in lots of places. Not recommended for children.

Finding the trailhead: From the town of Granite Falls, drive 7.1 miles east on WA 92, the Mountain Loop Highway. Park on the right (south) side of the highway beside the brick trail sign structure. **GPS: N48 06.617' / W121 51.401'**

Plants You Might See

Claytonia perfoliata, Miner's lettuce, Montiaceae
Cornus sericea, Redosier dogwood, Cornaceae
Dicentra formosa, Bleeding heart, Papaveraceae
Geranium robertianum, Stinky Bob, Geraniaceae
Geum macrophyllum, Large-leaved avens, Rosaceae
Polystichum munitum, Sword fern, Polypodiaceae
Rubus parviflorus, Thimbleberry, Rosaceae
Rubus spectabilis, Salmonberry, Rosaceae
Sambucus racemosa, Red elderberry, Adoxaceae
Typha latifolia, Cattail, Typhaceae

The Hike

The wooden sign announcing the Old Robe Trail has a history of being vandalized. The brick structure around it resembles an old bread oven. There are some warning signs at the trailhead: One says that shooting guns is not allowed; the other informs pet owners that this is a dangerous trail for unleashed dogs.

Find the wide trail behind the signs and begin walking through a maturing forest of, mostly, Western hemlock. There's also a lot of Rocky Mountain maple (*Acer glabrum*). The ground is so moist, it is covered by many species of moss. Plenty of Small-flowered alumroot (*Heuchera micrantha*), Deer fern (*Blechnum spicant*), and Bracken fern (*Pteridium aquilinum*) can be found. Everybody's least favorite, the spiny and prickly Devil's club (*Oplopanax horridus*), can be found where the sun manages to make its way to the forest floor.

Quickly come to some more signs. These tell you the trail is dangerous for children and is closed after 1.2 miles. A waytrail, marked by a painted 4-by-4 post, off to your right (west) leads to a nicely situated picnic bench. Beyond the signs the trail switchbacks down the hill for 0.4 mile and ends in a lovely old Red alder grove.

In another 0.1 mile you come to signs announcing park hours, no camping and no fires, no alcohol and no motorized vehicles. All of this means that you are officially within the boundaries of Robe Historic Park. The trail here is wide and appears to be an old wagon road. It's pretty marshy too, so you're guaranteed of seeing mosquitoes

The mighty Stillaguamish River.

Tellima grandiflora, *Fringecup*. Dave Flotree/
Ellen Hauptmann

during spring and summer. Standing water means Red alder, Skunk cabbage (*Lysichiton americanus*), and Scouring rush (*Equisetum hyemale*) are in abundance.

In another 0.2 mile reach the South Fork Stillaguamish River. There are some grand-looking Bigleaf maples along the river, and a little further on you come to a delightful river view with a humongous Sitka spruce. The trail through here is constantly wet; it's in the flood zone of the river. Skunk cabbage and Scouring rush reappear and there is also a sedge (*Scirpus cyperinus*). You'll also see Fringecup (*Tellima grandiflora*) growing intertwined with another gorgeously subtle member of the Saxifrage family, Piggyback plant (*Tolmiea menziesii*).

The trail crosses a creek in 0.4 mile and shortly crosses another (seasonally dry). Some waytrails will take you quickly to a nice swamp, if that sort of thing pleases you. The walls of the canyon start to close in and narrow. This is the place highly experienced whitewater kayakers love. You'll see tall and wide hanging gardens of Maidenhair fern (*Adiantum pedatum*) festooned everywhere through the Robe Canyon gorge,

Adiantum pedatum, *Maidenhair fern*.

thriving in all the moisture seeping across the rock. It's likely you'll also be tripping over lots of Scouler's valerian (*Valeriana scouleri*) through here too.

The trail along this section is the old Monte Cristo Railroad bed. Tired of seeing their railroad washed away, the builders laid a concrete slab into which they embedded rails and ties. As you can see, it didn't work.

In another 0.1 mile come to the official end of the maintained trail. The way becomes rougher and rougher, requiring you to clamber over large rocks that have fallen from the gorge walls. In about 0.1 mile Monte Cristo Railroad tunnel 6 is reached. It's dark inside but lit well enough from either end to see your way through. Expect water and slippery rock. Another 0.1 mile and you're at the much shorter tunnel 5. A landslide makes further travel problematic. The adventurous can continue on another 0.2 mile to the collapsed tunnel 3 and a tall retaining wall

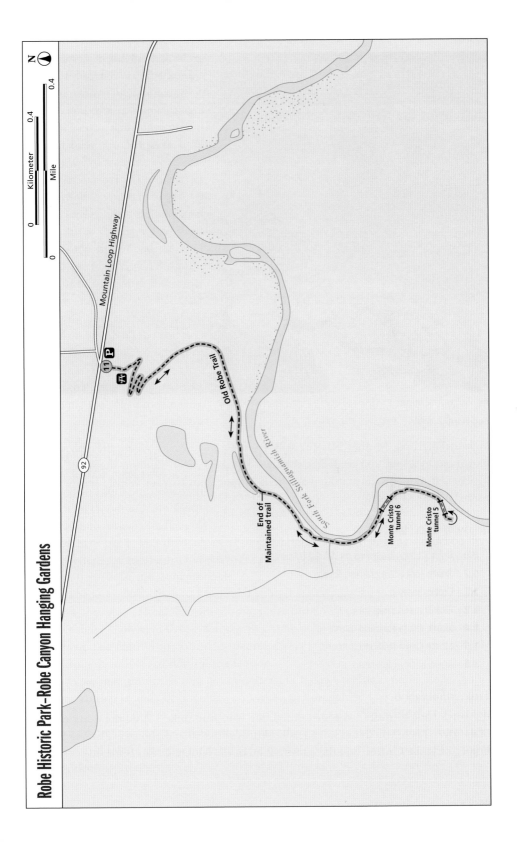

Robe Historic Park–Robe Canyon Hanging Gardens

Mountain Loop Highway

92

11

P

Old Robe Trail

End of
Maintained trail

South Fork Stillaguamish River

Monte Cristo
tunnel 6

Monte Cristo
tunnel 5

N

Kilometer
0   0.4

Mile
0   0.4

The mighty Stillaguamish is a wild, rip-snorting, fast and furious river cutting through a rocky and narrow defile.

built to hold back Mother Nature's will. There's a huge cavity where the wall was blown out by a slide and eroded by the river. Kayakers call it "Hole-in-the-Wall."

Back at tunnel 5, turn around and retrace your steps to your vehicle where it's parked on the Mountain Loop Highway.

Miles and Directions

0.0 Robe Canyon trailhead on WA 92 (Mountain Loop Highway).

0.7 South Fork Stillaguamish River.

1.1 Creek crossing.

1.2 End of maintained trail.

1.4 Monte Cristo Railroad tunnel 6.

1.5 Monte Cristo Railroad tunnel 5.

3.0 Arrive back at trailhead.

Hike Information

It's worthwhile to make a detour to the Lime Kiln Trail (hike 10) on the other side of the river. There you'll find some reader boards with text and photos explaining the history of Robe Canyon and the construction of the Monte Cristo Railroad.

Southwest Washington Coast

The long spit of sand stretching northward from Cape Disappointment to Leadbetter Point is a unique geological feature. On the west, the sand holds back the Pacific Ocean and on the east, holds in Willapa Bay. On both extremes and in the middle, the Long Beach Peninsula helps support equally unique sand dune forests with their distinctive flora. There are also shallow ponds with both freshwater and saltwater marsh aquatic vegetation.

With an economy based on tourism and growing cranberries, the area is also filled with historical significance. In the north, Oysterville preserves its heritage as a former county seat and the center of an expansive nineteenth-century fishery. In the south, the area is significant for the visit in 1805 by Captain William Clark and eleven of his men, members of the Lewis and Clark Expedition, Voyage of Discovery.

North Head Lighthouse

12 North Head Lighthouse, Cape Disappointment State Park

There are plenty of reasons for this hike besides classic Pacific Northwest wildflowers. The biggest reason is to see, no, experience the impressive and massively huge Sitka spruce along the trail. The other reasons are historical: the North Head Lighthouse, a World War I gun battery, and the nearby November 18, 1805, campsite of Captain William Clark and eleven of his men while exploring this area.

Start: Across the road from the parking area with monuments and interpretive displays dedicated to the Lewis and Clark Expedition
Distance: 4.8 miles out and back
Hiking time: About 3–4 hours
Difficulty: Moderate
Trail surface: Forested path, short bit of gravel road and concrete path
Seasons: Year-round. Best wildflowers: April–May (July 2, 2015).
Other trail users: Trail runners
Canine compatibility: Leashed dogs allowed
Land status: Washington State Parks
Nearest town: Ilwaco

Services: Gas, food, lodging. Two campgrounds at Cape Disappointment State Park. A small restaurant with an extensive menu of pizza and seafood along with limited camper items is available at the Cape D Cafe opposite the park entrance.
Permit: Discover Pass
Maps: USGS Cape Disappointment; DeLorme Page 95 F-7
Trail contact: Cape Disappointment State Park
Special considerations: Potable water and toilets available 0.3 mile east of trailhead at the campground. Seasonally (primarily in winter) wet, muddy, and slippery trail with lots of big tree roots.

Finding the trailhead: From Ilwaco, drive south on the WA 100 loop road for 3.5 miles, following signs to Cape Disappointment. Turn right (west) into the park, passing through the entrance station. Make an immediate right (north) turn onto the main campground road and pass by Lake O'Neil. The unsigned trailhead parking is a gravel lot on your left (south) in 0.3 mile with several monuments and displays documenting Lewis and Clark's Voyage of Discovery. Cross the road, turn left (west), and find the trailhead in 0.1 mile. **GPS: N46 17.135' / W124 03.787'**

Plants You Might See

Carex obnupa, Slough sedge, Cyperaceae
Erythranthe guttata, Monkeyflower, Phrymaceae
Lysichiton americanus, Skunk cabbage, Araceae
Maianthemum racemosum, False Solomon's seal, Liliaceae
Marah oreganus, Manroot, Cucurbitaceae
Rubus parviflorus, Thimbleberry, Rosaceae
Tellima grandiflora, Fringecup, Saxifragaceae
Tolmiea menziesii, Piggy-back plant, Saxifragaceae
Vancouveria hexandra, Inside-out flower, Berberidaceae

The Hike

The trail begins beside a colorful map of Cape Disappointment State Park and an interpretive display showing how the cape's shoreline has changed since 1805 when it was first mapped by Captain William Clark. Proceed north through an old-growth forest of Sitka spruce and old, tall Red alder. This first stretch of trail has several interpretive signs covering the Lewis and Clark Expedition. The understory consists of tall and robust Salal (*Gaultheria shallon*) and Sword fern (*Polystichum munitum*). The understory has carpets of False lily-of-the-valley (*Maianthemum dilatatum*). Being so close to the shallow and marshy Lake O'Neil, expect to make donations of blood to the local mosquito population.

The trail rises gently, passing many fine specimens of Sitka spruce. Watch your step where the spruce roots cross the trail. It's easy to trip. The tree is easily recognized by its bark; it looks as if someone has gone through the forest and glued corn flakes on the trunks of all the trees!

In 1.1 miles is a bench. No views to distant shores here, but there are plenty of big spruce to take your breath away. The path can be in poor repair, with frequent muddy spots; these places have been partially bridged with planks or lumber. The way is also frequently overgrown.

In another 0.4 mile come to stairs and a boardwalk, complete with handrails, to bridge an ephemeral creek. Keep an eye out for typical streamside and moist-ground

Cape Disappointment area.

COMMON NAMES FOR PLANTS

Botany students in their taxonomy classes are taught to identify unknown plants using dichotomous keys in regional or state floras. At the end of what can be a long process, observing the unknown's characteristics and measuring this or that feature, the student arrives at the (hopefully) correct name in the form of genus+species. This is called the "Latin" name, or "scientific" name, or (more properly) the "botanic" name.

The amateur botanist and wildflower enthusiast flips through a field guide, comparing illustrations and photographs to that same unknown, and fairly soon comes up with the correct "common," or "vernacular," name.

Neither method is more correct than the other, since the purpose of identifying the unknown is the same: The thirst for knowledge has been satiated; a mystery has been solved.

Take time to stop and appreciate the flowers along the trail.

Beginning with a name, we start learning something new about the world around us.

Vernacular names don't reveal the relationships between different species as do botanic names, so plant taxonomists don't like to use them. Wildflower enthusiasts may be interested in these relationships, but if all they want to do is satisfy their curiosity about what to call that unknown, common names are perfectly fine.

A problem everyone has with common names is that they aren't standardized. They can change from one area to another. For instance, what we call Fireweed (*Chamerion angustifolium*) in Washington is called Great willow-herb in Canada and Rosebay willowherb in Great Britain. Then again, Fireweed was once called *Epilobium angustifolium* by taxonomists. So, who is to complain about inconsistent common names?

Some people don't like botanic names. They say they can't get their tongues around the Latin words. But they have no issue with Chrysanthemum, or Rhododendron, or Anemone—all of which are both a common name and a botanic name.

There are also loads of plants with no common name. In these cases, nature books and field guides make up a vernacular name by adopting or slightly modifying the botanic name. For instance, *Angelica genuflexa* translates to Kneeling angelica. *Balsamorhiza serrata* becomes Serrate balsamroot. Botanically speaking, *Saxifraga mertensiana* becomes Merten's saxifrage, vernacularly speaking. And so on and so forth. It turns out there is no reason to avoid using common *or* botanic names!

vegetation like Field chickweed (*Cerastium arvense*), Bleeding heart (*Dicentra formosa*), Horsetail (*Equisetum* spp.), Large-leaved avens (*Geum macrophyllum*), Small-flowered alumroot (*Heuchera micrantha*), Pacific waterleaf (*Hydrophyllum tenuipes*), buttercups (*Ranunculus* spp.), Hooded lady's tresses (*Spiranthes romanzoffiana*), and some violets (*Viola* spp.).

In 0.2 mile there are some breaks in the trees along with views to the Pacific Ocean. The trail then climbs abruptly and in 0.2 mile reaches the paved parking lot for North Head Lighthouse. If you don't need to use the vault toilets here, turn left (west) and make you way down along a wide gravel road for 0.2 mile to the lighthouse. On your right are two large homes that housed lighthouse keepers and their families back in the days before lighthouses were automated.

The views from the lighthouse are stupendous, though it can be a bit breezy at times. The trail down here is actually a loop; the return route is a concrete path once used by the lighthouse keepers. What a nice commute to work! The way back passes by the Lighthouse Keeper's Store with a gift shop on one side and displays on the other. It's well worth a visit.

Retail therapy and historical interest satisfied, find your way back to the trail in the parking lot and reverse your route to the North Head trailhead. But when you get there, don't go right to your car and drive away. Read the displays about the Lewis and Clark Expedition and then hike up the steep 0.2-mile trail to McKenzie Head. Captain William Clark climbed up here in 1805 (from the beach side) and commented on the lack of vegetation, except for some "coarse grass." The grass is still here, but the head is now completely forested, demonstrating that change does exist in the natural world.

Gaultheria shallon, *Salal.*

On top you'll also find some interpretive signs plus Battery 247, part of coastal fortifications built during the nineteenth and twentieth centuries to protect the entrance to the Columbia River from foreign warships in time of war. The guns are gone, but the gearing to make them move is still there. The interior of the fortification can be explored; a flashlight is

Clarkia amoena, *Farewell-to-spring.*

North Head Lighthouse, Cape Disappointment State Park

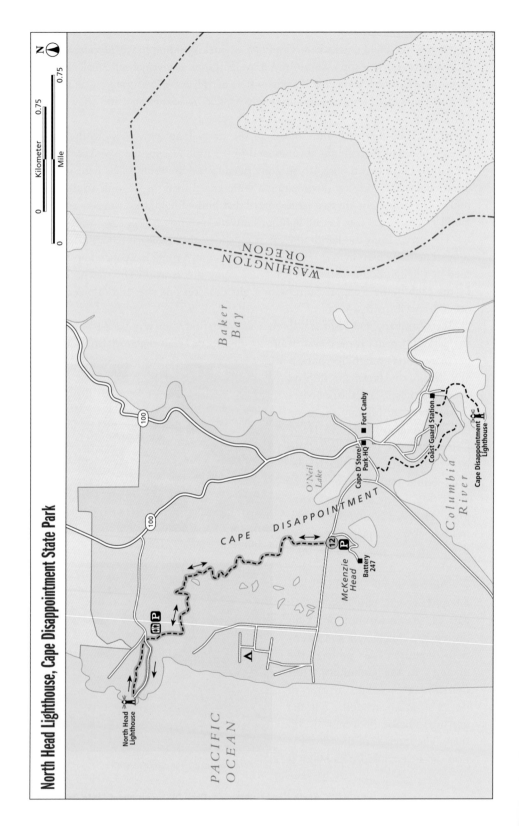

N

0   Kilometer   0.75

0   Mile   0.75

PACIFIC OCEAN

North Head Lighthouse

100

100

Baker Bay

O'Neil Lake

CAPE DISAPPOINTMENT

Cape D Store/ Park HQ

Fort Canby

Coast Guard Station

12

McKenzie Head

Battery 247

Columbia River

Cape Disappointment Lighthouse

WASHINGTON

OREGON

a good idea. Once done with McKenzie Head, make your way back down the hill to your car and, now, you may drive away.

Miles and Directions

0.0 North Head Lighthouse trailhead.

1.1 Bench.

1.5 Boardwalk creek crossing.

1.9 North Head parking lot.

2.1 North Head Lighthouse.

4.4 Arrive back at trailhead.

4.6 Top of McKenzie Head / Battery 247.

4.8 Return to parking area.

Other Nearby Hiking Options

The Discovery Trail on the north end of Cape Disappointment State Park connects the town of Ilwaco to the Pacific Ocean via Beards Hollow. The Coastal Forest Trail is a short loop on the park's east side with views of Baker Bay. From the Lewis and Clark Interpretive Center, it is a short walk to visit coastal fortifications and the Cape Disappointment Lighthouse.

Hike Information

Guided tours of the North Head Lighthouse are available; small fee for ages 18 and up (free for children). North Head vacation rentals for the old lighthouse keeper houses can be made by calling (888) 226-7688 or online at https://Washington.going tocamp.com.

13 Martha Jordan Birding Trail, Leadbetter Point State Park

This is one of those hidden trails not many hikers know about because it hasn't been written up anywhere and it doesn't appear on maps—not even the Leadbetter State Park map. It isn't the most spectacular hiking experience—there are no sweeping vistas, and most of the way is on a road—but the rewards are manifest. First is the opportunity of see one of Washington's sensitive-listed plants, *Hydrocotyl ranunculoides*, along with a huge freshwater pond. Second, the newest section of trail meanders through a mature sand dune forest of Sitka spruce and Beach pine, affording an opportunity to experience this amazing ecosystem up close and personal.

Start: Parking lot for Martha Jordan Birding Trail, Leadbetter Point State Park
Distance: 3.0 miles out and back
Hiking time: About 2-3 hours
Difficulty: Easy
Trail surface: Gravel road, forested path, sand dune
Seasons: Year-round. Best wildflowers: April–May (July 2, 2015).
Other trail users: None
Canine compatibility: Leashed dogs allowed

Land status: Washington State Parks, Leadbetter Point State Park
Nearest town: Ocean Park
Services: Gas, food, lodging
Permit: Discover Pass
Maps: USGS Oysterville; DeLorme Page 95 B-7
Trail contact: Leadbetter Point State Park
Special considerations: No water or toilets at trailhead. Vault toilets (no potable water) are located 0.9 mile farther north at the southern trailhead for the Dune Forest loop trail.

Finding the trailhead: From Ocean Park, drive north on WA 103 for about 8 miles to the entrance to Leadbetter Point State Park. Immediately after passing the park sign/boundary, turn left (west) into the large gravel parking lot. **GPS: N46 35.308' / W124 01.798'**

Plants You Might See

Berula erecta, Cut-leaved water parsnip, Apiaceae
Carex obnupa, Slough sedge, Cyperaceae
Oenanthe sarmentosa, Water parsley, Apiaceae
Potamogeton natans, Floating-leaved pondweed, Potamogetonaceae
Sambucus racemosa, Red elderberry, Adoxaceae

The Hike

At the south end of the parking area, find the trailhead beside the sign welcoming you to the Martha Jordan Birding Trail. In 0.1 mile the trail intersects a wide, gravel road and the way turns right (west). To the left (east) is a fancy, and locked, wrought-iron entry gate. Check out the amusing sign signaling that a Sasquatch has been sighted in the area.

Large freshwater ponds are common on the Long Beach Peninsula.

Follow the road into "Sherwood Forest" through overarching Red alder and Sitka spruce, passing two distinct (and one indistinct) roads coming in on the left (south). In 0.7 mile reach a large pond (which extends several miles south to Oysterville) on the left. Islands of dead Sitka spruce can be seen in the pond along with a massive population of Yellow pond-lily (*Nuphar polysepalum*) that appears to occupy the water's entire surface. When the plants are in bloom, it's like looking across a vast bobbing and swaying yellow carpet.

The only access to the water's edge occurs at a break in the hedge-like vegetation. Spot the metal grate covering a channel, which allows water from the pond to intermingle with the wetland to the north. Mosquitoes are fierce here in spring and summer; you've been warned! Look for Float-ing water pennywort (*Hydrocotyl ranunculoides*) along the shore. The leaves are three-lobed, kidney-bean-shaped, and brilliantly green, the stems floating in the water or creeping across the muddy shore. The small white flowers are arranged in umbels (like the stays of an umbrella) and are unimpressive.

The road ends in 0.3 mile at an impressive gate with artistic overtones and a couple of NO TRESPASSING signs. Turn right (north) onto

Picea sitchensis, Sitka spruce, is common on the coast but not inland.

Martha Jordan Birding Trail, Leadbetter Point State Park

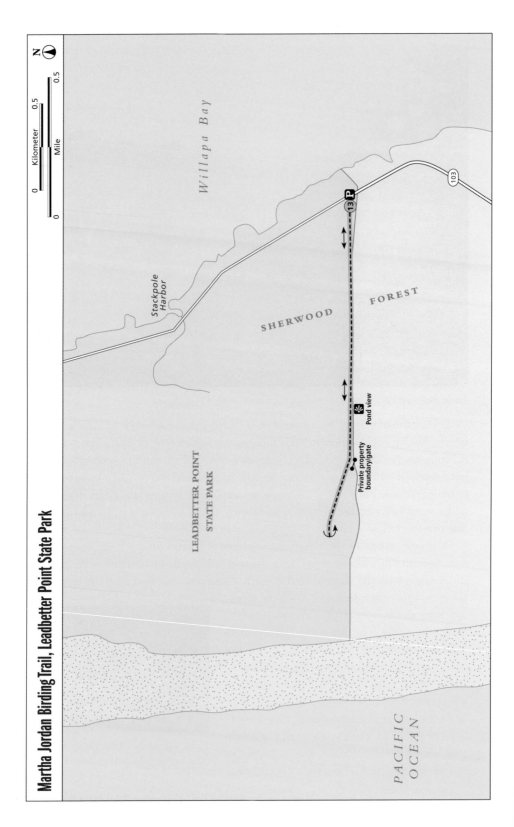

a forested path that bridges several wet areas with boardwalks. There are some big Sitka spruce here along with a vigorous growth of Salal (*Gaultheria shallon*), Bracken fern (*Pteridium aquilinum*), and Sword fern (*Polystichum munitum*).

Hydrocotyle ranunculoides, *Floating water pennywort*.

In 0.2 mile the trail crosses a wet area on a long boardwalk. The way then narrows considerably; in 2015 this stretch of trail had all the appearance of having recently been constructed. Wind through a forest of Sitka spruce and climb a thickly vegetated sand dune. Over the top, the trees change to Beach pine and the path dead-ends in a thicket of vegetation after 0.5 mile without ever reaching the road shown slightly farther west on some maps. One can expect this trail to penetrate deeper into the forest in future years.

Time to turn around and retrace your way back to the parking lot and your car.

Miles and Directions

0.0 Parking lot for Martha Jordan Birding Trail, Leadbetter Point State Park.

0.7 Access to pond.

1.0 Private property boundary.

1.5 Trail dead-ends.

3.0 Arrive back at parking lot.

Other Nearby Hiking Options

There are four other much better known and established trails on Leadbetter Point. The 2.9-mile round-trip Dune Forest Trail takes hikers through a Sitka spruce and Beach pine forest and along the sandy beach fronting Willapa Bay. In Willapa National Wildlife Refuge, the 1.1-mile Bay Loop Trail traverses sandy beach, salt marsh, and forest, while the 3.6-mile round-trip Bearberry Trail remains in forest until popping out on the beach facing the Pacific Ocean. The Bearberry Trail can be combined with the Weather Beach Trail to make a 3.5-mile loop. All four trails can be soggy, or even underwater, during the rainy season.

Hike Information

Hydrocotyl ranunculoides can also be found south of Leadbetter Point at Loomis Lake State Park and may also exist in other wetlands on the Long Beach Peninsula. It is a native of North and South America as well as Africa but ironically is considered a weed in Great Britain and Australia, where it clogs waterways. It is listed as a sensitive species in Washington because the plant's distribution here is so limited.

South Cascades and Columbia River Gorge

I f ever there was an area of Washington with an incredible juxtaposition of weather and flora, it would have to be the South Cascades and the Columbia River Gorge. Experiencing the transition from wet coastal influence to dry interior is visual, overridingly palpable, and nearly instantaneous as you make your way east. As fast as the climate in the Gorge changes, so it seems does the flora. But careful study will uncover how plants from the wet and dry sides of the mountains intertwine like lovers' fingers.

Dramatic as a west–east journey through the Gorge can be, it's nothing like hiking from the Columbia River up any number of peaks where thick forest gives way to bald hills. It's on these bald hills where Gorge wildflowers come into their own in spring and, if your timing is right, your eyes will be overwhelmed by acres and acres of yellows, blues, reds, and greens—that, and awe-inspiring views of the mighty "River of the West" making its way to the sea.

Columbia River Gorge and Deltoid balsamroot (Balsamorhiza deltoidea).

14 Dog Mountain

Here is a place famous not only for its incredibly steep trail, but for its incredible display of wildflowers. In fact, the summit of Dog Mountain is one big field of flowers. It's hard to describe, there are so many species and so many colors. Best you make an effort to get to Dog Mountain as soon as you can. Oh, and the views up and down the Gorge are fantastic. On cloudless days, you can also see a lot of volcanoes.

Start: Dog Mountain (Trail 147) trailhead, Columbia River Gorge National Scenic Area
Distance: 7.3-mile loop
Hiking time: About 4–6 hours (all day if you need to stop with your flower guides and examine every bloom!)
Difficulty: Moderate to difficult
Trail surface: Forested path
Seasons: Spring, summer, and fall. Best wildflowers: May–July (June 4, 2015).
Other trail users: Trail runners; mountain bikers on some sections
Canine compatibility: Leashed dogs allowed

Land status: Columbia River Gorge National Scenic Area
Nearest town: Stevenson
Services: Gas, food, lodging
Permit: Northwest Forest Pass
Maps: Green Trails #430 Hood River, OR; USGS Mount Defiance; DeLorme Page 111 F-8
Trail contact: Columbia River Gorge National Scenic Area
Special considerations: Vault toilet and trash cans at trailhead. No potable water at trailhead. Poison oak, ticks, rattlesnakes, exposure.

Finding the trailhead: In Washington, from east or west, drive on WA 14 to milepost 53. From Portland, drive east on I-84 to exit 44 and cross the Columbia River on the Bridge of the Gods (toll required). Turn right (east) onto WA 14 and drive 12 miles to milepost 53. The large parking area is on the north side of the road. **GPS: N45 41.956' / W121 42.497'**

Plants You Might See

Adenocaulon bicolor, Pathfinder, Asteraceae
Anemone deltoidea, Columbia windflower, Ranunculaceae
Aquilegia formosa, Red columbine, Ranunculaceae
Delphinium nuttallii, Nuttall's larkspur, Ranunculaceae
Gilia capitata, Globe gilia, Polemoniaceae
Holodiscus discolor, Oceanspray, Rosaceae
Lilium columbianum, Leopard lily, Liliaceae
Microseris nutans, Nodding microseris, Asteraceae
Phlox diffusa, Spreading phlox, Polemoniaceae
Sedum spathulifolium, Broad-leafed stonecrop, Crassulaceae
Trillium ovatum, Trillium, Liliaceae

The Hike

The Dog Mountain Scenic Trail, Trail 147, begins at the east end of the parking lot beside the reader board. In 0.1 mile reach the vault toilet. From here the trail climbs very steeply through a dry Douglas fir forest with an understory of very healthy Poison oak along with Bigleaf maple, Garry oak (*Quercus garryana*), Snowberry (*Symphoricarpos albus*), Hazelnut (*Corylus cornuta*), Thimbleberry (*Rubus parviflorus*), and Oregon grape (*Mahonia nervosa*). As you can see, it's not all Poison oak! In 0.4 mile come to a junction of the Dog Mountain Scenic Trail and the Old Route. The old way up the mountain is steeper than what you've already done and lacks any of the views yet to come, so stay on the scenic trail.

Gallardia aristata, *Common blanket flower.*

Dog Mountain is just far enough east to have dry south-facing slopes. This means a thinner forest, less ground coverage by understory shrubs, and more light reaching the forest floor—all of which equates to a much more well-developed herbaceous layer. And for the wildflower hunter, this translates into one amazing bloom after another as the trail ascends to the meadows atop Dog Mountain. Not only are

Great views and great wildflowers can be found on Dog Mountain.

Cephalanthera austinae, *Phantom orchid.*

Dichelostemma congestum, *Ookow.*

such familiar species as Twinflower (*Linnaea borealis*) or Inside-out flower (*Vancouveria hexandra*) found, but you can expect to find the nodding blue heads of Brodiaea (*Dichelostemma congestum*), the papery blooms of Wild onion (*Allium acuminatum*), and the purple-spotted petals of Farewell-to-spring (*Clarkia amoena*), among many more.

There is a section of trail where the ground cover is almost entirely Oregon grape. Here can be found the most unusual Phantom orchid (*Cephalanthera austiniae*). Though it's a flowering plant, Phantom orchid lacks chlorophyll and is completely white, receiving nutrition by parasitizing fungi found in the soil, which in turn are parasitizing the roots of some nearby conifer. But the tree makes out well in the deal because the fungus helps the conifer absorb water and nutrients from the soil.

In 1.7 miles up the trail you pop out of the forest to a small side-of-the-hill dry meadow and great views of the Gorge. This is also your first inkling of what is to come, as the ground is covered by the big gray floppy mule-ear leaves and sunflower-like blooms of Carey's balsamroot (*Balsamorhiza careyana*). There's another equally impressive though not as large member of the sunflower family here: Common blanketflower (*Gaillardia aristata*). It has yellow petals, toothed at the tips, and

Balsamorhiza careyana, *Carey's balsamroot.*

a nearly black center. Look also for Harsh paintbrush (*Castilleja hispida*) and Nine-leaf lomatium (*Lomatium triternatum*). In 0.4 mile come to an unsigned trail junction where the scenic trail is met again by the Old Route up Dog Mountain. From here the trail becomes so steep, you'll be wishing for stairs . . . or a ladder. After 0.4 mile of this, come to Puppy Dog Mountain—not a mountain, really, but a broad platform

Achillea millefolium, *Yarrow, is widely distributed throughout western Washington.*

that overlooks the Gorge. There used to be a fire tower here, but the structure was dismantled in 1967 and hauled away. The flower displays here are truly stunning. When authors wax eloquent about "riotous cacophonies" of color, this is what they are talking about.

After 0.3 mile of walking through flower gardens, come to a weathered sign; turn right (east) and reach the summit of Dog Mountain in 0.2 mile. It can be windy up here, and if you're not prepared, take shelter in the copse of trees on top of the mountain. Views to three volcanoes are possible along with what looks like the entire lower Columbia River Valley.

It's up to you to decide what to do next. You can retrace your steps down the way you came, perhaps mixing it up by taking the Old Route. Or, return to the main trail and turn right (north) to walk along the Dog Mountain ridge. In 0.2 mile you run out of wildflower gardens and enter the forest.

Another 0.8 mile brings you to a trail junction. Turn left (south) and begin a long decline to the Columbia. Because this forest is on a north-facing slope, everything is a little bit wetter than on the scenic trail, but you'll see all the same, and familiar, species. It will just look more lush. In 2.8 miles reach the end of the trail in the Dog Mountain parking lot.

Miles and Directions

0.0　Dog Mountain (Trail 147) trailhead and parking lot off WA 14.

0.1　Vault toilet.

0.5 - Scenic trail / Old Route lower trail junction.

2.2　First Gorge view.

2.6　Dog Mountain Scenic Trail / Old Route upper trail junction.

3.0　Puppy Dog Mountain.

3.3　Dog Mountain Scenic Trail / Summit Trail junction.

3.5　Dog Mountain summit.

4.5　Augspurger Trail / Augspurger Mountain Trail junction.

7.3　Arrive back at Dog Mountain parking lot.

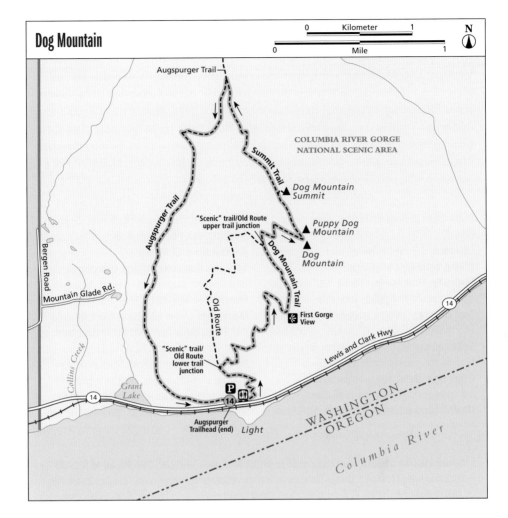

Hike Information

You can always tell how popular a hiking area is by the size of the parking lot. Dog Mountain's lot can accommodate a hundred cars. An early start is therefore recommended in order to have a bit of peace and quiet on the summit. Weekdays are preferred to weekends.

15 Hamilton Mountain

If not for Dog Mountain, a little farther eastward, this would have to be the best place for seeing wildflowers on western Washington's side of the Columbia River Gorge. From the bottom of the trail to its top, there is over 2,000 feet of vertical relief and this is best expressed in the sheer numbers of flower species to be found. And then, there are the views up and down the Gorge! Even the roar from Bonneville Dam can be heard above the whoosh-whoosh of traffic far below on WA 14. Waterfall lovers—and who isn't?—also have two big falls to enjoy.

Start: Beacon Rock State Park, lower picnic area

Distance: 7.3-mile lollipop

Hiking time: About 5–8 hours

Difficulty: Moderate to difficult, with many steep sections and a little exposure

Trail surface: Forested path, rocky, hard-pack and gravel road

Seasons: Spring, summer, and fall. Best wildflowers: May–July (June 3, 2015).

Other trail users: Trail runners; mountain bikers and equestrians on some sections

Canine compatibility: Leashed dogs allowed

Land status: Washington State Parks Department, Beacon Rock State Park

Nearest town: Stevenson

Services: Gas, food, lodging. Camping at Beacon Rock State Park.

Permit: Discover Pass

Maps: Green Trails #428 Bridal Veil, OR, and #429 Bonneville Dam, OR; USGS Beacon Rock; DeLorme Page 110 G-5

Trail contact: Beacon Rock State Park

Special considerations: Potable water and flush toilets available at trailhead. Watch for ticks and Poison oak. There have been reports of rattlesnakes.

Finding the trailhead: From Vancouver, or points east in Washington, take WA 14 to Beacon Rock State Park. From Portland or Hood River and points east in Oregon, cross the Columbia River on the Bridge of the Gods (toll required) and head west on WA 14 to Beacon Rock State Park. A hundred feet east of the park headquarters, turn north on an unsigned road. In 0.4 mile turn right (east) into the large and mostly paved lower picnic area for Beacon Rock State Park. If the lower lot is full, drive farther up the road to the upper picnic area parking area. **GPS: N45 37.955' / W122 01.190'**

Plants You Might See

Achillea millefolium, Yarrow, Asteraceae

Achlys californica, Vanilla leaf, Berberidaceae

Apocynum androsaemifolium, Dogbane, Apocynaceae

Aquilegia formosa, Red columbine, Ranunculaceae

Aruncus dioicus, Goat's beard, Rosaceae

Asarum caudatum, Wild ginger, Aristolochiaceae

Fritillaria lanceolata, Chocolate lily, Liliaceae

Lilium columbianum, Leopard lily, Liliaceae

The Hike

The trail starts behind the parking lot reader board, then jogs past the children's play area and group picnic site to another reader board and a trail sign for Hamilton Mountain Trail. Ascend steeply through a thick forest of large Douglas fir and a well-developed understory of Oregon grape (*Mahonia nervosa*), Vine maple (*Acer circinatum*), Sword fern (*Polystichum munitum*), Bigleaf maple, Red alder, Thimbleberry (*Rubus spectabilis*), False lily-of-the-valley (*Maianthemum dilatatum*), Pathfinder (*Adenocaulon bicolor*), Twinberry (*Linnaea borealis*), Snowberry (*Symphoricarpos albus*), Bracken fern (*Pteridium aquilinum*), and everybody's less-than-favorite, Poison oak (*Toxicodendron diversilobum*).

In 0.5 mile comes a trail junction. Off to the left (west) is a spur to the upper picnic area; continue straight (north). In 0.4 mile cross over a steep creek on a fine, old-fashioned wood and log bridge. Another 0.1 mile past that is a very short spur trail to a viewpoint for Hardy Falls, mostly unseen through the closed-in forest. And 0.1 mile past that is a spur trail to view Rodney Falls. The main trail drops to the right (east) and crosses Hardy Creek. After making the crossing, the trail rises to the Hamilton Mountain summit trail junction in 0.1 mile.

This trail has a reputation for climbing like it's nobody's business, and this is where that reputation was earned. Climb through the forest on ever-increasing steep and short switchbacks until achieving the lower ridge of Hamilton Mountain. The way

Lupinus latifolius, *Broad-leaf lupine.*

Toxicodendron diversilobum, *Poison oak.*

BEACON ROCK

Beacon Rock, the park's namesake, has a 2-mile round-trip trail that starts at the highway and ends on the rock's summit. The "trail," with some serious drop-offs to the ground far, far below, is actually a series of paved paths, boardwalks, and wooden planks with ironwork bridges and stairways. A guardrail is provided most of the way up for the faint of heart.

The first route up Beacon Rock was built in 1935 by Henry J. Biddle. This was before Washington State Parks purchased the property and when Biddle owned all the land around here. Not to worry: The trail has been repaired and rebuilt over the years, though the current way up still follows Biddle's original route.

Beacon Rock and the Columbia River.

grows rocky and feels vertical, the views throughout the Gorge ever more expansive, and a great number of wildflowers make an appearance—so many, in fact, there's no way to mention them all. Some of what you'll see include Self-heal (*Prunella vulgaris*), Anemone (*Anemone deltoidea*), Harsh paintbrush (*Castilleja hispida*), Broad-leaved stonecrop (*Sedum spathulifolium*), Taper-tip onion (*Allium acuminatum*), the white form of Heart-leaf buckwheat (*Eriogonum compositum*), and Woodland star (*Lithophragma glabrum*).

In 1.7 miles from the previous trail junction, reach the summit of Hamilton

Lilium columbianum, *Leopard lily.*

Mountain. Take a look around. It's pretty shrubby up here, so leave the top of the mountain and continue to the left (north) for 0.3 mile through a section overgrown with shrubby Garry oak (*Quercus garryana*), Thimbleberry (*Rubus parviflorus*), Baldhip rose (*Rosa gymnocarpa*), Red alder, and Oceanspray (*Holodiscus discolor*), with Harsh paintbrush (*Castilleja hispida*), Mountain ash (*Sorbus sitchensis*), and many others. Enter the forest for 0.5 mile and emerge onto an exposed and wide ridge. The ridge is 0.2 mile long and at its northern end is a trail junction of the Hamilton Mountain and Hardy Creek Trails.

Don't forget to admire the views before leaving the ridge! There are three choices to make. On the right a path leads to a sign that says "Dead End." Don't take that one. The middle option is a 4WD road. Nope. Find the other 4WD road farthest west and south. From here the trail doesn't exactly plunge earthward, and it's safe to say the way is less steep than the route up. But that isn't saying much because the pitch is enough that you'll find gravity heavily

Castilleja hispida, *Harsh paintbrush*.

in charge. This is the Hardy Creek Trail; both mountain bikers and equestrians are allowed.

In 0.1 mile ignore Dons Cutoff (foot traffic only) on the right (northwest). With the trail's pitch finally showing signs of alleviating, saunter downward through the forest and into the Hardy Creek drainage. Keep your eyes peeled for large stands of Cow parsnip (*Heracleum lanatum*). Look for attractive whitish inflorescences ranging in size from a salad to a dinner plate on 6-foot-tall plants. The rough stems are occasionally streaked with red, which makes Cow parsnip resemble Poison hemlock (*Conium maculata*). All parts of Poison hemlock are toxic; if in doubt, consult Socrates.

In 0.8 mile reach another trail junction. Dons Cutoff finds its way here, having come the long way around. But the way home is to follow directions left (south) to the Equestrian Trail and trailhead option. This leads to another trail junction in 0.2 mile where the Equestrian Trail and Hardy Creek Trail part company. There is a picnic table here if you need a place to sit and eat. Or, maybe just sit. Leave this pretty glen, and once more you are hiking on a forested path rather than a rocky, cobbled road and your feet will feel the difference.

Apocynum androsaemifolium, *Dogbane*.

Now begin a lovely forest walk. Always to the right (west) will be the roaring and roiling sound of Hardy Creek—heard but never seen. After 0.9 mile reach a familiar

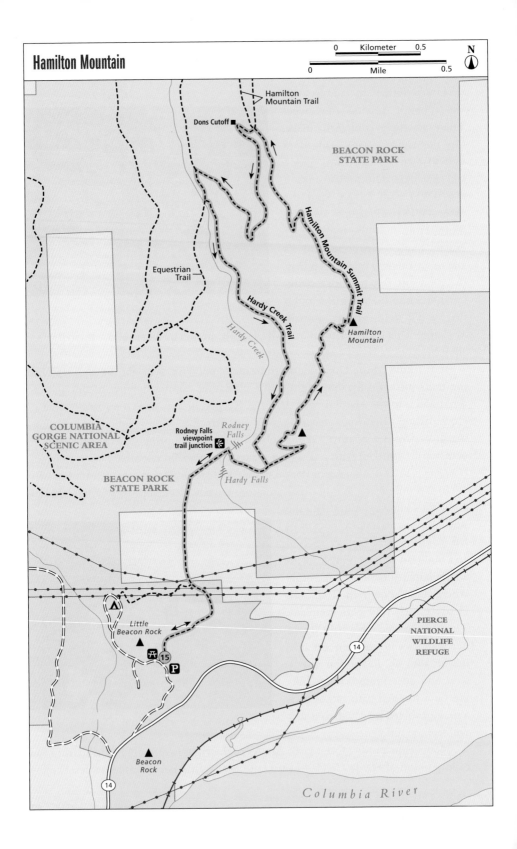

Hamilton Mountain

0   Kilometer   0.5

0   Mile   0.5

N

Hamilton
Mountain Trail

Dons Cutoff ■

BEACON ROCK
STATE PARK

Hamilton Mountain Summit Trail

Equestrian
Trail

Hardy Creek Trail

Hardy Creek

Hamilton
Mountain ▲

Rodney
Falls

COLUMBIA
GORGE NATIONAL
SCENIC AREA

Rodney Falls
viewpoint
trail junction

▲

Hardy Falls

BEACON ROCK
STATE PARK

PIERCE
NATIONAL
WILDLIFE
REFUGE

Little
Beacon Rock

🏕 15

P

14

Beacon
Rock ▲

14

Columbia River

place. It's the Hamilton Mountain summit trail encountered so early in the day. Drop down to the crossing of Hardy Creek and meet the Rodney Falls viewpoint trail junction. It's only a couple hundred yards uphill to the viewpoint and it's well worth the effort, no matter how tired you may be by this point. Watch your step, though. The way is muddy and slippery.

If it's a hot day, linger on the viewing platform at the "Pool of the Winds" to take advantage of the cooling spray. If it isn't a hot day, work your way back down to

Look in coastal meadows, low- to mid-elevation forests, and subalpine meadows for Lilium columbianum, *Tiger lily.*

the main trail and think about the parking lot, your car, and the drive home. You're on well-trodden ground now, and the plants will look familiar. It's 1.3 miles from here to the end of the trail.

Miles and Directions

0.0 Hamilton Mountain trailhead in Beacon Rock State Park lower picnic area.

0.5 Spur trail to upper picnic area.

0.9 Cross over steep creek.

1.0 Hardy Falls viewpoint.

1.1 Rodney Falls viewpoint trail junction.

1.2 Hamilton Mountain summit trail.

2.9 Hamilton Mountain summit.

3.9 Hamilton Mountain / Hardy Creek Trail junction.

4.0 Dons Cutoff.

4.8 Trail junction.

5.0 Hardy Creek Trail / Equestrian Trail junction.

5.9 Hamilton Mountain summit trail.

6.0 Rodney Falls viewpoint trail junction.

7.3 Arrive back at trailhead.

16 Gillette Lake

For such a short trail, the way up to Gillette Lake packs a wildflower wallop. One reason for this is that the forest is maturing second-growth with plenty of light breaks. Another reason is that the trail crosses two clear-cuts. One is nearly thirty years old, and the other is less than five. Removing an entire forest is anathema, of course, but it allows a plethora of pioneering species like shrubs and herbs to colonize the newly cleared land while the conifers slowly recover their dominance. This makes for interesting plant-watching. Also, you end up at a lake, quite an unusual end point for such a low-elevation trek.

Start: Tamanous Trailhead
Distance: 6.0 miles out and back
Hiking time: About 3–4 hours
Difficulty: Moderate
Trail surface: Forested path, rocky
Seasons: Year-round. Best wildflowers: May–June (June 2, 2015).
Other trail users: Trail runners, equestrians
Canine compatibility: Leashed dogs allowed
Land status: Columbia River Gorge National Scenic Area; Washington State Department of Natural Resources

Nearest town: Stevenson
Services: Gas, food, lodging
Permit: Northwest Forest Pass
Maps: Green Trails #429 Bonneville Dam, OR; USGS Bonneville Dam OR-WA; DeLorme Page 110 G-6
Trail contact: Columbia Gorge National Scenic Area
Special considerations: No potable water at trailhead. Vault toilet at trailhead. Picnic tables available. Watch for Poison oak, ticks, and rattlesnakes.

Finding the trailhead: From Portland, take I-84 east to exit 44, Cascade Locks. Pay your fare and cross over the Bridge of the Gods toll bridge, then turn left (west) on WA 14. In 1.5 miles find the massive BONNEVILLE TRAILHEAD, COLUMBIA RIVER GORGE SCENIC AREA sign on the north side of the highway. This takes you to the paved parking lot for the Tamanous Trailhead, opposite the Bonneville Visitor Center (entrance to the visitor center is 1 mile west). From Vancouver, drive 48 miles east on WA 14 to the BONNEVILLE TRAILHEAD, COLUMBIA RIVER GORGE SCENIC AREA sign and Tamanous Trailhead on the left (north) side of the highway, opposite the Bonneville Visitor Center. **GPS: N45 39.021' / W121 56.014'**

Plants You Might See

Achillea millefolium, Yarrow, Asteraceae
Aquilegia formosa, Red columbine, Ranunculaceae
Claytonia sibirica, Candy flower, Montiaceae
Lilium columbianum, Leopard lily, Liliaceae
Prunella vulgaris, Self-heal, Lamiaceae
Trillium ovatum, Trillium, Liliaceae
Vancouveria hexandra, Twinflower, Berberidaceae

The Hike

Beyond the toilet and reader boards, find the trailhead, a wide gravel road, at the north end of the large parking lot. In 100 feet the road continues straight ahead, but

veer slightly right to continue on the forested path of Trail 27. The trees here are Douglas fir, Western red cedar, and Bigleaf maple, some of impressive size for a second-growth forest. The understory has Thimbleberry (*Rubus spectabilis*), Oceanspray (*Holodiscus discolor*), Oregon grape (*Mahonia nervosa*), Sword fern (*Polystichum munitum*), and Poison oak (*Toxicodendron diversilobum*).

Prunella vulgaris, *Self-heal.*

There are plenty of herbs alongside the trail, including Piggy-back plant (*Tolmiea menziesii*), Fringecup (*Tellima grandiflora*), and Stinky Bob (*Geranium robertianum*). Of note is Pathfinder (*Adenocaulon bicolor*). The tops of Pathfinder's triangular leaves are a nice shade of green, but the undersides are silvery or white. There is a story that people once used this color differential to mark their way along the trail for those who followed. Kind of like leaving cairns, signposts, or bread crumbs along the way. Or, so the story goes.

Linnaea borealis, *Twinflower.*

In 0.5 mile come to a junction of Trail 27 and the Pacific Crest Trail (PCT). Turn left (northwest) and join the PCT. You're now on your way to Canada. Reach a parcel of DNR land within the scenic area and pass though an old clear-cut with its thick jumble of understory plants and herbaceous species. You'll not only see the deep forest plants already viewed, but a few others like False lily-of-the-valley (*Maianthemum dilatatum*), Large-leaf lupine (*Lupinus polyphyllus*), and Mock orange (*Philadelphus lewisii*). There are also plenty of the lovely white blooms with yellow centers

▶ **The Cascade Mountains get their name from a waterfall that used to exist where the Columbia River flowed over several steep steps of rock created by multiple flows of lava. Those cascades now lie beneath Bonneville Dam.**

Aquilegia formosa, *Columbine.*   Anemone deltoidea, *Anemone.*

of Columbia wind flower (*Anemone deltoidea*). All this diversity is due to disturbance. It's one "advantage" to clear-cuts: They are equal opportunity providers of abundant sunlight.

The trail winds through this clear-cut and crosses an old road after another 0.5 mile. It reenters the forest and after 1.0 mile comes to a much newer clear-cut: more DNR land. Cross another logging road in 0.4 mile and continue northward, towards the power lines.

Before the last bit of trail drops down to Gillette Lake, there are nice views to the Gorge and Bonneville Dam. In the rocks beside the trail are plants that enjoy a less wet environment. You'll be able to find the tall yellow inflorescences of Western wallflower (*Erysimum capitatum*), Broad-leafed stonecrop (*Sedum spathulifolium*), Silver-leaf phacelia (*Phacelia hastata*), and some Saskatoon (*Amelanchier alnifolia*). Also in the rocks is Parsley fern (*Cryptogramma crispa*), an odd little fern that bears both fertile (i.e., spore-bearing) and non-fertile fronds.

Lilium columbianum, *Leopard lily.*

Gillette Lake itself is an unassuming body of greenish water. There are a couple of horribly impacted campsites alongside the trail and an even worse one located on the lakeshore. The PCT continues northward, but arrival at the lake means it's time to turn around and head back, retracing your steps to the trailhead.

Gillette Lake

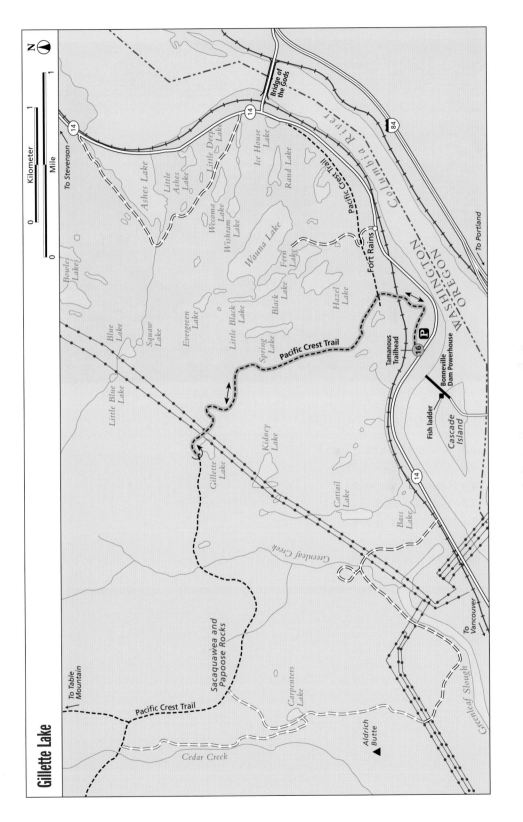

Prunella vulgaris, *Self-heal, favors disturbed soils in moist places at the forest's edge.*

Miles and Directions

0.0 Tamanous Trailhead.

0.5 Trail 27 / Pacific Crest Trail junction.

1.0 Cross old logging road.

2.0 Large clear-cut.

2.4 Cross newer logging road.

3.0 Gillette Lake.

6.0 Arrive back at trailhead.

17 Catherine Creek

Sometimes you want a wildflower hike that can be done early in the year that reflects a long winter of no walking activity of any kind. In short: a trail with very little up, not much distance, and plenty to see. Welcome to Catherine Creek. Being on the less wet side of the Gorge, Catherine Creek dries up early in the spring, and you can expect the hills to be brown and most of the flowers to be gone by June. Not that there is a lack of things to see during the summer—just less. Whenever you're in the Columbia River country, this is a great place to stop and break the road warrior monotony of travel or take a quick hike to stretch your legs.

Start: Coyote Wall and Catherine Creek Trail System on north side of Old Highway 8.
Distance: 3.7-mile loop with an out-and-back.
Hiking time: About 2–3 hours
Difficulty: Mostly easy, with a few short moderate sections
Trail surface: 4WD road, rocky trail, some pavement
Seasons: Spring and fall. Best wildflowers: March–April (June 5, 2015).
Other trail users: Trail runners; equestrians (May–November)
Canine compatibility: Leashed dogs allowed

Land status: USFS, Columbia River Gorge National Scenic Area
Nearest town: Lyle
Services: Gas, food, lodging
Permits: None
Maps: USGS Lyle; DeLorme Page 111 F-11
Trail contact: Gifford Pinchot National Forest
Special considerations: No potable water at trailhead. Chemical toilets located across the street. Garbage can by trailhead. Watch for Poison oak, ticks, rattlesnakes, and exposure to heat and sun.

Finding the trailhead: Eastbound from Bingen, follow WA 14 about 4.6 miles to milepost 71 and Old Highway 8 (CR 1230). Turn left (northeast) at Rowland Lake and drive 1.4 miles to the gravel Coyote Wall and Catherine Creek Trail System parking lot on the north side of the road. There is no left-turn lane from WA 14 to Old Highway 8, which makes this a hazardous maneuver. Caution is advised.

Westbound from Lyle, follow WA 14 for about 0.3 mile and turn right onto Old Highway 8 (CR 1230). This turn is right after crossing the Klickatat River. Follow Old Highway 8 for 4.8 miles to the gravel Coyote Wall and Catherine Creek Trail System parking area on the north side of the road. **GPS: N45 42.630' / W121 21.729'**

Plants You Might See

Balsamorhiza deltoidea, Balsamroot, Asteraceae
Calochortus macrocarpus, Sagebrush mariposa lily, Liliaceae
Cryptogramma densa, Indian's-dream fern, Pteridaceae
Delphinium distichum, Two-spike larkspur, Ranunculaceae
Dodecatheon conjugens, Desert shooting star, Primulaceae
Dodecatheon poeticum, Narcissus shooting star, Primulaceae

Erythranthe guttata, Common monkeyflower, Phrymaceae
Lewisia rediviva, Bitterroot, Montiaceae
Micranthes integrifolia, Northwest saxifrage, Saxifragaceae
Penstemon richardsonii, Richardson's penstemon, Plantaginaceae
Prunus emarginata, Bitter cherry, Rosaceae
Toxicoscordion venenosus, Death camas, Melanthiaceae
Triteleia grandiflora, Brodiaea, Asparagaceae
Triteleia hyacinthina, Fool's onion, Asparagaceae

The Hike

From the parking area, pass through the opening in the barbed-wire fence onto a 4WD road. It immediately splits, left and right. To enjoy a view of the Gorge with Mount Hood rising into the sky beyond, turn left (west). The rough road crosses a grassland and heads towards a copse of Ponderosa pine and some impressive Garry oak (*Quercus garryana*). In the shade of the trees is a most bodacious clump of Poison oak (*Toxicodendron diversilobum*).

Past the peak flowering time, when the ground is brown and the grasses dried out, you'll be treated to Bluedicks (*Brodiaea coronaria*). The large and flat-topped blossoms of Buckwheat are everywhere, along with Yarrow (*Achillea millefolium*), one of Washington's most ubiquitous plants. In the shady places not occupied by Poison oak is Saskatoon (*Amelanchier alnifolia*).

Reach the bluff view in 0.8 mile. Then, turn around and head back to the trailhead to where the 4WD originally split left and right. It's possible to find your own shortcuts (there are plenty of volunteer trails) and obviate the need to double back, but the tall grass might be hiding the odd rattlesnake here and there.

From the trailhead, take the right side of the split road. It's marked 1230/020 on a flexible sign. This appears to be a county road marking. This 4WD road surmounts a small rise in 0.3 mile and drops down into Catherine Creek. Despite the dryness of the area, you will find some familiar wet western Gorge plants such as Oceanspray (*Holodiscus discolor*), Mountain ash (*Sorbus sitchensis*), Manroot (*Marah oreganus*), Bigleaf maple (*Acer macrophylla*), and Mock orange (*Philadelphus lewisii*).

If the creek is dry, pick your way over the cobbles to the other side. Should there

Delphinium distichum, *Two-spike Larkspur.*

be water in the creek, look to your left and see the bridge. Come to a trail junction in 0.1 mile and continue straight (north) on a trail where mountain bikes are not allowed. In another 0.2 mile is an old corral; you can figure out for yourself how this property was once used. Just beyond that, as the trail begins to climb through stately Ponderosa pine and Garry oak, you'll see the collapsed structure that probably once represented the dreams and aspirations of the person who built the corral.

Triteleia hyacinthina, *Fool's onion.*

Walk uphill for 0.4 mile, passing under a power line, to a trail junction. Turn right, leaving the 4WD road behind for a narrow path that climbs up the east bluff overlooking Catherine Creek. Reach the top in 0.2 mile, with a pole fence and some nice views of Mount Hood and the Gorge across a forest of pine. The trail

Brodiaea coronaria, *Bluedicks.*

ends here but a well-defined social trail continues south, following the fence line. From here you can return the way you came or continue on. The way is a bit rougher from here, so let that be your guide.

The fence line ends in 0.2 mile and you get an idea of why that pole fence is here in the first place. There is a natural arch in the lava flow below you that makes up the bluff above Catherine Creek. You saw that same pole fence below, where the corral is located. The fence is to discourage people from climbing over the bluff and possibly injuring themselves or disturbing the rock.

From here the social trail gets rougher and follows the descending slope southward, cutting in and out of gullies, acclivities, and declivities. It does this for 0.5 mile before reaching Old Highway 8. Once you get close to the road, avoid the temptation to slide down to the pavement. Pretty soon the path will take you there. Turn right (west) and follow the pavement 0.2 mile to the parking lot and your car. Watch out for oncoming traffic.

Catherine Creek

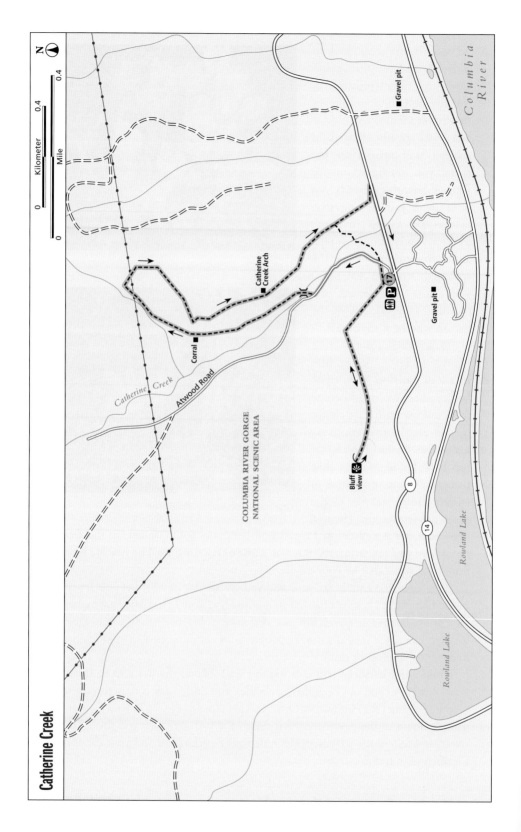

N

Kilometer
0   0.4

Mile
0   0.4

Columbia River

Gravel pit

Catherine Creek

Atwood Road

Corral

Catherine Creek Arch

COLUMBIA RIVER GORGE NATIONAL SCENIC AREA

Bluff view

Gravel pit

P 17

8

14

Rowland Lake

Rowland Lake

Miles and Directions

0.0 Catherine Creek trailhead and parking area on north side of Old Highway 8.

0.8 Bluff view.

1.6 Return to trailhead.

2.0 Trail junction 1.

2.2 Old corral.

2.6 Power line / trail junction 2.

2.8 Mount Hood view.

3.0 Fence ends.

3.5 Join Old Highway 8.

3.7 Arrive back at trailhead and parking area.

Other Nearby Hiking Options

Across Old Highway 8 from the trailhead are two paved ADA-accessible loop trails. The easiest and shortest of the two leads to Catherine Creek Falls. Confusingly, the signage also refers to these two as the Catherine Creek Trail.

Alpine Lakes Wilderness

S andwiched between I-90 on the south and WA 2 on the north, the Alpine Lakes Wilderness is a wilderness next door to millions of people in western Washington. Within its boundaries lie diversity of ecosystem and habitat that offers plant hunters everything they could ever want between lowland forest and alpine peaks.

The wilderness was established in 1976 after years of efforts to establish a national park had failed. The Middle Fork Snoqualmie River Road (FR 56) deeply penetrates the wilderness and provides access to beautiful scenery nearly unrivaled anywhere in the state. With this thought in mind, a $15 million road construction project was begun in 2015 to rehabilitate the road, encourage lower speeds, formalize pullouts at key recreation sites, replace three failing bridges and numerous culverts, and widen and pave the once narrow, often rutted, and always dusty and/or muddy road. All this and maintain the forested character of the road corridor too.

Ingalls Lake and Mount Stewart.

18 Ira Spring Trail Wildflower Garden

Motorists making their way over Snoqualmie Pass on I-90 have their eyes glued to the roadway, as they should. But their passengers in springtime should be looking to the north, towards Bandera Mountain, because, even as far away as the interstate, can be seen the bold purple of a field of Fireweed interspersed with the bright cream blossoms of Beargrass and the vibrant orange of Paintbrush. Hikers can enjoy all this glory and more in one of the most striking spring wildflower gardens in the Alpine Lakes Wilderness. The trail up is a stiff climb, but the rewards are fantastic. Besides all the flowers there are views west to Seattle and beyond to the Olympic Mountains. Across the Snoqualmie Valley is the craggy spire of McClellan Butte, and farther away is the ice- and snow-laden bulk of Mount Rainier.

Start: Trailhead for Ira Spring Trail #1038

Distance: 6.8 miles out and back

Hiking time: About 4–8 hours, with a possible overnight stay at Mason Lake

Difficulty: Strenuous, steep trail with talus

Trail surface: Forested path, old road, rocky

Seasons: Summer and fall. Best wildflowers: June–August (May 30, 2015).

Other trail users: None

Canine compatibility: Leashed dogs allowed

Land status: USDAFS Mount Baker–Snoqualmie National Forest, Snoqualmie Ranger District; Alpine Lakes Wilderness

Nearest town: North Bend

Services: Gas, food, lodging

Permits: Northwest Forest Pass, Wilderness Permit (free at trailhead)

Maps: Green Trails #206 Bandera Mountain; USDAFS Mount Baker–Snoqualmie National Forest; Alpine Lakes Wilderness; DeLorme Page 64 A-4

Trail contact: Mount Baker–Snoqualmie National Forest, Snoqualmie Ranger District

Special considerations: Talus; exposure to sun. No potable water at trailhead or on trail. Vault toilet at trailhead.

Finding the trailhead: From Seattle, drive east on I-90 to exit 45 (Lookout Point Road / FR 9030 and FR 9031). Turn left (north) at the stop sign and pass under the interstate. Bear left (west). The pavement ends and becomes a narrow hard-pack dirt road. Pass the road to Talapus Lake and Trail 1039 in 0.3 mile. Continue on FR 9031 and after 1.6 miles pass an old logging road on the right (north), now blocked off from traffic. There is another logging road at 2.5 miles which was constructed in 2012. In 3.3 miles reach the large trailhead parking lot. On busy days the lot can be full with overflow parking along the road. Pay attention to areas posted No Parking. They're serious. **GPS: N47 25.486' / W121 35.013'**

Plants You Might See

Geum macrophyllum, Large-leaved avens, Rosaceae

Mahonia nervosa, Oregon grape, Berberidaceae

Rubus parviflorus, Thimbleberry, Rosaceae

Rubus spectabilis, Salmonberry, Rosaceae

Rubus ursinus, Trailing blackberry, Rosaceae

Tellima grandiflora, Fringecup, Saxifragaceae
Tolmiea menziesii, Piggy-back plant, Saxifragaceae
Trientalis latifolia, Western starflower, Primulaceae

The Hike

The trail begins a few feet beyond the vault toilet and reader board on the west side of the parking lot. Late arrivals with caloric deficit will be interested in the picnic tables nearby.

The Ira Spring Trail could also be called "Starts with a Bang" because the wide path (actually an old road) begins steeply and only gets more so the higher up you go.

The forest here is Douglas fir, Western hemlock, and Western red cedar with a well-developed understory. Tall, mature Red alder can be found where the sun breaks through this old-growth forest.

There is lots to see on the ground under these big trees. Keep your eyes peeled for the creeping stems and diminutive blooms of Twinflower (*Linnaea borealis*). There is also plenty of False lily-of-the-valley (*Maianthemum dilatatum*), Wild ginger (*Asarum caudatum*), Trillium (*Trillium ovatum*), Star-flowered false Solomon's seal (*Maianthemum stellatum*), and the horrid-smelling Stinky Bob (*Geranium robertianum*).

On hot days it doesn't pay to tarry too long in the cool forest. The big wildflower show is up ahead anyway, high and exposed. But the show also consists of unrelenting access to that evil yellow sky orb some call the sun. Still, it's difficult to ignore the drooping purple blooms of Bleeding heart (*Dicentra formosa*), not to mention the white tower

The Ira Spring Trail is a veritable garden of wildflowers in early spring.

Valeriana sitchensis, *Valerian.*

Maianthemum stellatum, *Star-flowered false Solomon's seal.*

HOW TO BOTANIZE

People who enjoy looking for, or collecting, or photographing plants out in nature call their activity "botanizing." It's a natural verb to use for a field of study called botany: the science of plant biology.

It doesn't take much in the way of specialized equipment to botanize, though it's entirely possible to go way over the top with what you bring. Isn't that true with everything? If you're looking for wildflowers with an interest in identifying what you find, a field guide of some kind is necessary. There is a list of flower finders and field guides in Appendix C. Some of the books are floras for our region with dichotomous keys and extensive technical and scientific descriptions. Others are simple guides that help you identify what you see based on color or habitat. Still others fall somewhere in between on a sliding scale between the technical and the simple. Like most plant hunters, you will probably start with basic guides, and as your knowledge of botany progresses, search out the more difficult and complete guides because they will provide you with more information.

You'll see some photographic botanizers carrying gear that runs the gamut from point-and-shoot cameras to tripod-mounted single-lens-reflex digital cameras with macro lenses. And more! It is entirely possible to take wonderful images with lesser camera gear, but the professional photographer won't be satisfied with anything but the best.

The most serious botanizers are professional botanists working at a university or college botany department herbarium. Although, truth be told, there are plenty of amateurs to give the professionals a run for their money in terms of knowledge and expertise. These botanizers carry not only their flora, camera, interest, and love of wildflowers and other plants, but a "plant press" into which will go "collections." Collections consist of plants to be brought home, pressed, dried, and mounted to special paper. Collections are made for further study or to trade with other botanists and herbaria in other regions of the world.

of flowers poking out of a spreading carpet of large foliage that is Vanilla leaf (*Achlys californica*).

Within the first 0.5 mile, cross two creeks. The second one is Mason Creek. In the past this was a dangerous crossing in early spring. Thanks to a cooperative effort by the Ira Spring Trust, the Mountains to Sound Greenway Trust, the Forest Service, and other partners, in 2015 a log bridge was built across the creek. Enter the Alpine Lakes Wilderness in 0.2 mile with no appreciable change in the forest composition except for an occasional spindly Sitka spruce alongside the trail; the upward pitch continues.

Phylodocce empetriformis, *Red mountain-heather*

Cornus unalaschkensis, *Bunchberry.*

In 0.3 mile the trail does finally change. It splits from the old road which peters out, on the right, in a mass of deadfall, rejuvenating forest, and scattered boulders. Take the left side of the split and begin climbing in earnest. Hard to believe a trail could get steeper, but it does. As the trail climbs, the forest thins a bit and begins to dry out. Along with a Mountain hemlock here and there can be seen the beginning of what is to come: Beargrass (*Xerophyllum tenax*), Fireweed (*Chamerion angustifolium*), Bunchberry (*Cornus unalaschkensis*), and Harsh paintbrush (*Castilleja hispida*) make their first appearance. It only gets better the higher you go.

Before reaching a talus slope, a good deal of darkish rocks above and below the trail becomes common. In these rocks can be seen the dome of white flowers that indicate Valerian (*Valeriana sitchensis*), the flat-top cream-colored inflorescences of Red elderberry (*Sambucus racemosa*), and the smaller, less frequent albino flower domes of Sitka mountain ash (*Sorbus sitchensis*). Mountain ash and Valerian look similar from a distance, but the former is shrubby with serrated pinnately compound leaves and the latter is a tall herb with oppositely arranged simple leaves.

A mile from Mason Creek, leave the forest for good and come to Bandera Junction. To the right (east) the trail continues another 1.0 mile to the false summit preceding Bandera Mountain. Too much bushwhacking after that precludes all but

the hardiest souls from continuing. Our trail turns to the left (north) and the wildflower garden of the Ira Spring Trail comes fully into its own. If you get here at the right time (usually mid to late July), the entire hillside is given over to Beargrass, Fireweed, Paintbrush, and a dozen other colorful species.

The odd-looking and scaly green plant that appears to be crawling over and around the rocks is called Running clubmoss (*Lycopodium clavitum*).

Achlys californica, *Vanilla leaf.*

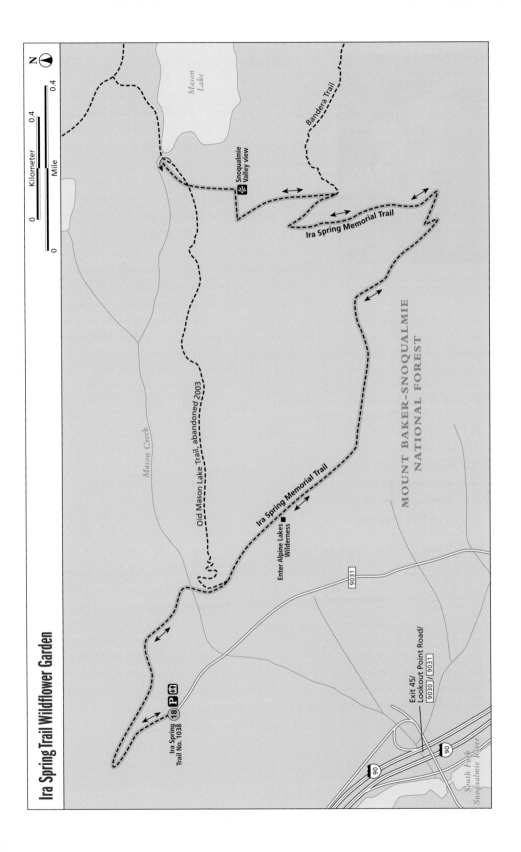

Ira Spring Trail Wildflower Garden

N

Kilometer
0   0.4   0.4
Mile

Mason Lake

Bandera Trail

Snoqualmie Valley view

Ira Spring Memorial Trail

Mason Creek

Old Mason Lake Trail, abandoned 2003

Ira Spring Memorial Trail

Enter Alpine Lakes Wilderness

MOUNT BAKER-SNOQUALMIE NATIONAL FOREST

Ira Spring Trail No. 1038

18 P

9031

Exit 45/ Lookout Point Road/ 9030 / 9031

90

90

South Fork Snoqualmie River

Lupinus latifolius, *Broad-leaf lupine.*

It's a primitive vascular plant older than the ferns. In its glory days before the Age of Dinosaurs, *Lycopodium* evolved into large trees. All representatives of this vestigial group of plants are now little more than inconspicuous herbs. They don't have flowers, they produce cones—similar to pines and firs, except much smaller.

A mile past Bandera Junction, the trail reaches a ridgetop that provides the best views yet of Snoqualmie Valley, Puget Sound, and Mount Rainier. The trees are a mix of Mountain hemlock, Grand fir, and Subalpine fir. Growing among the rocks is Mountain heather (*Phyllodoce empetriformis*) with its urn-shaped pink or rose-colored flowers. Follow the trail over the ridge for a 0.4-mile descent though a nearly pure Mountain hemlock forest to Mason Lake. There is camping at the north end of the lake, and trails take off in various directions to other exciting destinations. Through with exploring the lake's environs? Turn around and retrace your steps back to the trailhead and your motor transport.

Miles and Directions

0.0 Ira Spring trailhead.
1.0 Trail splits.
2.0 Bandera Junction.
3.0 Snoqualmie Valley view.
3.4 Mason Lake.
6.8 Arrive back at trailhead.

Other Nearby Hiking Options

From Mason Lake, backpackers can head off in all directions to such places as Thompson Lake, Mount Defiance, Kulla Kulla Lake, Pratt Lake, and beyond. The world is your oyster!

Hike Information

The trail memorializes photographer, author, and environmental activist Ira Spring. One of his projects, conducted with Volunteers for Outdoor Washington, was to successfully lobby the Forest Service to close the original trail, built in 1958 to enable fire crews to access Mason Lake. The current footpath was completed in 2003, replacing the old route that went 1,700 feet straight up Mason Creek. Imagine how badly eroded it was!

19 Ollalie Meadow–Twin Lakes Loop

It's hard to believe sometimes that anything special could be found in a forest so close to the large metropolitan area of Seattle and greater Puget Sound, a major ski resort, and an interstate highway. Ollalie Meadow, with its diverse displays of wildflowers, demonstrates the value of keeping an open mind on that subject. And so does the loop trail to Twin Lakes, which should more properly be called "The Greater Snoqualmie Huckleberry Garden" since the entire route is one long huckleberry patch. During the fall you can easily pick your fill from the four species of *Vaccinium* ssp. that line the trail.

Start: Pacific Crest Trail (Forest Trail 2000) trailhead at Windy Pass
Distance: 6.8-mile lollipop with an additional out-and-back
Hiking time: About 4–6 hours
Difficulty: Moderate to strenuous, with some route finding and one particularly long and steep downhill section
Trail surface: Forested path, gravel road
Seasons: Spring, summer, and fall. Best wildflowers: June–August (June 16, 2015).
Other trail users: None
Canine compatibility: Leashed dogs allowed

Land status: Okanogan-Wenatchee National Forest
Nearest town: North Bend
Services: Gas, food, lodging
Permits: None
Maps: Green Trails #207S Snoqualmie Pass Gateway; USGS Snoqualmie Pass; DeLorme Page 71 F-10, G-10
Trail contact: Okanogan-Wenatchee National Forest, Cle Elum District
Special considerations: No water or toilet at trailhead. Devil's club, a long and steep downhill section of trail, and some route finding due to deadfall on trail.

Finding the trailhead: From I-90, take exit 54 (Hyak) and head south on Hyak Drive, crossing WA 906. Also signed Hyak Drive E., the narrow but paved road proceeds for 0.9 mile, reaching a sewage oxidation pond on the left (east) before turning to a good gravel road that shortly forms a junction with FR 9070. Drive 4.3 miles on this occasionally rough road, passing the trailhead to Mount Catherine, and in another 0.3 mile finding parking at Windy Pass alongside FR 9070.
GPS: N47 22.388' / W12 26.816'

Plants You Might See
Arnica latifolia, Mountain arnica, Asteraceae
Aruncus dioicus, Goatsbeard, Rosaceae
Blechnum spicant, Deer fern, Polypodiaceae
Chamerion angustifolium, Fireweed, Onagraceae
Dodecatheon jeffreyi, Jeffrey's shooting star, Primulaceae
Fragaria vesca, Wild strawberry, Rosaceae
Menyanthes trifoliata, Buckbean, Menyanthaceae
Parnassia fimbriata, Fringed grass-of-Parnassus, Saxifragaceae

Piperia unalascensis, Alaska rein-orchid, Orchidaceae

Rhododendron albiflorum, White rhododendron, Ericaceae

Senecio triangularis, Arrowleaf groundsel, Asteraceae

Spiranthes romanzoffiana, Hooded lady's tresses, Orchidaceae

Viburnum edule, Highbush cranberry, Adoxaceae

The Hike

FR 9070 bisects the Pacific Crest Trail. Find the trail sign pointing to Stampede Pass and enter a copse of dwarf Mountain hemlock, a forest regenerating from logging activity. The predominant shrubs here are all huckleberries of some sort. You'll see Mountain huckleberry (*Vaccinium membranaceum*), Cascade huckleberry (*V. deliciosum*), and Oval-leafed huckleberry (*V. ovalifolium*). Grouseberry (*V. scoparium*) has also been reported from the area. If you're here during autumn, it's highly likely you won't get much hiking done, as you'll easily be overwhelmed by all the berry-picking possibilities. Buck up, though! The entire Twin Lakes loop trail is one long huckleberry patch that make the pickings seem endless.

In 0.1 mile is a small pond—really a bog. Here, and in other wet areas along the trail, early in the season you'll find Sticky asphodel (*Triantha occidentalis*), plenty of Marsh marigold (*Caltha leptosepala*), and the delicately bloomed Canby's licorice root

Take time to stop and appreciate the flowers along the trail.

Achlys californica, *Vanilla leaf.*

Aquilegia formosa, *Columbine.*

Clintonia uniflora, *Queen's cup.*

Cornus unalaschkensis, *Bunchberry.*

Polygonum bistortoides, *Bistort.*

Xerophyllum tenax, *Beargrass.*

Tolmiea menziesii, *Piggy-back plant.*

Spirea densiflora, *Rosy spirea.*

Senecio triangularis, *Arrowleaf groundsel.*

Mertensia paniculata, *Tall bluebells.*

Pedicularis groenlandica, *Elephant's head.*

Eriophorum polystachion, *Narrow-leaved cottongrass.*

Ligusticum canbyi, *Canby's licorice-root.*   Caltha leptosepala, *Marsh marigold.*
DAVE FLOTREE/ELLEN HAUPTMANN

(*Ligusticum canbyi*). On the edges of the pond is shrubby Rosy spirea (*Spiraea densiflora*) with its fabulously pink to deep rose clustered flower heads. There is also Sitka mountain ash (*Sorbus sitchensis*). This pond and the other ponds located upslope from here are home to many species of sedge, rush, and grass.

The trail enters a deep, dark forest of mature Mountain hemlock and climbs at a very nice incline. In early summer the shady trailside is overflowing with Queen's cup (*Clintonia uniflora*), Trillium (*Trillium ovatum*), and Vanilla leaf (*Achlys californica*). Where the sun breaks through the canopy, expect to see Red columbine (*Aquilegia formosa*) and Tall bluebells (*Mertensia paniculata*). There's also Bistort (*Polygonum bistortoides*); the inflorescence resembles a wooly sheep that has been run up a flagpole.

The trail crosses several branches of upper Cold Creek, and the sounds of I-90 fade away to whispers and then to nothingness in the quiet of the hemlock forest. After 1.5 miles is an avalanche chute—a great place to stop and look around. There is a lot of Beargrass (*Xerophyllum tenax*), Green false hellebore (*Veratrum viride*), Broad-leaf lupine (*Lupinus latifolius*), Rosy spirea, and so much more poking out of the rocks. Also notice the damage wrought to the trees by winter's sliding snows.

In another 0.7 mile come to a shallow pond, perfect for resting, meditation, and eating lunch. Leaving the pond the trail climbs a bit, passing a succession of boggy areas, chockablock with Marsh marigold, Pink mountain heather (*Phyllodoce empetriformis*), and plenty of . . . You guessed it! Huckleberries. A further 0.6 mile brings you to a junction of the PCT

Arnica latifolia, *Mountain arnica*

Drosera rotundifolia, *Sundew.*

and Cold Creek Trail. Turn left (north). The PCT continues 0.7 mile south to Mirror Lake, then Oregon, terminating in the deserts of California.

The Cold Creek Trail plunges 1,400 vertical feet over the next 1.7 miles to reach Twin Lakes. It's so steep in areas, it seems stairs would be in order. An area of deadfall two-thirds of the way down covers the ground with some large Mountain hemlock logs, obliterating the trail. Pick your way through it all, ignoring a significant waytrail that goes uphill, and reacquaint yourself with the real trail going down.

Twin Lakes has a shallow shoreline where the Cold Creek Trail comes in. To cross over to the other side, you can either use the log (caution advised, it's a long way down from the log to the creek) or work your way around the shore. In 0.1 mile cross an old access road; the trail continues on the other side. Cold Creek Trail rises through a forest of Western hemlock for 1.0 mile to hit FR 9070. Turn left (north) and in 0.3 mile return to your car.

To complete the hike, take the PCT for 0.4 mile towards Snoqualmie Pass. Walk though a regenerating forest with Beargrass, Rosy spirea, Bunchberry (*Cornus unalaschkensis*), and huckleberry to Ollalie Meadow. In the large meadow you'll find lots to see, including some very special plants such as Narrow-leaved cotton grass (*Eriophorum polystachion*). After this sedge-like plant has flowered and fruited, it produces tufts of what look like cotton balls. Also in the meadow is Elephant's head (*Pedicularis groenlandica*). Once you've seen this flower, you'll instantly know where the common name came from. Like other members of the genus, Elephant's head is a partial parasite, attacking the roots of nearby shrubs.

The real glory of Ollalie Meadow is a plant of such diminutive stature that it will go unseen by any and all who are not willing to get down on their hands and knees and search the damp areas. This is Sundew (*Drosera rotundifolia*). There are at least 194 species of the insectivorous Sundew (*Drosera* spp.). They are found in both the northern and southern hemispheres, with over 50 percent of the species occurring in Australia. The plants grow in habitats where the soil is moist and acidic, and light is plentiful. Insects are trapped by sticky, stalked glands on the Sundew's leaves. These glands secrete a mucilage that attracts the insects, snares them, and provides the enzymes that dissolve the creature's body. The liberated nutrients are then absorbed through the plant's leaves.

When ready to leave the meadow, retrace your steps to Windy Pass and your car.

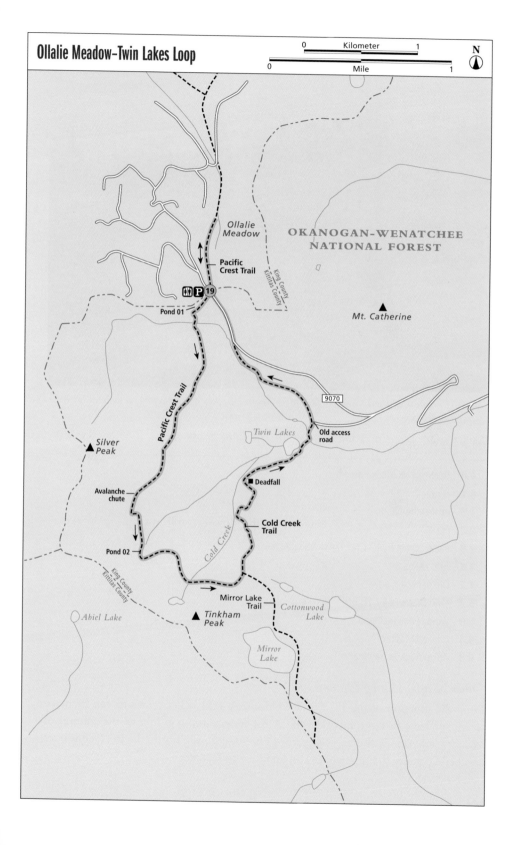

Ollalie Meadow–Twin Lakes Loop

0   Kilometer   1

0   Mile   1

N

Ollalie Meadow

Pacific Crest Trail

OKANOGAN–WENATCHEE NATIONAL FOREST

King County / Kittitas County

Mt. Catherine

P 19

Pond 01

9070

Twin Lakes

Old access road

Silver Peak

Pacific Crest Trail

Avalanche chute

■ Deadfall

Cold Creek Trail

Pond 02

Cold Creek

King County / Kittitas County

Abiel Lake

Mirror Lake Trail

▲ Tinkham Peak

Cottonwood Lake

Mirror Lake

Bogs and ponds might seem inviting for only biting insects, but they also provide habitat for some unusual plants.

Miles and Directions

0.0 Trailhead at Windy Pass.

0.1 Pond.

1.6 Avalanche chute.

2.3 Pond.

2.9 Pacific Crest Trail / Cold Creek Trail junction.

4.6 Twin Lakes.

4.7 Old access road.

5.7 Cold Creek Trail / FR 9070 junction.

6.0 Windy Pass trailhead.

6.4 Ollalie Meadow.

6.8 Arrive back at trailhead.

Other Nearby Hiking Options

From the junction of the PCT and Cold Creek Trail, side excursions can be make to Mirror Lake or Cottonwood Lake. A 2.4-mile round-trip hike to the summit of Mount Catherine is also accessible from FR 9070. To the north, the PCT continues another 6.5 miles to Snoqualmie Pass and then to Canada.

20 Kendall Katwalk

This is one of those classic Cascade Mountain hikes justifiably famous for lots of reasons. First and foremost are the wildflowers; you'll see plenty of them in the talus fields the trail traverses. And then there's views everywhere: northward to Mount Thompson and into the heart of the Alpine Lakes Wilderness, south to Mount Rainier, westward across the valley to Red Mountain and Guye Peak, east to Keechelus Lake. Finally, don't miss the Katwalk—a stretch of trail blasted out of a rock wall. All this makes the Kendall Katwalk one of the most popular hikes around Snoqualmie Pass, so be prepared for herds of people on sunny weekends.

Start: Parking area at Snoqualmie Pass for Pacific Crest Trail #2000
Distance: 11.0 miles out and back
Hiking time: About 6–8 hours
Difficulty: Moderate
Trail surface: Forested path, talus, rocky
Seasons: Spring and fall. Best wildflowers: June–August (July 11, 2015).
Other trail users: Trail runners, equestrians
Canine compatibility: Leashed dogs allowed
Land status: Mount Baker–Snoqualmie National Forest
Nearest town: North Bend

Services: Gas, food, lodging
Permit: Northwest Forest Pass
Maps: Green Trails #207S Snoqualmie Pass Gateway; USGS Snoqualmie Pass; DeLorme Page 71 F-10
Trail contacts: Alpine Lakes Protection Society; Middle Fork Snoqualmie, Mount Baker–Snoqualmie National Forest, North Bend Office
Special considerations: Dangerous snow crossing and possibility of avalanches on the Katwalk in early season. Vault toilet at trailhead. No potable water at trailhead.

Finding the trailhead: From I-90, take exit 52 (West Summit) and turn left (north) at the end of the ramp, passing under the freeway and onto Alpental Road. After 0.1 mile take the first right, an unmarked road. The road splits in another 0.1 mile, and on the left is parking for people with stock and on the right is parking for people. **GPS: N47 25.672' / W121 24.802'**

Plants You Might See

Aconitum columbianum, Monkshood, Ranunculaceae
Anaphalis margaritacea, Pearly everlasting, Asteraceae
Asarum caudatum, Wild ginger, Aristolochiaceae
Erigeron glacialis, Subalpine daisy, Asteraceae
Erythranthe guttata, Yellow monkeyflower, Phrymaceae
Erythranthe lewisii, Lewis's monkeyflower, Phrymaceae
Goodyera oblongifolia, Rattlesnake plantain, Orchidaceae
Lilium columbianum, Leopard lily, Liliaceae
Rhododendron albiflorum, White rhododendron, Ericaceae
Trillium ovatum, Trillium, Liliaceae
Veratrum viride, Green false hellebore, Liliaceae

Find the trail between the vault toilet and reader board at the east end of the large, paved parking area. Despite its size, the lot fills up early on weekends—on sunny days or not.

In 100 feet come to a sturdy picnic table. To the right (south) the Pacific Crest Trail takes off for Snoqualmie Pass and Mexico. Bear left (east) and quickly intersect the horse trail coming from the equestrian trailhead. The moss-lined trail proceeds under

a forest of Western and Mountain hemlock, Pacific silver fir, Devil's club (*Oplopanax horridus*), Bunchberry (*Cornus unalaschkensis*), and several kinds of huckleberry (*Vaccinium* spp.). This first stretch of trail is moist, and you can expect to see Marsh marigold (*Caltha leptosepala*), Deer fern (*Blechnum spicant*), Queen's cup (*Clintonia uniflora*), Small-flowered alumroot (*Heuchera micrantha*), False Solomon's seal (*Maianthemum racemosum*), Fringecup (*Tellima grandiflora*), and Piggyback plant (*Tolmiea menziesii*).

The trail climbs steadily but not too steeply for 2.5 miles, passes into the Alpine Lakes Wilderness, and makes three prominent switchbacks before reaching a junction with the Commonwealth Basin Trail.

Aconitum columbianum, *Monkshood.*

Bear right (northeast) through a forest that is increasingly dominated by Mountain hemlock and Subalpine fir.

In another 1.8 miles the trail traverses a series of talus fields and avalanche slopes below Kendall Peak, which could collectively be considered "wildflower heaven" on account of the vast numbers of species encountered. Early in the spring you'll see the flat-topped cream-colored blossoms of Red elderberry (*Sambucus racemosa*).

Aquilegia formosa, *Columbine.*

Campanula rotundifolia, *Common harebell.*

Erythranthe lewisii, *Lewis's monkeyflower.*   Chamerion angustifolium, *Fireweed.*

Erythanthe gutatta, *is called Yellow monkey-*   Castilleja miniata, *Scarlet paintbrush.*
flower because the face of the flower resembles
the face of a monkey… or so they say!

By summer these will have changed to clusters of red berries. In purple fields of Fireweed (*Chamerion angustifolium*), look for Sitka burnet (*Sanguisorba sitchensis*)—the inflorescences resemble bunches of bottle brushes poking up out of the ground.

Other spring beauties alongside the trail include Common harebell (*Campanula rotundifolia*), Partridgefoot (*Luetkea pectinata*), Sickletop lousewort (*Pedicularis racemosa*), and Davidson's penstemon (*Penstemon davidsonii*). In and among the rocks in the talus field you'll find some shrubs including White mountain heather (*Cassiope mertensiana*), Red mountain heather (*Phyllodoce empetriformis*), and Ground juniper (*Juniperus communis*).

Leaving wildflower heaven behind, the trail climbs through an "airy" section that will have you thinking, "This must be the Katwalk," but it's only a precursor of precipitous views to come. In 0.7 mile, in a copse of dwarf Mountain hemlock, you'll come to a waytrail that leads up the highly exposed route to Kendall Peak. Soon, you'll know you're at the Katwalk after another 0.5 mile when you see a sign nailed to a tree that warns equestrians, "Dismount. Check ahead. Proceed with caution."

The actual Kendall Katwalk is about 0.3 mile in length and wide enough for two hikers to walk astride or pass in opposite directions, though the exposure will have

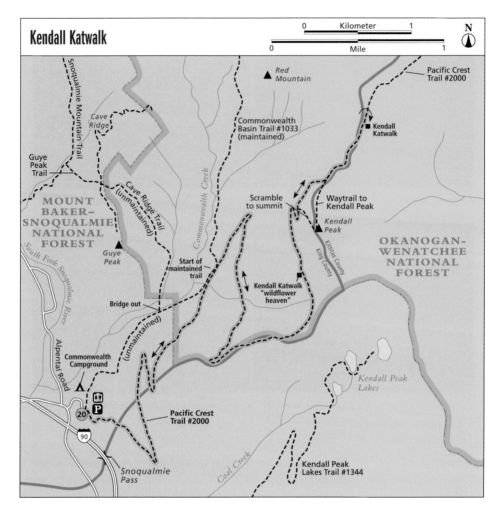

Kendall Katwalk

Kilometer 0 — 1
Mile 0 — 1

N

Red Mountain

Pacific Crest Trail #2000

Snoqualmie Mountain Trail

Cave Ridge

Commonwealth Basin Trail #1033 (maintained)

Kendall Katwalk

Guye Peak Trail

Cave Ridge Trail (unmaintained)

Commonwealth Creek

Scramble to summit

Waytrail to Kendall Peak

Kendall Peak

MOUNT BAKER– SNOQUALMIE NATIONAL FOREST

South Fork Snoqualmie River

Guye Peak

Start of maintained trail

Kendall Katwalk "wildflower heaven"

Kittitas County

King County

OKANOGAN– WENATCHEE NATIONAL FOREST

Bridge out

(unmaintained)

Alpental Road

Commonwealth Campground

Kendall Peak Lakes

20

P

Pacific Crest Trail #2000

90

Snoqualmie Pass

Coal Creek

Kendall Peak Lakes Trail #1344

most hikers hugging the cliff and wishing for a handrail. Should you encounter a horse and rider, find a secure spot on the cliff side of the trail and be still, allowing the bigger animals to pass. Continue on as long as you like after the Katwalk before turning around and retracing your steps to the parking area.

Miles and Directions

0.0 Pacific Crest Trail parking area at Snoqualmie Pass.

2.5 Trail junction to Commonwealth Basin.

4.3 Kendall Katwalk "wildflower heaven."

5.5 Kendall Katwalk.

11.0 Arrive back at trailhead.

Other Nearby Hiking Options

There is an unmarked path around the 5-mile mark that leads up the side of Kendall Peak to the summit. Some technical climbing skills are required. Watch for loose rock. There's a bit of exposure at the ridgeline, so this route is not for the faint of heart. But, what is?

Continue on past the Katwalk to Canada on the PCT if you like. For a shorter backpacking trip with more great scenery and wildflowers, plus alpine lakes, arrange a car shuttle and hike the 75 miles or so to Stevens Pass.

Hike Information

Asarum caudatum, *Wild ginger.*
DAVE FLOTREE/ELLEN HAUPTMANN

When the Pacific Crest Trail was created, it adopted many extant routes along its way, all of which were eventually linked by new trail construction. One such adopted route was the old Cascade Crest Trail that left Snoqualmie Pass and continued north through Commonwealth Basin, over Red Pass, and through the Middle Fork Snoqualmie Valley to many points north. However, this well-watered route was lacking in scenic grandeur, so a new trail was created in the late 1970s to closely follow the spine of the mountains in order to maximize awesome views. Trail builders found it easier to blast a trail out of the mountainside than find a way around it, and the Kendall Katwalk was born.

21 Tonga Ridge

It's uncommon to see more than three dominant conifer species in our western forests. The Tonga Ridge Trail offers six, including two unusual sightings. There's the uncommonly seen Alaska yellow cedar along with Engelmann spruce—not usually seen west of the Cascade Mountains. All this plus views, views, views, and a stroll through a heather-land subalpine meadow. Pretty good for a trail that allows your automobile to do the hard work of gaining all the elevation! Huckleberry lovers will also be happy in autumn to find four different species to delight their taste buds. Timing your visit to beat the birds and the bears to this berry cornucopia is always a challenge.

Start: Tonga Ridge Trail parking area at the end of FR 310

Distance: 6.0 miles out and back

Hiking time: About 4–5 hours

Difficulty: Easy

Trail surface: Forested path

Seasons: Summer and fall. Best wildflowers: June–August (June 13, 2015).

Other trail users: None

Canine compatibility: Leashed dogs allowed

Land status: Alpine Lakes Wilderness

Nearest towns: Gold Bar and Skykomish

Services: Gas, food, lodging

Permits: Northwest Forest Pass, Wilderness Permit (free at trailhead)

Maps: Green Trails #176S Alpine Lakes–Stevens Pass; USGS Skykomish; DeLorme Page 71 C-12

Trail contact: Mount Baker-Snoqualmie National Forest, Wild Sky Wilderness. Alpine Lakes Wilderness

Special considerations: No potable water at trailhead. Pit toilet with no privacy screen at trailhead.

Finding the trailhead: Find FR 68 (Foss River Road) 0.4 mile east of the Skykomish Ranger Station on WA 2 and turn south. In 1.1 miles the pavement ends at a fork in the road. Turn right (south). This good gravel road, FR 68, continues for 2.3 miles to another fork (sometimes signed, sometimes not). Turn left (south) on FR 6830, which switchbacks up above the Foss River for 6.5 miles until reaching a junction with FR 310. Turn right (south) and proceed 1.3 miles to the trailhead at the end of the road. Parking is extremely limited; be considerate and leave room for others. **GPS: N47 40.728' / W121 15.890'**

Plants You Might See

Holodiscus discolor, Oceanspray, Rosaceae

Picea engelmannii, Engelmann spruce, Pinaceae

Sambucus racemosa, Red elderberry, *Adoxaceae*

Vaccinium membranaceum, Black huckleberry, Ericaceae

Vaccinium ovalifolium, Oval-leafed blueberry, Ericaceae

The Hike

The Tonga Ridge Trail (#1058) starts behind a reader board at the far end of the parking lot (really, a wide spot in the road that terminates at the trailhead). To the right (west) a short trail leads down to a rudimentary pit toilet badly in need of repair. Perhaps Northwest Forest Pass funds can be used here?

You begin in a forest of mostly Western hemlock with the occasional Douglas fir thrown in. Two trees you won't see are Big-leaf maple and Red alder. The reason for this is twofold. First: elevation. The trail takes off at 4,300 feet—beyond the normal range of both species. Second: This is an old-growth forest. By the time a forest like this reaches its maturity, it has outlasted the lifespan of Bigleaf maple and Red alder.

The trail does most of its climbing in the first mile. The hemlocks are large and grow close together and effectively shade out any shrubs or herbs except for the odd spot here and there. Later on, as the forest thins, look for Bracken fern (*Pteridium aquilinum*), Broad-leaf lupine (*Lupinus latifolius*), Tall bluebells (*Mertensia paniculata*), Small-flowered penstemon (*Penstemon procerus*), and

Sanguisorba sitchensis, *Sitka burnet.*

Harsh paintbrush (*Castilleja hispida*) in the sun breaks.

You'll see a lot of Sitka mountain ash (*Sorbus sitchensis*) along the trail from beginning to end. Spot its odd-pinnately compound leaves, dome of closely clustered white flowers, and (in the fall) red berries. These fruits are bitter but edible. Birds like them, but history has shown they don't appear to need sugar to enjoy the fruit of their labors.

After 1.1 miles the trail enters the Alpine Lakes Wilderness, and in 0.2 mile more, a short spur trail on the left (east) takes you to a nice mountain view. Two miles from the trailhead you reach a waytrail to the summit of Mount Sawyer. If you've gone too far, you quickly come to a depression, now a meadow, just off the east side of the

Cassiope mertensiana, *White mountain-heather.*

Erigeron glacialis, *Sub-alpine daisy.*

trail. This small, yet deep, declivity is marked on older maps as "Lake Sawyer." In any event, the unsigned 0.8-mile waytrail for the summit of Mount Sawyer is nearby. Look for a cairn of rocks (not always there) and a steep, beaten, dirt path on the east side of the trail. Views from the peak are stupendous. Don't forget to look around your feet for Spreading phlox (*Phlox diffusa*) and Davidson's penstemon (*Penstemon davidsonii*).

Another 1.0 mile brings you to Sawyer Pass and a great place to stop for lunch. Besides its thick-growing carpet of Cascade huckleberry (*Vaccinium deliciosum*), this subalpine meadow is home to White rhododendron (*Rhododendron albiflorum*), Pink mountain heather (*Phyllodoce empetriformis*), and White mountain heather (*Cassiope mertensiana*).

Despite the draw of views and wildflowers, the real stars of the Tonga Ridge Trail are the conifers. Lowland hikers will recognize both Western hemlock and Douglas fir. But these two species quickly drop from the plant list as you get farther from the trailhead. Then, Mountain hemlock becomes the most prevalent tree seen. Its cones are plumper, though about the size and shape of those found on Douglas fir, and lack the extruding little "mouse tail" found with *Pseudotsuga menziesii* cones. Mountain hemlock foliage, viewed head-on, resembles clustered explosions of bright green fireworks.

Lupinus latifolius, *Broad-leaf lupine.*

There are two true firs seen along the trail. The first is Pacific silver fir. It's a tall, stout, straight-growing tree. But for being susceptible to heart-rot, this fir would have been suitable for ship's masts during the age of sail. The lower branches are flattish with 1¼-inch-long needles that are bluntly pointed or notched at their tips. Upper branches have erect needles. Like all true firs, the long cones of Pacific silver fir point up (not down, as with other conifers) and disintegrate on the tree. You won't see them cluttering the forest floor.

Another fir that grows with increasing density along the trail and all over the slopes of Mount Sawyer is Subalpine fir. Firs can be

Tonga Ridge

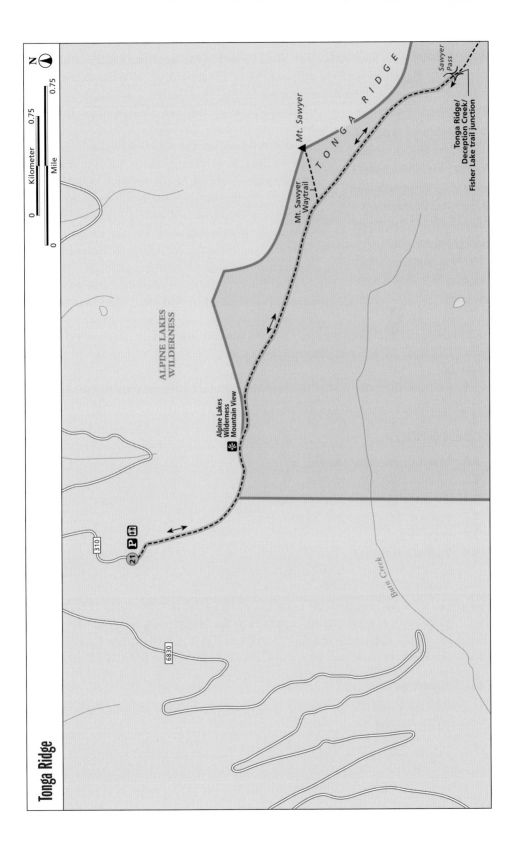

N

Kilometer
0   0.75   0.75

Mile
0

ALPINE LAKES
WILDERNESS

TONGA RIDGE

Mt. Sawyer

Mt. Sawyer
Waytrail

Sawyer
Pass

Tonga Ridge/
Deception Creek/
Fisher Lake trail junction

Alpine Lakes
Wilderness
Mountain View

310

21

6830

Burn Creek

difficult to tell apart from each other when viewed in the hand, but Subalpine fir is never confusing when seen from a distance. These firs are dark in color, slender, erect, and nearly perfectly Christmas-tree shaped.

▶ **Mount Sawyer is named for a Forest Service ranger, George Sawyer, who worked many years in the Skykomish Ranger District. There was a fire lookout on Tonga Ridge throughout the 1920s, which was probably built in response to a 1914 fire in the area.**

The real prize on this trail is having the opportunity to see so many individuals of Alaska yellow cedar (*Xanthocyparis nootkatensis*). The tree isn't especially rare along its distribution from northern California through southeast Alaska, but it is decidedly uncommon. Some observers see a yellowish cast to the thin, scaly, fluted bark, and some see gray in color. The cones are globose and small, like the tree's cousins in the Juniper family; the foliage is flattened—almost as if ironed—like true cedars and false cedars such as Western red cedar. This beautiful tree almost appears sorrowful. Its branches sweep and bow low to the ground, as if carrying the weight of the world on its shoulders. The appearance of sorrow is accentuated because this year's dead brown foliage is retained until next year, giving the overall effect in color of a tree in mourning.

To return to the parking area, turn around at Sawyer Pass and retrace your steps though the wonderful garden of Tonga Ridge conifers.

Miles and Directions

0.0 Tonga Ridge Trail #1058 trailhead.

1.1 Alpine Lakes Wilderness boundary.

1.3 Alpine Lakes Wilderness mountain viewpoint.

2.0 Waytrail to Mount Sawyer and "Sawyer Lake."

3.0 Sawyer Pass.

6.0 Arrive back at trailhead.

Other Nearby Hiking Options

From Sawyer Pass an unsigned trail continues south for 1.8 miles to Fisher Lake. The Tonga Ridge Trail, which is signed, continues to the Deception Creek Trail #1059. This route can be followed north for 5.5 miles to WA 2 and Deception Falls State Park. A much longer route continues south, deep into the Alpine Lakes Wilderness.

Hike Information

The round-trip length of this trail has been variously reported as being anywhere between 5.5 miles and 8 miles long.

22 Gold Creek Pond

It's only a mile of walking on an asphalt trail. And the pond is a gravel pit left over from the construction of I-90 that Conservation Northwest and the Forest Service are restoring to a natural habitat with 6,000 locally adapted native plants. With all that you'd think Gold Creek Pond hardly worth the effort of an hour's drive from Seattle. But you'd be wrong, because Gold Creek Pond is wildflower paradise! And a wonderful place for birding too. You can spend an hour here or an entire day.

Start: Parking lot for Gold Creek Pond
Distance: 1-mile lollipop
Hiking time: About 1–4 hours
Difficulty: Easy
Trail surface: ADA-approved asphalt
Seasons: Spring, summer, and fall. Best wildflowers: May–July (May 28, 2015).
Other trail users: None
Canine compatibility: Leashed dogs allowed
Land status: Mount Baker–Snoqualmie National Forest
Nearest town: North Bend
Services: Gas, food, lodging
Permit: Northwest Forest Pass

Maps: Green Trails #207S Snoqualmie Pass Gateway; USGS Chikamin Peak; Mount Baker–Snoqualmie National Forest, Alpine Lakes Wilderness; DeLorme Page 65 A-6
Trail contacts: Okanogan-Wenatchee National Forest, Cle Elum Office; Mount Baker–Snoqualmie National Forest, North Bend Office; Alpine Lakes Protection Society; Middle Fork Snoqualmie
Special considerations: No fishing or swimming allowed in Gold Creek Pond. No bicycles allowed on trail. Roadsides in the area have been treated with herbicides to control weeds.

Finding the trailhead: From I-90, take exit 54. Turn north and pass under the freeway. In 0.1 mile make a right turn onto FR 4832. In 1 mile turn left on FR 142 to Gold Creek trailhead parking (signed). The paved parking lot is after 0.3 mile of hard-pack gravel road. **GPS: N47 23.801' / W121 22.758'**

Plants You Might See

Achlys californica, Vanilla leaf, Berberidaceae
Amelanchier alnifolia, Saskatoon, Rosaceae
Cornus sericea, Redosier dogwood, Cornaceae
Cornus unalaschkensis, Bunchberry, Cornaceae
Dicentra formosa, Bleeding heart, Papaveraceae
Fragaria virginiana, Wild strawberry, Rosaceae
Linnaea borealis, Twinflower, Linnaeaceae
Lonicera involucrata, Twinberry, Caprifoliaceae
Maianthemum dilatatum, False lily-of-the-valley, Liliaceae
Maianthemum racemosum, False Solomon's seal, Liliaceae
Maianthemum stellatum, Star-flowered false Solomon's seal. Liliaceae
Mertensia paniculata, Tall bluebells, Boraginaceae

Phleum pratense, Timothy, Poaceae

Pteridium aquilinum, Bracken fern, Polypodiaceae

Rubus spectabilis, Salmonberry, Rosaceae

Sambucus racemosa, Red elderberry, Adoxaceae

Sorbus sitchensis, Sitka mountain ash, Rosaceae

Thalictrum occidentale, Western meadow-rue, Ranunculaceae

Trillium ovatum, Trillium, Liliaceae

Viola palustris, Marsh violet, Violaceae

Viola sempervirens, Trailing yellow violet, Violaceae

The Hike

The ADA-approved asphalt Gold Creek Pond trail begins west of the vault toilet and behind the reader board. There are lots of signs to read here, mostly telling you what you cannot do. On the positive side, one sign says that the Audubon Society has designated this trail as the "Sun and Sage Loop," part of the "Great Washington Birding Trail."

Viola sempervirens, *Trailing yellow violet.*

Mertensia paniculata, *Tall bluebells.*

Perhaps because this 1-mile loop trail has been reclaimed from abuse, monitored for weedy plants, and consciously revegetated with natives, there is a remarkable diversity of things to see. Oh, there're the usual forest trees: Douglas fir, Mountain hemlock, Red alder, and a few Black cottonwood (*Populus trichocarpa*) here and there. But there is also a smattering of Western white pine and Lodgepole pine. All of Gold Creek Pond, for its minuscule size, offers a palate of color and species diversity to entice any wildflower lover. Despite the brevity of walking, do take your time to savor every inch of this trail, for there is so much to see.

Leaving the parking lot, the trail splits in 0.1 mile. Peel off to the left (west), walking clockwise around the pond. Soon, reach a large picnic area with lots of pond

Sambucus racemosa, *Red elderberry.*

Fragaria virginiana, *Wild strawberry.*

Maianthemum stellatum, *Star-flowered false Solomon's seal.*

Trillium ovatum, *Trillium.* DAVE FLOTREE/ ELLEN HAUPTMANN

Achlys californica, *Vanilla leaf.*

Acer circinatum, *Vine maple.*

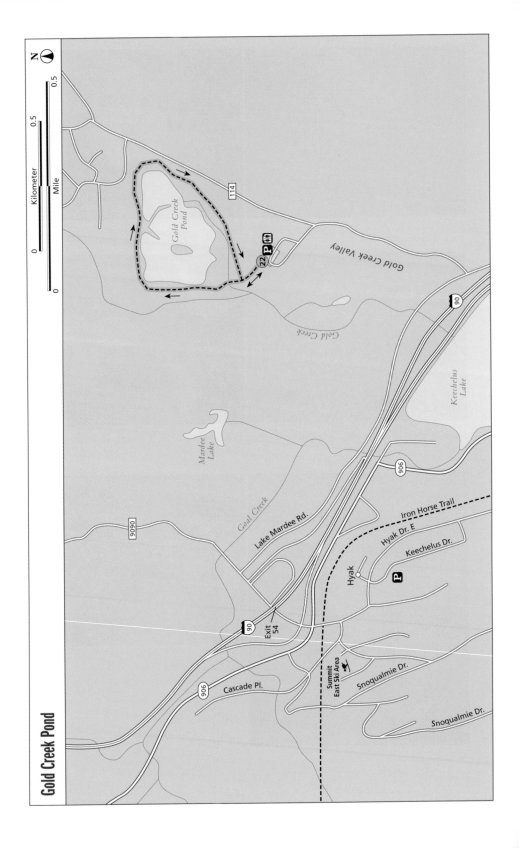

Gold Creek Pond

Gold Creek Pond

Gold Creek Valley

Gold Creek

Keechelus Lake

Mardee Lake

Goal Creek

Lake Mardee Rd.

Iron Horse Trail

Hyak Dr. E

Keechelus Dr.

Hyak

Exit 54

Summit East Ski Area

Snoqualmie Dr.

Snoqualmie Dr.

Cascade Pl.

N

Kilometer
0   0.5

Mile
0   0.5

views as well as a great look into the rocky mountain high country of the Alpine Lakes Wilderness, itself a botanical cornucopia defying description. There's a short spur trail halfway around the pond to the pond's shore, where you'll see Caltha-leaved avens (*Geum calthifolium*) and Large-leaved avens (*G. macrophyllum*).

Another 0.2 mile after that comes a bridge followed by another shorter bridge and a long boardwalk that traverses a wet meadow. Here you'll find a couple of different violets, lots of Bunchberry (*Cornus unalaschkensis*), and everything else you'd expect in such a wet place.

All too soon the trail finishes its circumambulation of Gold Creek Pond and the last bit of asphalt walking brings you to the parking lot.

Miles and Directions

0.0 Gold Creek Pond trailhead and parking lot.
0.1 Trail splits.
0.3 Cross bridge.
1.0 Arrive back at trailhead and parking lot.

Other Nearby Hiking Options

With a whole lot more effort and work, you can see almost all the same species from Gold Creek Pond, except huckleberries, by hiking to Margaret Lake or Lake Lillian. Both lakes are accessed by driving about 5 miles farther on down FR 4832 to its junction with the unsigned Road 4934 and a parking area that appears to have once been a log-loading platform.

Hike Information

Beginning in the late 1970s and ending in 1983, what is now Gold Creek Pond was a gravel pit for the construction of I-90. As part of revegetating the land surrounding Gold Creek Pond, there is active management for controlling weeds. Monitoring sites are marked with a piece of rebar, labeled and topped with a plastic cap. You are encouraged to leave these monitoring markers undisturbed.

23 Ingalls Lake

The Hollywood stars of this hike are the Larch trees at Ingalls Pass, and their draw is huge during autumn when these unusual deciduous conifers turn from green to gold. But springtime is great anywhere along this trail for wildflower hunters as you pass from forested slopes to subalpine and alpine meadows. The high and wild Ingalls Lake, with its dramatic view of Mount Stuart, is just one step away from desolation, and it would be that way but for the crowds of weekenders who flock to the lake's shores.

Start: Esmeralda Trailhead

Distance: 10.2 miles out and back

Hiking time: About 6–8 hours

Difficulty: Moderate to strenuous, with one difficult section

Trail surface: Forested path, rock, talus, scree

Seasons: Spring, summer, and fall. Best wildflowers: Late June–July (July 29, 2015). Best time to see Larches in fall color is late September–early October.

Other trail users: Bicyclers and equestrians on first 0.3 mile of trail

Canine compatibility: Leashed dogs only permitted from trailhead to Alpine Lakes Wilderness boundary at Ingalls Pass

Land status: Okanogan-Wenatchee National Forest, Alpine Lakes Wilderness

Nearest town: Cle Elum

Services: Gas, food, lodging. Camping at Beverly, along FR 9737 (vault toilet; no water).

Permits: Northwest Forest Pass, Wilderness Permit (free at trailhead)

Maps: Green Trails #209 Mount Stuart; USGS Mount Stuart; Alpine Lakes Wilderness; DeLorme Page 72 F-5

Trail contact: Okanogan-Wenatchee National Forest, Cle Elum Ranger District

Special considerations: Vault toilet at trailhead. No potable water at trailhead.

Finding the trailhead: Take exit 85 from I-90 to WA 970. In 9 miles turn north onto Teanaway Road. After 13.2 miles the pavement ends and the road splits; take the right fork to FR 9737 and follow this good but dusty gravel, and occasionally washboarded, road to Esmeralda Basin and Trail 1394. Watch for livestock along the road. The road forks in 1.3 miles; bear left. At 2.3 miles the road splits again; bear right. At 3.7 miles bear left at another fork in the road towards Trail 1394. At 4.0 miles, pass the small and primitive Beverly Campground with vault toilets but no water. At 8.1 miles reach the summer camp at Camp Wahoo, with horses and tent cabins. Immediately come to multiple signs informing you that you have entered a fee area and a self-service pay station. At 9.8 miles the road ends in a large, dirt parking lot. **GPS: N47 26.206' / W120 56.240'**

Plants You Might See

Anemone drummondii, Drummond's anemone, Ranunculaceae

Chaenactis thompsonii, Thompson's chaenactis, Asteraceae

Douglasia nivalis, Snow douglasia, Primulaceae

Elmera racemosa, Elmera, Saxifragaceae

Erythronium grandiflorum, Glacier lily, Liliaceae

Ipomopsis aggregata, Skyrocket, Polemoniaceae

Parnassia fimbriata, Fringed grass-of-Parnassus, Saxifragaceae
Physaria alpestre, Alpine twinpod, Brassicaceae
Sibbaldia procumbens, Creeping sibbaldia, Rosaceae
Tofieldia glutinosa, Bog lily, Liliaceae
Veronica cusickii, Cusick's speedwell, Plantaginaceae

The Hike

Three trails leave from the Esmeralda Trailhead, behind the reader boards on the east end of the parking lot, opposite the vault toilet. They are the Esmeralda Basin Trail #1394, Longs Pass Trail #1229, and our trail, Ingalls Way #1390. This is a dry forest with Douglas fir, Grand fir, Western white pine, and Lodgepole pine with an understory of Kinnikinnick (*Arctostaphylos uva-ursi*) and Huckleberry (*Vaccinium* sp.). Most wildflowers are gone by midsummer—victims to sun and heat—but late in the season you can still see Yarrow (*Achillea millefolium*) and Pearly everlasting (*Anaphalis margaritacea*). There are scattered Mountain hemlock here and there.

With short switchbacks, the trail climbs the hillside and in 0.3 mile reaches a trail junction with the Esmeralda Basin Trail; turn right (north) and continue climbing through the thinning forest with broken views into the North Fork Teanaway River valley. In another 1.5 miles come to the junction of Ingalls Way and Longs Pass Trail

Mount Rainier from the Ingalls Lake trail.

Oreamnos americanus, *mountain goats, can be a nuisance at Ingalls Pass.*

#1229 in an open, dry meadow. Here you begin to see Subalpine fir as well as Sky pilot (*Polymonium viscosum*), which can be found growing in the shadow of any large rock or environmental shelter. Sky pilot is renowned for its repugnant odor, but it's interesting to note that researchers in Colorado have found that not *all* the plants stink.

In this meadow, and in other dry meadows and seeps farther up the trail, you'll be able to find Elephant's head (*Pedicularis groenlandica*), Marsh marigold (*Caltha leptosepala*), Partridgefoot (*Luetkea pectinata*), and many others including Northern buckwheat (*Eriogonum compositum*), Common harebell (*Campanula rotundifolia*), and Large-leaved lupine (*Lupinus polyphyllus*).

After 3.2 miles from the trailhead, come to a nice, but small, wet meadow at a switchback in the trail. As this will be your last shady spot for quite some time, contemplate taking a long rest if the day has been a hot one. Protected by trees on one side, in the meadow you'll find specimens of the lovely blue Explorer's gentian (*Gentiana calycosa*), Jeffrey's shooting star (*Dodecatheon jeffreyi*), and Green false hellebore (*Veratrum viride*). Oh, and an amazing view of Mount Rainier to the south.

Ingalls Lake and Mount Stewart, Alpine Lakes Wilderness.

From the meadow it's a steep 0.2 mile to the Alpine Lakes Wilderness boundary and Ingalls Pass. Dogs must turn back at this point. At the top you'll see a sign for the Ingalls Way Alternate Trail #1390.2 that says "Ingalls Lake" with an arrow. Pass it by and continue straight on "Ingalls Way Tr. No. 1390.1." The pass isn't marked, and you won't realize you've crossed over until doing so. Keep a weather eye out for Mountain goats. They frequent the pass and the stretch of trail between here and Ingalls Lake and have been known to make a nuisance of themselves to hikers.

After crossing Ingalls Pass the predominate tree you see is Subalpine larch (*Larix lyallii*). Most of the trees are rather spindly 10- to 20-footers, but there are a few larger and impressive individuals. Larches are deciduous—unusual for conifers.

Descending from Ingalls Pass, the trail crosses through talus and in 0.7 mile reaches Headlight Creek and a spur trail leading in 0.1 mile to a primitive toilet. The camping here is poor to fair and crowded, but the views across the canyon to Mount Stuart are worth any overnight inconveniences. There is a carpet of Red mountain heather here (*Phyllodoce empetriformis*).

The trail now wanders through the rocks and the trees, poking around as if indecisive of how to best approach Ingalls Lake. Don't be surprised if you lose the trail from time to time; there are plenty of large cairns marking the way, though. In 0.6 mile there is a trail junction. To the left (north), Ingalls Way Trail continues to the lake. To the right, Ingalls Way Alternate #1390.2 (east, then south) makes its way back to Ingalls Pass.

For the next 0.4 mile, the trail continues to wander but with a little more purpose than before; it goes up and down but generally up. Just when you think you're never going to see the lake, the trail charges up a rocky slope, you crest the hill, and *viola!* You're there.

The scene is sublime. Directly across is Mount Stuart. Above you is the impressive hunk of Ingalls Peak. The lake is a pretty shade of blue set in a rock basin. Most of the vegetation surrounding the lake is right there with you, though a copse of trees is visible directly across the way. It looks like all there is to see here are various sedges (*Carex* sp.), but when you start paying attention, you'll find Maidenhair fern (*Adiantum pedatum*), Muskflower (*Erythranthe moschata*), Alpine aster (*Aster alpigenus*), Subalpine daisy (*Erigeron glacialis*), and some sort of Rush (*Juncus* sp.).

Penstemon richardsonii, *Richardson's penstemon.*

Gentiana calycosa, *Explorer's gentian.*

▶ Larches have a higher rate of photosynthesis than other conifers and therefore lose more water via transpiration. Living in an extreme habitat where winters are long and cold, the energy investment of growing new needles every year could be offset by eliminating the mechanical and moisture stress of keeping leaves.

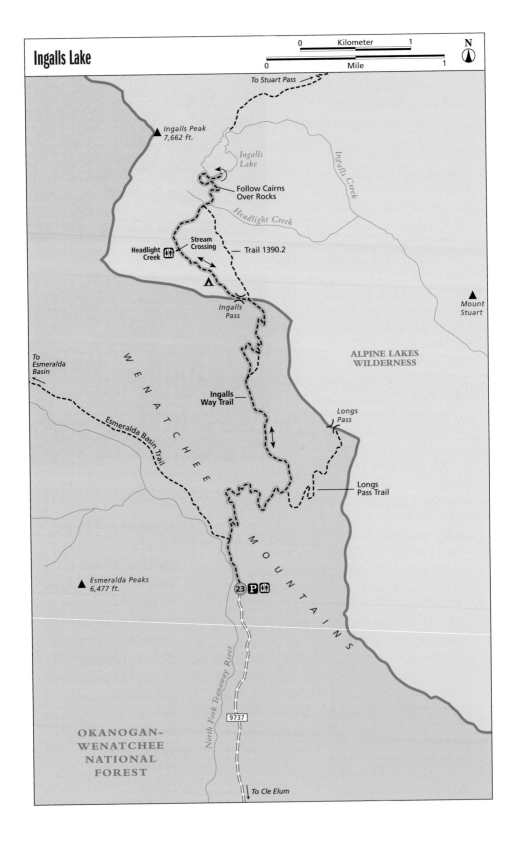

Ingalls Lake

0 Kilometer 1
0 Mile 1

N

To Stuart Pass

Ingalls Peak
7,662 ft.

Ingalls
Lake

Ingalls Creek

Follow Cairns
Over Rocks

Headlight Creek

Stream
Crossing

Headlight
Creek

Trail 1390.2

Ingalls
Pass

Mount
Stuart

W E N A T C H E E

To Esmeralda
Basin

ALPINE LAKES
WILDERNESS

Esmeralda Basin Trail

Ingalls
Way Trail

Longs
Pass

Longs
Pass Trail

M O U N T A I N S

Esmeralda Peaks
6,477 ft.

23 P

North Fork Teanaway River

9737

OKANOGAN-
WENATCHEE
NATIONAL
FOREST

To Cle Elum

To return to the parking area, reverse your route. No camping is allowed at the lake.

Miles and Directions

0.0 Esmeralda Trailhead.

0.3 Esmeralda Basin / Ingalls Way trail junction.

1.8 Ingalls Way / Longs Pass trail junction.

3.2 Meadow / Mount Rainier view.

3.4 Alpine Lakes Wilderness / Ingalls Pass.

4.1 Headlight Creek / toilet trail junction.

4.7 Ingalls Way Trail #1390 / Trail #1390.2 junction.

5.1 Ingalls Lake.

10.2 Arrive back at trailhead.

Other Nearby Hiking Options

It's 0.7 mile from the Ingalls Lake trail to Longs Pass and Trail #1229, which offers a difficult 4-mile alternate route to Ingalls Lake via Stuart Pass on Trail #1215. The Esmeralda Basin Trail #1394 takes hikers deeper into the Alpine Lakes Wilderness.

Erigeron glacialis, *Sub-alpine daisy.*

Hike Information

Mountain goats (*Oreamnos americanus*) frequent Ingalls Pass and can pester hikers. Make sure you read and understand the suggested human behaviors, posted at the trailhead, to deal with these animals.

Olympic Peninsula

Rain forest is not a term that comes to mind when speaking of North America, but what else can you call a place like the west side of the Olympic Mountains where rainfall can exceed 120 inches a year? Yet, on the northern edge of the Olympics, rainfall is as low at 24 inches per year. In the high mountains, winter rains turn to snow and glaciers can be found! The result of this variation in precipitation accounts for a variety of vegetation. Not only that, where mid-elevation old-growth forests reach towards timberline are sunny expanses with exhilarating displays of wildflowers in meadows, across rocky slopes, and along lakeshores. The Olympic Peninsula is an amazing place.

Olympic National Park with Mount Olympus in the background.

24 Mount Townsend

The views from the summit of Mount Townsend (6,280 feet) have rightly been called "sweeping." To the north can be seen Port Angeles and Sequim, with the Strait of Juan de Fuca and Vancouver Island in the background. From east to south is Puget Sound, downtown Seattle, and Mount Baker along with the entire crest of the Cascade Mountains all the way to Mount Rainier. And to the west are the high peaks of the Olympic Mountains. Not bad for a wildflower hike that also includes two kinds of Rhododendron, numerous species of pine and fir, and a pretty outstanding subalpine flora. It's a lot of work, though: The trail climbs 2,900 feet in slightly more than 4 miles to the south summit of Mount Townsend.

Start: Mount Townsend Trail (Forest Service Trail #839) trailhead
Distance: 8.4 miles out and back
Hiking time: About 6–8 hours
Difficulty: Moderate to strenuous
Trail surface: Forested path, rocky
Seasons: Spring and summer. Best wildflowers: July–August (July 17, 2015).
Other trail users: Trail runners
Canine compatibility: Leashed dogs allowed
Land status: Olympic National Forest, Buckhorn Wilderness
Nearest town: Quilcene

Services: Food
Permits: Northwest Forest Pass, Wilderness Permit (free at trailhead)
Maps: Green Trails #168S Olympic Mountains East and #136 Tyler Peak; USGS Mount Townsend; *Trails Illustrated Olympic National Park*; USFS Olympic National Forest and Olympic National Park; Custom Correct Buckthorn Wilderness; DeLorme Page 68 A-6
Trail contact: Olympic National Forest, Hood Canal Ranger District
Special considerations: Vault toilet at trailhead. No potable water at trailhead or on trail.

Finding the trailhead: From the Hood Canal Ranger District office in Quilcene, drive west on US 101 for 1 mile and bear right (west) onto Penny Creek Road. Drive through the quarry on a good two-lane asphalt road. In 1.4 miles the road splits and you veer left (south) onto graveled FR 27 (shown on some maps as Big Quilcene River Road). In 1.1 miles you reach a Y; bear right (west), continuing on FR 27, a narrow, one-lane, paved road. Several gravel roads intersect FR 27; keep to the pavement. After 9.2 miles come to a road junction to the lower Mount Townsend trailhead. Bear right (northwest) and drive 1.2 miles of pavement to one last road junction. Leave FR 27 by turning left (west) onto a potholed and washboarded dirt road. In 1 mile the road ends at the parking area for the upper Mount Townsend parking area. **GPS: N47 51.365' / W123 02.151'**

Plants You Might See

Arctostaphylos uva-ursi, Kinnikinnick, Ericaceae
Campanula scouleri, Scouler's harebell, Campanulaceae
Castilleja miniata, Scarlet paintbrush, Orobanchaceae
Clintonia uniflora, Queen's cup, Liliaceae
Cornus unalaschkensis, Bunchberry, Cornaceae

Eriogonum umbellatum, Sulfur buckwheat, Polygonaceae

Goodyera oblongifolia, Rattlesnake plantain, Orchidaceae

Linnaea borealis, Twinflower, Caprifoliaceae

Luina hypoleuca, Silverback luina, Asteraceae

Mahonia nervosa, Oregon grape, Berberidaceae

Phlox diffusa, Spreading phlox, Polemoniaceae

Pterospora andromedea, Pinedrops, Ericaceae

Vaccinium spp., Huckleberry (five kinds), Ericaceae

The Hike

Find the trail behind the reader board at the west end of the parking area. The way begins steeply though a shady forest with the sound of Townsend Creek on the left (south). The first 1.7 miles of trail are through a mixed conifer forest of both Western and Mountain hemlock with a heavy dose of Pacific rhododendron (*Rhododendron macrophylum*) in the understory. Also scattered throughout this forest are Douglas fir and Western red cedar. Look for the occasional Alaska yellow cedar (*Xanthocyparis nootkatensis*); spot this tree by its straight trunks and its distinctive yellowish-gray bark. In 0.3 mile sharp eyes will see a benchmark on the right (north) side of the trail, celebrating the sesquicentennial of Jefferson County.

A field of wildflowers reaches to the summit of Mount Townsend.

Solidago multiradiata, *Goldenrod, a harbinger of autumn.*

Silene parryi, *Parry's catchfly. Note the glandular hairs, probably the reason for the name "catchfly."*

Pterospora andromedea, *Pinedrops, is a saprophyte, lacks chlorophyll, and lives in a parasitic relationship with mycorrhizal fungi.*

Castilleja miniata, *Scarlet paintbrush.*

Pedicularis racemosa, *Sickletop lousewort.*

Luina hypoleuca, *Silverback luina.*

Dasiphora frucicosa, *Shrubby cinquafoil.*

Anticlea elegans, *Death camas.*

Campanula rotundifolia, *Common harebell.*

Chimaphilia umbellata, *Pipsissewa.*

Orthocarpus imbricatus, *Mountain owl-clover.*

Eriogonum umbellatum, *Sulphur buck-wheat.* DAVE FLOTREE/ELLEN HAUPTMANN

Rhododendron macrophyllum, *Pacific rho-dodendron.* DAVE FLOTREE/ELLEN HAUPTMANN

The trail continues to climb through a thinning forest with views developing into the Townsend Creek drainage and towards the complex of ridges called Welch Peaks. Down in the valley below it's possible to separate the various species of conifer by their color and shape. The most prominent one is the dark green Subalpine fir with its tight, classic, evergreen shape, but the droopy branches of both Western red cedar and Alaska yellow cedar are also easy to pick out. The puffy branches and light green foliage indicate Western white pine and Lodgepole pine; this last one also begins to make an appearance alongside the trail. With the addition of Pacific silver fir, Grand fir, and Western yew (*Taxus brevifolia*), the Townsend Creek drainage is uniquely rich in conifers.

This lower stretch of trail can also be rich in species of wintergreen including Pipsissewa (*Chimaphila umbellata*) and five kinds of *Pyrola*. It's also easy to see lots of members of the Saxifrage family, including Small-flowered alumroot (*Heuchera micrantha*).

In 2.6 miles come to a junction. Left (south) leads to the small camping area at Camp Windy. The main route continues right (north) on a series of tight and steep switchbacks through dry meadows. Here you'll find Common harebell (*Campanula rotundifolia*) and plenty of early spring and lower elevation plants such as Vanilla leaf (*Achlys californica*), Harsh paintbrush (*Castilleja hispida*), Field chickweed (*Cerastium arvense*), and Thimbleberry (*Rubus parviflorus*), among others. Though not as showy as the Western rhododendron at the trail's beginning, you will also start seeing White rhododendron (*Rhododendron albiflorum*).

> A quiet bay at the northeast end of the Olympic Peninsula was christened Port Townshend in 1792 by Captain George Vancouver to honor his friend, George Townshend. With time the *h* was dropped and many other features on the landscape picked up the name. A fire lookout graced the north peak of Mount Townsend from 1933 until 1962, when it was destroyed.

Another 0.4 mile brings the trail junction to Silver Lake. Bear right (north) and continue uphill. Hard to believe the trail could get any steeper, but it does. Past this point the forest thins appreciatively and soon there are fewer and fewer trees, though timberline is elusive. On the other hand, the increase in solar radiation means ever-greater floral displays and species diversification. In addition to what you've already seen, expect to see Pearly everlasting (*Anaphalis margaritacea*), Fireweed (*Chamerion angustifolium*), Oval-leaf buckwheat (*Eriogonum ovalifolium*), and Wooly eriophyllum (*Eriophyllum lanatum*).

Traversing a sunny hillside and yet more switchbacks, the trail finally reaches the long ridge that is Mount Townsend after an additional 0.7 mile. In 0.2 mile come to a spur trail on the right (east) that leads to the south summit of Mount Townsend. The main trail continues left (north) towards the north summit, though you can also reach it from the south summit. The taller of the two summits, by about 70 feet, is the south.

At the right time of year, there can be loads of wildflowers all over Mount Townsend—enough to keep you occupied for hours! Keep your eyes sharp for the

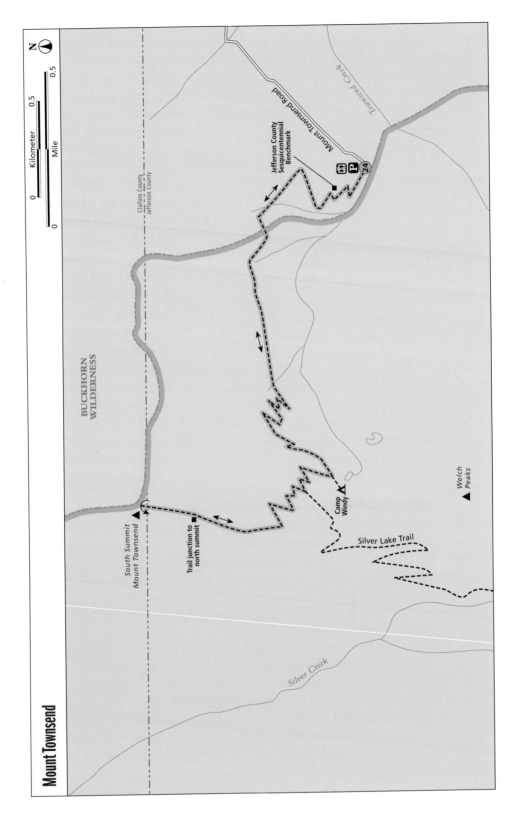

Mount Townsend

N

| 0 | 0.5 | Kilometer |
| 0 | 0.5 | Mile |

BUCKHORN WILDERNESS

Clallam County
Jefferson County

Townsend Creek

Townsend Creek

Mount Townsend Road

Jefferson County
Sesquicentennial
Benchmark

24

South Summit
Mount Townsend

Trail junction to
north summit

Camp
Windy

Welch
Peaks

Silver Lake Trail

Silver Creek

unusual Shrubby cinquefoil (*Dasiphora fruticosa*), Northern goldenrod (*Solidago multiradiata*), Mountain owl-clover (*Orthocarpus imbricatus*), Parry's catchfly (*Silene parryi*), and a Death camas not found at lower elevations (*Anticlea elegans*).

Enjoy the 360-degree view and the wildflowers. It can be windy up here, and the ground squirrels are habituated to handouts. Please, don't encourage them. To return to the trailhead, turn around and retrace your steps.

Miles and Directions

0.0 Mount Townsend Trail #839 trailhead.

0.3 Benchmark noting the sesquicentennial of Jefferson County.

2.6 Trail junction to Camp Windy.

3.0 Trail junction to Silver Lake.

3.9 Trail to north summit and beyond.

4.2 South summit of Mount Townsend.

8.4 Arrive back at trailhead.

Other Nearby Hiking Options

A lower trailhead for Mount Townsend begins 1.2 miles and 400 vertical feet below the upper trailhead. From the south summit of Mount Townsend, continue on to the north summit. You can also keep hiking on the Little Quilcene Trail #835 for an extensive multi-night trip through the Buckhorn Wilderness into Dungeness Valley and Wolf Valley. A side trip from the Mount Townsend trail leads 2.9 miles to Silver Lake, where camping is fair to poor but the wildflowers (in season) are as stunning as the setting.

One of our most ubiquitous wildflowers, Achillea millefolium, *common yarrow, is also one of the most lovely.*

25 Mount Ellinor

It's impossible to conceive of how steep this trail is until you're on it. Suffice to say it's like climbing nearly 4 miles up then down from one flight of stairs to another. But there are rewards aplenty—not only in flowers, but in views.

Start: Parking area for upper trail (the "summer" trail) to Mount Ellinor
Distance: 3.6 miles out and back
Hiking time: About 3-5 hours
Difficulty: Strenuous; difficult to follow in places
Trail surface: Forested path, rocky, talus
Seasons: Spring and summer. Best wildflowers: July–August (July 21, 2015).
Other trail users: None
Canine compatibility: Leashed dogs allowed
Land status: Olympic National Forest, Mount Skokomish Wilderness
Nearest town: Hoodsport

Services: Gas, food. Camping at Staircase Campground.
Permit: Northwest Forest Pass
Maps: Green Trails #168S Olympic Mountains East; Custom Correct Enchanted Valley–Skykomish and Mount Skykomish–Lake Cushman; USGS Mount Washington; USFS Olympic National Forest and Olympic National Park; DeLorme Page 68 E-5
Trail contacts: Olympic National Forest, Hood Canal Ranger District, Mount Skokomish Wilderness
Special considerations: Vault toilet at trailhead. No potable water at trailhead. Hot and dry slope; carry plenty of water.

Finding the trailhead: Leave US 101 in Hoodsport, turning west onto WA 119 (North Lake Cushman Road). In 9.4 miles WA 119 ends; turn right onto FR 24 and follow this gravel and washboarded road for 1.6 miles. At FR 2419 turn left and reach the lower trailhead in 4.7 miles (parking limited). For the upper trailhead, proceed another 1.7 miles on a poor road, still suitable for passenger cars, and turn left on FR 2419-014. The upper trailhead is in 1 mile at the end of the road. **GPS: N47 30.618' / W123 14.858'**

Plants You Might See

Achlys californica, Vanilla leaf, Berberidaceae
Antennaria alpina, Alpine pussytoes, Asteraceae
Campanula piperi, Olympic harebell, Campanulaceae
Chamerion angustifolium, Fireweed, Onagraceae
Gentiana amarella, Northern gentian, Gentianaceae
Heracleum lanatum, Cow parsnip, Apiaceae
Rhododendron albiflorum, White rhododendron, Ericaceae
Sorbus sitchensis, Sitka mountain ash, Rosaceae

The Hike

Find the trail at the west end of the parking area, behind the picnic table and two reader boards. The forest here is primarily Western hemlock with some Douglas fir. There are even a few Western white pines. The understory alongside the trail consists of Twinflower (*Linnaea borealis*), Oregon grape (*Mahonia nervosa*), and lots of Beargrass (*Xerophyllum tenax*). In 100 feet the trail makes a sharp switchback and quickly ascends to a second reader board where hikers are invited to register as well as contribute stories about their encounters with Mountain goats.

Everything said about the steepness of this trail from the parking area to Mount Ellinor's summit is entirely true, but what else would you expect when you gain over 2,400 feet in a scant 1.8 miles? In this forested section, where the trees are giants, the trail ascends on steps built with 6-inch-diameter logs. There is Woodland beardtongue (*Nothochelone nemorosa*) here along with Pipsissewa (*Chimaphila umbellata*) and Scouler's harebell (*Campanula scouleri*).

In 0.3 mile the lower trail comes in on your left (south); continue your upward trek. In another 0.4 mile the "summer" trail is met by the "winter" trail coming in on the right (east). This route is not recommended by the Forest Service for use unless covered with snow due to the large amount of loose rock along its route. In any event, continue straight ahead. The trail *really* begins to climb now.

A typical hiking day in the Pacific "Northwet."

The female flowers of Alnus rubra, *Red alder, look like tiny pine cones when they dry out.*

Male flowers of Alnus rubra, *Red alder.*

Campanula scouleri, *Scouler's harebell.*

Aquilegia formosa, *Columbine.*

You can see why they call Linnaea borealis *Twinflower.*

In 0.5 mile leave the deep, dark forest behind and come to a talus slope bordered on both sides by gravely subalpine meadows. As you climb ever upward, look for Common harebell (*Campanula rotundifolia*), Subalpine daisy (*Erigeron glacialis*), Pearly everlasting (*Anaphalis margaritacea*), Jeffery's shooting star (*Dodecatheon jeffreyi*), and the ubiquitous Yarrow (*Achillea millefolium*). Jammed in the cracks of smaller talus you'll find the lime green fronds of Oak fern (*Gymnocarpium dryopteris*).

Wildflower hunters can stop, contented, anywhere along this ridiculously steep, rocky, and difficult-to-follow section of trail and revel not only in beauteous blooms, but views to Hood Canal and far-distant peaks. Hikers motivated by reaching the summit of Mount Ellinor, push on! Though, on hot summer days, you'll be wishing you brought more drinking water, a broad-brimmed hat, and loads of sunscreen.

The talus tops out at a ridge where, once again, you enter a forest. Follow the narrow path as it winds and climbs to cross the ridge once more. Here you will encounter the many paths of the "winter" trail as it crosses a steep slope of consolidated scree. It's easy to pick out the main path, though, which reaches the summit and 360-degree views. It feels like you're sitting on top of the world!

You'll likely encounter Mountain goats (*Oreamnos americanus*) on, or around, the summit. The goats were introduced to the Olympic Mountains during the 1920s. Their grazing, wallowing, and trampling severely impact the native flora. The goats are a nuisance to hikers, especially around the summit of Mount Ellinor, where the animals frequent places where people have urinated. If you must go, then go

▶ While employed by the United States Coast Survey, surveyor and Nottingham, England, native George Davidson named Mount Ellinor in 1853 for Ellinor Fauntleroy. The Brothers were also named by Davidson after Ellinor's two brothers, Arthur and Edward. Davidson named Mount Constance after Ellinor's oldest sister. Not surprisingly, Ellinor Fauntleroy and George Davidson were married in 1858.

on rocks and not vegetation; goats will tear apart plants, seeking the salt in urine. Mountain goats have sharp hooves and sharper horns and might defend themselves by charging if they are surrounded or too closely approached by inquisitive people. Keep your distance!

Retrace your route to return to the trailhead. If you thought the trail was steep coming up, just wait until you start heading down. Watch your step through the talus; there are plenty of opportunities to slip and slide on loose rocks, recalling that childhood board game of Chutes and Ladders.

Miles and Directions

0.0   Mount Ellinor upper trailhead.

0.3   Lower trail / upper trail junction.

0.7   Junction with "winter" trail.

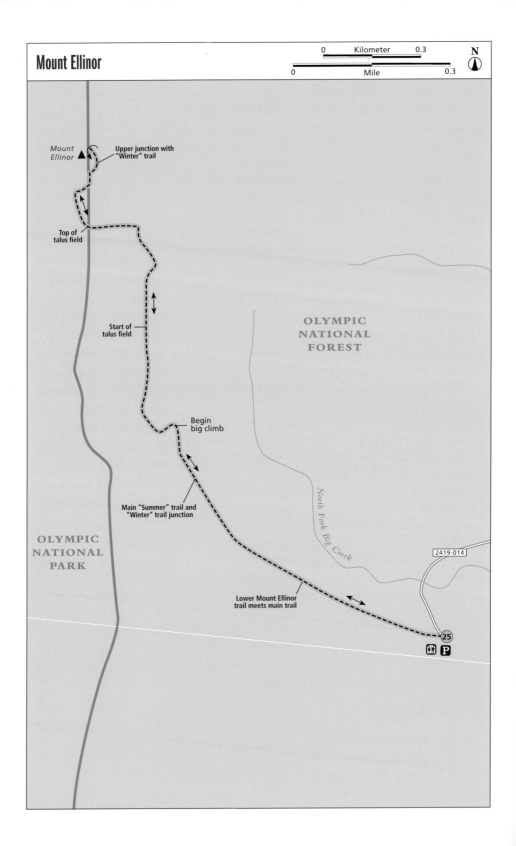

Mount Ellinor

0 Kilometer 0.3
0 Mile 0.3

N

Mount Ellinor ▲ Upper junction with "Winter" trail

Top of talus field

Start of talus field

Begin big climb

Main "Summer" trail and "Winter" trail junction

OLYMPIC NATIONAL FOREST

North Fork Big Creek

2419-014

Lower Mount Ellinor trail meets main trail

OLYMPIC NATIONAL PARK

25

Like most peaks in the Olympics, Mount Ellinor is a cloud-catcher. Be prepared by bringing proper clothing.

1.2 Begin talus.

1.8 Summit of Mount Ellinor.

3.6 Return to trailhead.

Other Nearby Hiking Options

The 1.7-mile lower trail begins 900 feet below the upper trail and climbs moderately through the forest. No Northwest Forest Pass is required.

26 Elk Mountain–Badger Valley Loop

The difference in habitat between the two halves of this hike is startling. You begin on rocky, treeless, and windswept Elk Mountain, where what little vegetation is there barely holds onto its perch. Then, the trail dips precipitously through a forest of Subalpine fir, across gurgling springs riotous in colorful wildflowers, to a large meadow before climbing once again to the desolation of Elk Mountain.

Start: Parking area at Obstruction Point
Distance: 4.8-mile loop
Hiking time: About 3–4 hours
Difficulty: Easy to difficult, with steep grades and one bit of route finding
Trail surface: Dirt, forested path, scree, rock
Seasons: Spring and summer. Best wildflowers: June–July (July 27, 2015).
Other trail users: None
Canine compatibility: Dogs not permitted
Land status: Olympic National Park
Nearest town: Port Angeles

Services: Gas, food, lodging. Camping in Olympic National Park at Heart O' the Hills.
Permit: National Park Service entrance fee
Maps: Green Trails #134S Elwah North Hurricane Ridge; USGS Mount Angeles, Maiden Peak, and Wellesley Peak; Custom Correct Gray Wolf-Dosewallips; *Trails Illustrated Olympic National Park*; DeLorme Page 54 G-3
Trail contact: Olympic National Park
Special considerations: Vault toilet at trailhead. No potable water at trailhead. Water and flush toilets available at Hurricane Ridge Visitor Center.

Finding the trailhead: From Port Angeles, drive 18 miles south to the Hurricane Ridge Visitor Center parking lot on Hurricane Ridge Road. At the east side of the parking lot, find Obstruction Point Road. Drive 7.4 miles on this poor-to-fair, occasionally washboarded, gravel road to its terminus at the Obstruction Point parking area. **GPS: N47 55.098' / W123 22.949'**

Plants You Might See

Agoseris glauca, Mountain agoseris, Asteraceae
Arnica mollis, Hairy arnica, Asteraceae
Arnica ovata, Sticky-leaf arnica, Asteraceae
Caltha leptosepala, Marsh marigold, Ranunculaceae
Dasiphora fruticosa, Shrubby cinquefoil, Rosaceae
Eremogone capillaris, Mountain sandwort, Caryophyllaceae
Hedysarum occidentale, Western sweet vetch, Fabaceae
Phyllodoce empetriformis, Red mountain heather, Ericaceae
Platanthera dilatata, White bog orchid, Orchidaceae
Polygonum bistortoides, Bistort, Polygonaceae
Senecio triangularis, Arrow-leaved groundsel, Asteraceae
Silene acaulis, Moss campion, Caryophyllaceae
Silene parryi, Parry's catchfly, Caryophyllaceae

The trail begins at the west end of the parking lot, behind the vault toilet, reader board, and interpretive signs. A large sign points right (south) to Grand Lake and left (north) to Badger Valley. Go left. Backpackers should note that no fires are allowed past this point and all cooking must be done on stoves.

The trail traverses a forlorn landscape, but it is not completely devoid of vegetation even though it may look that way at first. Little and big patches of green demonstrate that, where there is ground, a plant will take root. Common harebell (*Campanula rotundifolia*), Pearly everlasting (*Anaphalis margaritacea*), Cliff anemone (*Anemone multifida*), Western pasqueflower (*A. occidentalis*), and Washington's ever-present Yarrow (*Achillea millefolium*) are easily found in and among the shale and flinty rocks. You might also be surprised to find a sagebrush called Mugwort (*Artemisia ludoviciana*).

WEEDS

Plenty of stunning wildflowers that contribute immensely to coloring western Washington landscapes are not, sadly, native to our region. We usually lump all these plants under the term "weeds." Tops on this list are Scot's broom (*Cytisus scoparius*), Foxglove (*Digitalis purpurea*), and California poppy (*Eschscholtzia californica*). The first two are European imports, and the third one, though native to North America and Mexico, is not native to Washington.

Common foxglove.

We use the term "weed" in a pejorative sense for plants that are growing unwanted in a particular place. Plants that are not native to a region, especially those that have escaped cultivation or have invaded important agricultural lands, are universally reviled as "weeds." But plenty of native plants are considered "weeds" or "weedy" when found growing where people don't want them to be. For instance, Red alder is considered a weedy species in forests following logging because it crowds out the more-desirable Douglas fir and Western hemlock. And Devil's club (*Oplopanax horridus*) is an invasive native plant that grows like a weed, taking over huge amounts of real estate in disturbed sites.

California poppy.

Fog rolls up Badger Valley.

This first section of trail crosses the western haunch of Obstruction Peak, and the view down Badger Valley is a real breath-taker, especially because the narrow trail drops so precariously in that direction. In 0.3 mile pass the unmarked junction with the Badger Valley Trail, and 0.3 mile past that a short waytrail quickly ascends the ridge to a dynamite view of the Olympic Mountains.

The trail now begins to climb steadily up the southern side of Elk Mountain. In wet spots there is Explorer's gentian (*Gentiana calycosa*). In the more common drier areas, look for Spreading phlox (*Phlox diffusa*), Oval-leaf buckwheat (*Eriogonum*

ovalifolium), Silver lupine (*Lupinus lepidus*), and the aptly named Rockslide larkspur (*Delphinium glareosum*). There is also plenty of Ground juniper (*Juniper communis*) which, being a gymnosperm, is a far cry from a wildflower. But there is plenty of it, and its berries are used to flavor gin, so it is worth mentioning. It's also the only circumboreal conifer in the northern hemisphere, so that's also a good reason to be familiar with it.

Gentiana calycosa, *Explorer's gentian.*

Elk Mountain–Badger Valley Loop

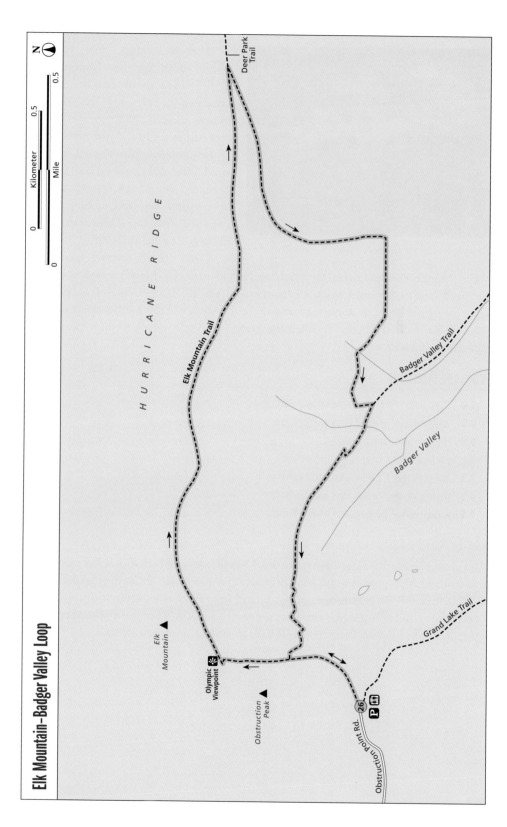

Anaphalis margaritaceae, *Pearly everlasting.*

After 2.2 miles turn right (south) onto the Elk Mountain Trail. Straight ahead (east) the trail continues 6 miles to Deer Park (where there is road access). Our trail begins to drop down the side of the mountain, passes into a scattered Subalpine fir forest, and, as it becomes fainter, gets steeper and steeper until you start wishing for stairs and a handrail. This stretch of trail can be quite difficult!

Cross over several springs where Monkeyflower (*Erythranthe guttata*) and Yellow fireweed (*Epilobium luteum*) can be found, and in 1.5 miles reach a large meadow and the Badger Valley Trail. Turn right (west) and begin to climb, regaining all the elevation you just lost but doing it in 0.8 mile. At the trail junction turn left (east), and in 0.3 mile return to the Obstruction Point trailhead.

Miles and Directions

0.0 Obstruction Point parking area trailhead.

0.3 Badger Valley / Grand Pass trail junction.

0.6 Olympic Mountains viewpoint.

2.2 Elk Mountain / Deer Park trail junction.

3.7 Badger Valley / Elk Mountain trail junction.

4.5 Badger Valley / Grand Pass trail junction.

4.8 Arrive back at parking area and trailhead.

Other Nearby Hiking Options

Also along Obstruction Point Road are the 3.8-mile out-and-back Cox Valley primitive trail and a 1.8-mile out-and-back primitive trail to PJ Lake. From the parking lot at Obstruction Point, a trail takes off for Grand Lake and farther south to Cameron Creek. A 9.1-mile loop trail, suitable as an overnight backpacking trip, can also be made from Obstruction Point to Grand Lake to Badger Valley and return.

27 Elwah Valley Restoration

Admittedly, at first blush there isn't much to see along this new trail except for a valley devastated by being underwater for nearly ninety years. Yet, that's exactly why this trail is in this book. It's a work in progress. Over the years, as the Elwah Valley recovers from having its dam removed—and with the able assistance of a coterie of scientists, land managers, Lower Elwah Klallam tribal members, citizens of Port Angeles, and many volunteers—what was once the bottom of a reservoir will become a natural valley once again. There will be salmon in the Elwah River migrating up-canyon to spawn. There will be trees, and shrubs, and, yes, wildflowers. We all have an opportunity to witness this recovery. Come back to the Elwah Valley on a yearly basis. Bring your camera to document the change. And bring your flower books too. Because every year there will be something different to experience.

Start: Glines Canyon Spillway Overlook on Olympic Hot Springs Road
Distance: 3.6 miles out and back
Hiking time: About 2–3 hours
Difficulty: Easy
Trail surface: Gravel, hard-packed ground
Seasons: Year-round. Best wildflowers: April–August (August 5, 2015).
Other trail users: None
Canine compatibility: Dogs not permitted
Land status: Olympic National Park
Nearest town: Port Angeles

Services: Gas, food, lodging. Camping available in Olympic National Park at the Altair and Elwah Campgrounds.
Permit: National Park Service entrance fee
Maps: Green Trails #134S Hurricane Ridge-Elwah North; USGS Elwah and Hurricane Hill; *Trails Illustrated Olympic National Park*; DeLorme Page 53 E-12
Trail contact: Olympic National Park
Special considerations: Vault toilet at trailhead. No water at trailhead. No shade.

Finding the trailhead: From US 101, 8 west of Port Angeles, turn left (south) on Olympic Hot Springs Road and follow it beyond the national park entrance station for 5.6 miles to the Glines Canyon Spillway Overlook parking area. **GPS: N48 00.165' / W123 36.031'**

Over the Years, Plants You Might See

Achlys californica, Vanilla leaf, Berberidaceae
Collinsia grandiflora, Large-leaved blue-eyed Mary, Plantaginaceae
Dicentra formosa, Bleeding heart, Papaveraceae
Dichelostemma congesta, Ookow, Liliaceae
Gaultheria shallon, Salal, Ericaceae
Holodiscus discolor, Ocean spray, Rosaceae
Linnaea borealis, Twinflower, Caprifoliaceae
Mahonia nervosa, Oregon grape, Berberidaceae
Polystichum munitum, Sword fern, Polypodiaceae

Sambucus racemosa, Coast red elderberry, Adoxaceae
Tolmiea menziesii, Piggy-back plant, Saxifragaceae
Trientalis latifolia, Western starflower, Primulaceae
Trillium ovatum, Trillium, Liliaceae
Vaccinium spp., Huckleberries, Ericaceae
And so many more as time goes by . . .

The Hike

On the edge of this hike, above where the former Lake Mills shoreline existed, you will find Douglas fir, Western hemlock, Western red cedar, and Red alder. Sadly, for shade seekers, during the occasional few weeks of sun and hot weather in the Pacific Northwest, you will quickly leave all four behind. At least, for now. There is no telling how cool and shady this hike will be in another generation or so. Keep your fingers crossed!

The Park Service knows this as the "revegetation trail," a new trail constructed so the folks responsible for replanting the exposed floodplain of the Elwah River would have access to the river. It's proved so popular with people visiting the area that everybody seems to know about it!

The Elwah River. Over the years the riverbed will be completely revegetated.

Find the trail at the west end of the paved parking lot, by the wooden rail fence. The first stretch is graveled, but it quickly becomes a wide and beaten path.

Remnants of the former Glines Canyon Dam is the predominate view, but you quickly are able to see where the reservoir formerly existed. It isn't pretty: an expanse that stretches upriver, filled by fallen trees and desolation. Take heart! 'Tis only a scene of the past merging into the present. The future holds so much more.

In 0.4 mile cross Stuckey Creek on a well-placed log. You're in full sun now, so if it's a sunny day, you'll be wishing for protection from that "evil orb." It won't get any cooler, so come prepared. The trail slowly descends. As you go lower and lower, you're getting deeper and deeper into the sediments that used to lie beneath the reservoir of Lake Mills.

In another 0.2 mile the trail comes to a terrace, and you're able to walk to the edge and survey the entire drainage. Be careful of the edge, though. The lake-bottom sediments are steep and unstable here. When the reservoir was first emptied, before you was one flattish plain. Now, it's been eroded by the Elwah—untamed as it is—into numerous river terraces. The river itself is below, with its braided channels reminiscent of what you see at the foot of glaciers.

In another 0.5 mile the way begins to get sketchier and sketchier, and the "official" revegetation trail ends. But it's a well-beaten path, so you can follow footprints on the terrace for as far upriver as

▷ Over the winter of 1889–90, the *Seattle Press* sponsored the first exploration of the Elwah River Valley. There were five men along, led by James Christie. With them were four dogs, two mules, and 1,500 pounds of supplies. The group planned to live off the land, and it nearly killed them. When they finally emerged from the mountains six months after plunging into the snowiest and harshest winter in recent memory, the men were dressed in rags and on the verge of starvation.

Trientalis latifolia, *Western starflower.*
<small>DAVE FLOTREE/ELLEN HAUPTMANN</small>

The Elwah River. Over the years the riverbed will be completely revegetated.

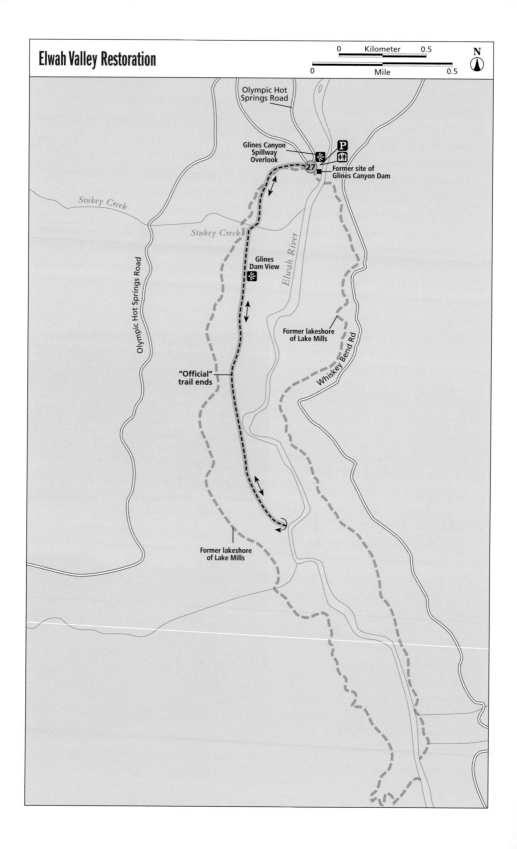

Elwah Valley Restoration

Olympic Hot Springs Road

Glines Canyon
Spillway
Overlook

Former site of
Glines Canyon Dam

27

Stukey Creek

Stukey Creek

Glines
Dam View

Elwah River

Former lakeshore
of Lake Mills

Whiskey Bend Rd

Olympic Hot Springs Road

"Official"
trail ends

Former lakeshore
of Lake Mills

Kilometer

Mile

N

0   0.5

0   0.5

you want to go. In 1.4 miles from the trailhead, you go around the opposite corner of Windy Arm and can no longer see the dam site downstream.

Undoubtedly it will change over time, but in 1.6 miles from the trailhead, the lay of the land allows you to cut your way down easily and safely through two separate terraces, then through a boulder field, and then in a further 0.2 mile, reach the Elwah River. From this point it is possible to continue sauntering upstream, either along the river (which would be really hard on account of all the boulders) or back up on the terrace for as far as you would want to go. Otherwise, turn around and head back the way you came.

Miles and Directions

- **0.0** Glines Canyon Spillway Overlook trailhead.
- **0.4** Cross Stuckey Creek.
- **0.6** View of drainage.
- **1.1** "Official" revegetation trail ends.
- **1.4** Windy Arm.
- **1.8** Reach the Elwah River.
- **3.6** Arrive back at trailhead.

Other Nearby Hiking Options

The 3.8-mile out-and-back Smokey Bottom Trail leads to Boulder Creek and winds through the forest above former Lake Mills. To access, continue for 0.3 mile past the Glines Canyon Spillway Overlook on an unmarked gravel spur road to a small parking lot with a picnic bench. No water; no toilet.

To reach the Elwah River Gorge below where Glines Canyon Dam once stood, drive 0.3 mile down (north) Olympic Hot Springs Road from the Glines Canyon Spillway Overlook to a gravel road, sometimes gated. Turn right (east). Follow the road down 0.3 mile to the river, a large turnaround, and a kayak launch spot in a beautiful forest glade of Douglas fir and mature Red alder.

Hike Information

Taking down the Glines Canyon Dam (built in 1927, removed in 2014), following elimination of the Lower Elwah Dam (built in 1913, removed in 2012), is the largest dam-removal project in the United States. The combined effect is to allow all five species of Pacific salmon to return to over 70 miles of Elwah River habitat. It's also to restore a watershed to its natural state—something unthinkable a hundred years ago . . . or even twenty years ago. People sometimes *do* think beyond themselves.

28 Hurricane Hill

It's not called "Hurricane Hill" for nothing! Wind gusts of over 75 miles per hour have been clocked at the visitor center on nearby Hurricane Ridge. Winters can bring 30 to 35 feet of snow, with drifts lingering on into summer. Is it any wonder the trees not sheltered by the lee side of the mountain are stunted and show signs of having been blasted and broken? With such a stark environment, it's surprising that over 125 different species of plants have been found up here! You'll see lots of familiar "faces" on Hurricane Hill, but they will all be shaped by the dangerous world they must live in.

Start: Parking area at end of Hurricane Hill Road

Distance: 3.2 miles out and back

Hiking time: About 2–3 hours

Difficulty: Easy

Trail surface: Asphalt, dirt

Seasons: Spring, summer, and fall. Best wildflowers: July–August (August 5, 2015).

Other trail users: None

Canine compatibility: Dogs not permitted

Land status: Olympic National Park

Nearest town: Port Angeles

Services: Gas, food, lodging. Camping available in Olympic National Park at Heart O' the Hills campground.

Permit: National Park Service entrance fee

Maps: Green Trails #134S Elwah North Hurricane Ridge; USGS Mount Angeles; Custom Correct Hurricane Ridge; *Trails Illustrated Olympic National Park*; DeLorme Page 54 G-3

Trail contact: Olympic National Park

Special considerations: Closest toilet and potable water to trailhead are located at the picnic areas 0.5 mile south and east on Hurricane Hill Road.

Finding the trailhead: From Port Angeles, drive 18 miles south to the Hurricane Ridge Visitor Center parking lot on Hurricane Ridge Road. At the west side of the parking lot, find Hurricane Hill Road and proceed 1.5 miles to the parking lot at road's end. Overflow parking, and an access trail, is available 0.5 mile south and east at the picnic areas. **GPS: N47 59.370' / W123 31.846'**

Plants You Might See

Agoseris aurantiaca, Orange agoseris, Asteraceae

Anemone occidentalis, Mountain pasqueflower, Ranunculaceae

Antennaria microphylla, Rosy pussy-toes, Asteraceae

Arnica parryi, Nodding arnica, Asteraceae

Artemisia ludoviciana, Western mugwort, Asteraceae

Aster paucicapitatus, Olympic Mountains aster, Asteraceae

Campanula rotundifolia, Common harebell, Campanulaceae

Castilleja hispida, Harsh paintbrush, Orobanchaceae

Delphinium glareosum, Rockslide larkspur, Ranunculaceae

Delphinium menziesii, Mountain larkspur, Ranunculaceae

Eriogonum ovalifolium, Oval-leaf buckwheat, Polygonaceae
Eriophyllum lanatum, Oregon sunshine, Asteraceae
Erythronium montanum, Avalanche lily, Liliaceae
Luetkea pectinata, Partridgefoot, Rosaceae
Lupinus latifolius, Broad-leaf lupine, Fabaceae
Penstemon procerus, Small-flowered penstemon, Plantaginaceae
Phlox diffusa, Spreading phlox, Polemoniaceae
Silene parryi, Parry's silene, Caryophyllaceae

The Hike

Find the trail at the west end of the parking area behind the reader board. Don't let the fact that this is a paved trail dissuade you from making the trip up Hurricane Hill. For purists, plenty of people have walked to the side of the asphalt, creating a hard-packed dirt trail next to the pavement. In any event, the views are fantastic and so are the plants.

The forest here, what little there is of it, includes Subalpine fir, Douglas fir, Mountain hemlock, and a scattering of Western white pine. In the lee of the ridge, the trees are stout but tall. On the hill's summit they are krummholzed and chopped up by wind, snow, and ice.

View of Olympic National Park from Hurricane Hill.

Abies lasiocarpa, *Subalpine fir, on Hurricane Hill.*

In 0.5 mile come to a junction with the Little River Trail and continue straight ahead (northwest). A further 0.9 mile brings you to a broad saddle and the junction with the Elwah Trail. Continue straight again (north); your goal is the tree-covered summit 0.2 mile ahead.

From the top of Hurricane Hill is a 360-degree view that encompasses Port Angeles below you with the San Juan Islands plus Victoria and Vancouver Island beyond, the Cascade Mountains and Mount Baker to the east, and all of the Olympic Mountains south and west. In the foreground are the skeleton trees remaining from the 2003 Griff Fire.

Campanula scouleri, *Scouler's harebell.*

Once you're done with the view, turn around and retrace your footsteps to the trailhead. Any flowers you missed on the way up, you'll be able to see on the way down.

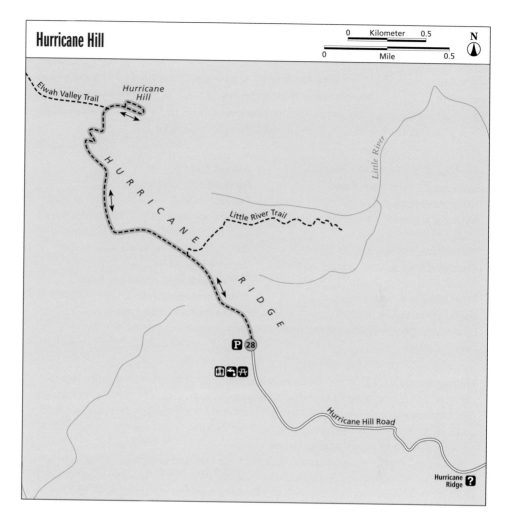

Miles and Directions

0.0 Hurricane Hill parking area and trailhead.

0.5 Little River Trail junction.

1.4 Elwah Valley Trail junction.

1.6 Hurricane Hill.

3.2 Arrive back at parking area and trailhead.

29 Tubal Cain Rhododendrons

This is a trail that has a lot going for it, but everything is overshadowed by a mile-long corridor of Pacific rhododendron. When the Rhodys are in bloom, you get to hike through a pink, rose, and purple-colored tunnel of flowers. By far this is one of the best places to see Rhododendrons on the Olympic Peninsula.

Start: Tubal Cain Trail (#840) trailhead
Distance: 8.2 miles out and back
Hiking time: About 4–6 hours
Difficulty: Moderate, with a few very steep pitches
Trail surface: Forested path, rocky
Seasons: Spring, summer, and fall. Best wildflowers: June–August (August 20, 2015).
Other trail users: None
Canine compatibility: Leashed dogs allowed
Land status: Olympic National Forest, Buckhorn Wilderness

Nearest town: Sequim
Services: Gas, food, lodging
Permits: None
Maps: Green Trails #168S Olympic Mountains East; USGS Mount Townsend; USFS Olympic National Forest and Olympic National Park; DeLorme Page 54 H-6
Trail contact: Olympic National Forest
Special considerations: No toilet or potable water at trailhead. Vault toilet located 3.5 miles away at Upper Dungeness Campground.

Finding the trailhead: On the eastern outskirts of the town of Sequim, turn south on Palo Alto Road. In 7.8 miles the road divides, with unpaved FR 28 going left and Palo Alto Road going right. Continue on the paved Palo Alto Road. At 8.1 miles the road forks. Turn right (south) onto FR 2880, signed Dungeness Forks Campground and Tubal Cain Trail. This narrow and unpaved road is not recommended for trailers or motor homes.

At 8.9 miles cross over the Dungeness River and reach the Dungeness Forks Campground. Continue forward (south) and at 9.8 miles come to a junction with FR 2870. Continue straight (south) on FR 2870 towards Dungeness Area Trails. At 12.4 miles is another road junction; FR 2870 continues to the right (south) and is signed for Dungeness Area Trails. At 17.3 miles FR 2870 continues straight (south) and a rough dirt road goes off to the right. At 18.8 miles FR 2870 crosses over the Dungeness River on two separate bridges, enters a US Fee Area with a self-service pay station, and meets the trailhead for the Dungeness Trail (#833), Lower Dungeness Trail (#8333), and a large parking area with a vault toilet.

The road makes a hairpin turn and continues northeast as FR 2860, passes through a gate (which may or may not be open or closed seasonally), and at 21.5 miles bridges Silver Creek. At 22.7 miles reach the trailhead parking for the Gold Creek Trail (#830) and Tubal Cain Trail (#840). The parking area is small and frequently full on busy weekends, with cars having to park alongside the road. Expect a minimum of 90 minutes to reach the parking area from US 101. As remote as this place feels, and is, it's surprising to receive such strong FM radio reception from Seattle stations. **GPS: N47 53.174' / W123 05.494'**

Plants You Might See

Aster foliaceus, Leafy aster, Asteraceae

Caltha leptosepala, Marsh marigold, Ranunculaceae

Calypso bulbosa, Fairy slipper, Orchidaceae

Campanula scouleri, Scouler's harebell, Campanulaceae

Cerastium arvense, Field chickweed, Caryophyllaceae

Corallorhiza maculata, Spotted coralroot, Orchidaceae

Corallorhiza mertensiana, Western coralroot, Orchidaceae

Eriophyllum lanatum, Oregon sunshine, Asteraceae

Erythranthe guttata, Common monkeyflower, Phrymaceae

Heuchera micrantha, Small-flowered alumroot, Saxifragaceae

Parnassia fimbriata, Fringed grass-of-Parnassus, Saxifragaceae

Piperia dilatata, White bog orchid, Orchidaceae

Pyrola secunda, One-sided wintergreen, Ericaceae

Trillium ovatum, Trillium, Liliaceae

Vancouveria hexandra, Twinflower, Berberidaceae

The Hike

The trail begins at the south side of the small parking area and in 100 feet brings you to a reader board. The forest here is a mix of Western hemlock, Douglas fir, and Western red cedar, with a jungle of Pacific rhododendron (*Rhododendron macrophyllum*) below. Also in the understory are Oregon grape (*Mahonia nervosa*), Bunchberry (*Cornus unalaschkensis*), Salal (*Gaultheria shallon*), Twinflower (*Linnaea borealis*), Baldhip rose (*Rosa gymnocarpa*), and Pipsissewa (*Chimaphila umbellata*). When they're all in bloom, the trail is splashed with color.

In 0.1 mile pass a large campsite on the right and the Silver Creek shelter on your left. The trail drops to the creek and crosses it on a sturdy log bridge. Enter the Buckhorn Wilderness in 0.4 mile.

The trail makes a turn and heads south, climbing at a comfortable rate and crossing several ephemeral streams along the way. The Rhodys are truly stupendous through here.

As you proceed, the Rhododendrons thin out as the forest canopy becomes closer and closer and darker and darker. Once you're 2.9 miles from the trailhead, they thin out into nothingness and disappear in a thicket of tall, slender Silver fir. This is your signal for approaching

Rhododendron macrophyllum, *Pacific rhododendron.*

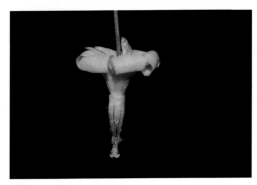

Vancouveria hexandra, *Inside-out flower.*
DAVE FLOTREE/ELLEN HAUPTMANN

the junction with the Tull Canyon Trail (#847) on your left (east). The junction is marked by a puny sign nailed to a tree.

The trail jumps up the hill and shortly comes a surprise: a rectangular horizontal hole in the rock, sign of an exploratory adit for some miners. Pass this by—all authorities render the same verdict: the mine is unsafe—and climb very steeply on a narrow trail through a Douglas fir forest with little to no ground cover except for the occasional patch of moss and foliose lichen. Climb, climb, climb and after 0.9 mile when it feels like you can climb no more, the trail levels out and you're at the site of Tull City, a grandiose name for the stuff that dreams are made of. All that remains of some miner's dreams are the rotting walls of two log cabins that now serve as a campsite for backpackers.

In the adjacent meadow are the remains of a B-17 that crashed into Dirty Face Mountain on January 19, 1952. The wreckage lies in shallow water most of the summer, surrounded by White rhododendron (*Rhododendron albiflorum*), Thimbleberry

A fallen B-17 Flying Fortress rests among a cornucopia of flowering shrubs and herbaceous plants. Please do not disturb the wreckage.

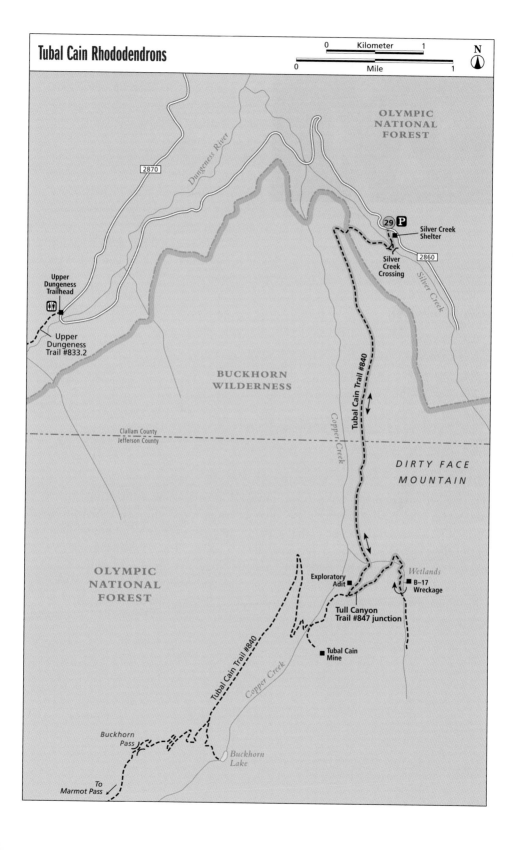

Tubal Cain Rhododendrons

0   Kilometer   1

0   Mile   1

N

2870

Dungeness River

OLYMPIC
NATIONAL
FOREST

29 P

Silver Creek
Shelter

Silver
Creek
Crossing

2860

Silver Creek

Upper
Dungeness
Trailhead

Upper
Dungeness
Trail #833.2

BUCKHORN
WILDERNESS

Copper Creek

Tubal Cain Trail #840

Clallam County
Jefferson County

DIRTY FACE
MOUNTAIN

OLYMPIC
NATIONAL
FOREST

Exploratory
Adit

Wetlands

B–17
Wreckage

Tull Canyon
Trail #847 junction

Tubal Cain
Mine

Tubal Cain Trail #840

Copper Creek

Buckhorn
Pass

Buckhorn
Lake

To
Marmot Pass

Linnaea borealis, *Twinflower*. Dave Flotree/
Ellen Hauptmann

(*Rubus parviflorus*), Fireweed (*Chamerion angustifolium*), Red elderberry (*Sambucus racemosa*), Cow parsnip (*Heracleum lanatum*), Pale larkspur (*Delphinium glaucum*), Yarrow (*Achillea millefolium*), the prickly-stemmed Swamp gooseberry (*Ribes lacustre*), Vanilla leaf (*Achlys californica*), Shrubby cinquefoil (*Dasiphora fruticosa*), the extremely densely hairy Variable willow (*Salix commutata*), and numerous others.

When you're done exploring the meadow for plants and B-17 wreckage (please leave behind anything you might be tempted to remove), retrace your steps to the trailhead.

Miles and Directions

- **0.0** Tubal Cain trailhead.
- **0.1** Cross Silver Creek.
- **0.4** Enter Buckhorn Wilderness.
- **2.9** Rhododendrons end.
- **3.2** Junction with Tull Canyon Trail.
- **4.1** Tull City mining camp and B-17 wreckage.
- **8.2** Arrive back at trailhead.

Hike Information

The crashed B-17 in the Tull Canyon meadow was returning through inclement weather to McChord Air Force Base after searching for Flight 324, a Northwest Airlines DC-4 that had ditched in the ocean off the coast of British Columbia. Three of the eight crewmen on the B-17 were killed in the accident. The aircraft was flying too low for mountainous conditions, and Air Force investigators determined the B-17 pilots had not corrected for high crosswinds and had been blown off-course. They impacted Dirty Face Mountain around the 5,900-foot level at 6:40 p.m. The wreckage then slid down the mountain into the Tull Canyon meadow.

Mount Rainier National Park

T his granddaddy of a volcano, spawning six major rivers and with a mantel of twenty-six glaciers, was named in 1792 by the English explorer Captain George Vancouver, to honor his friend, Rear Admiral Peter Rainier. At 14,411 feet, the stratovolcano Mount Rainier is the highest peak in the Cascade Mountains. Like overlapping napkins surrounding a corpulent diner, around the mountain can be found ancient trees and high alpine meadows overflowing with spring and summer wildflowers. Not to be missed are the huge tracts of undisturbed old-growth forests with trees so large, and growing so closely together, as to make high noon seem like the gloaming of the day.

Mount Rainier and Explorer's gentian (Gentiana calycosa).

It can be disconcerting to begin a hike where nearly all the walking is downhill. Berkeley Park is such a hike. Rather than tiring yourself out at the beginning of the day with some stiff uphill travel and then casually strolling your way home, getting to Berkeley Park is the opposite. Since you're moving away from Mount Rainier, most of the walking is downhill. That makes it easy to want to simply keep going—especially when there is so much to see both in scenery and in wildflowers! Berkeley Park isn't the largest alpine and subalpine meadow on Mount Rainier, but it can be a fairly easy jaunt since hikers may choose to turn around at any time.

Start: Northwest end of Sunrise parking area

Distance: 8.0 miles out and back

Hiking time: About 4–5 hours

Difficulty: Easy to moderate

Trail surface: Paved, rocky, forested path

Seasons: Spring and summer. Best wildflowers: June–August (July 25, 2015).

Other trail users: None

Canine compatibility: Dogs not permitted

Land status: Mount Rainier National Park

Nearest town: Enumclaw

Services: Gas, food, lodging. The White River Campground and picnic area is located 12 miles from the Sunrise Visitor Center, and there are hotel accommodations within the park at Paradise and Longmire.

Permit: National Park Service entrance fee

Maps: Green Trails #269S Mount Rainier; USGS Sunrise; *Trails Illustrated Mount Rainier National Park*; DeLorme Page 85 E-8

Trail contact: Sunrise Visitor Center, Mount Rainier National Park

Special considerations: Potable water and flush toilets located at trailhead.

Finding the trailhead: From the Sunrise–White River turnoff on WA 410, head west for 14 miles on Sunrise Road, passing through the Mount Rainier National Park White Canyon Entrance Station. The road ends at Sunrise in a large parking area. **GPS: N46 54.881' / W121 38.545'**

Plants You Might See

Antennaria microphylla, Rosy pussy-toes, Asteraceae

Chamerion angustifolia, Fireweed, Onagraceae

Eriogonum pyrolifolium, Alpine buckwheat, Polygonaceae

Phyllodoce empetriformis, Red mountain heather, Ericaceae

Spirea densiflora, Rosy spirea, Rosaceae

Valerian sitchensis, Valerian, Valerianaceae

Veratrum viride, Green false hellebore, Liliaceae

Veronica cusickii, Cusick's speedwell, Plantaginaceae

The Hike

The Berkeley Park Trail begins on a paved road at a reader board behind the Sunrise restrooms at the northwest end of the parking area. In 600 feet turn right (north) and leave the pavement behind. Begin ascending gently through Yakima Park on a very wide path, and in 0.1 mile turn left (west) onto the Sourdough Ridge Trail at a junction signed with eleven destinations, including Berkeley Park Camp. In another 0.2 mile turn left (west) at another trail junction towards Frozen Lake. In 0.3 mile continue straight (west) at another trail junction, away from the Huckleberry Creek Trail.

If you've been able to tear your eyes away from the dramatic vista of Mount Rainier long enough to look at your feet, you'll find the way strewn with Yarrow (*Achillea millefolium*), Erythanthe lewisii, *Lewis's monkeyflower.*
Common harebell (*Campanula rotundifolia*), Alpine aster (*Aster alpigenus*), Silver lupine (*Lupinus lepidus*), many kinds of sedge (*Carex* spp.), and lots, lots more.

Meadow and stream beyond Berkeley Park.

Eriogonum pyrolifolium, *Alpine buckwheat.*

Erythanthe lewisii, *Lewis's monkeyflower.*

Anemone occidentalis, *Western anemone.*

Cross a long talus field with an impressive rock wall and in 0.6 mile come to Frozen Lake, domestic water supply for all of Sunrise. Heed the signs to stay away from the reservoir and continue up the trail for 0.1 mile to a spur trail that leads, eventually, to Sunrise Camp and White River Campground. A further 0.1 mile brings you to "Four Corners" trail junction. Continue straight ahead (west), following the sign to (among others) Berkeley Park Camp. If you haven't already noticed, this is a marvelous place to begin spotting Sickle-top lousewort (*Pedicularis racemosum*), Western anemone (*Anemone occidentalis*), Bistort (*Polygonum bistortoides*), and Magenta paintbrush (*Castilleja parviflora*).

Continue another 0.3 mile to a junction with the Wonderland Trail; bear right (west) onto the Northern Loop Trail and enter Berkeley Park. There's plenty to see through here but, due to the fragile nature of the meadows, the Park Service doesn't like people venturing off-trail. Take your opportunities to explore by staying alongside the trail.

The trail now begins to drop away from this alpine meadow on its way to the subalpine meadow at Berkeley Park Camp. If you'd rather not lose a lot of elevation that you'll have to later regain, this is an excellent place to stop and turn around. But first, enjoy the views! Enjoy the blooms! Those who wish to continue on have another 2.3 miles to the camping area designated for the Berkeley Park area.

Berkeley Park Camp

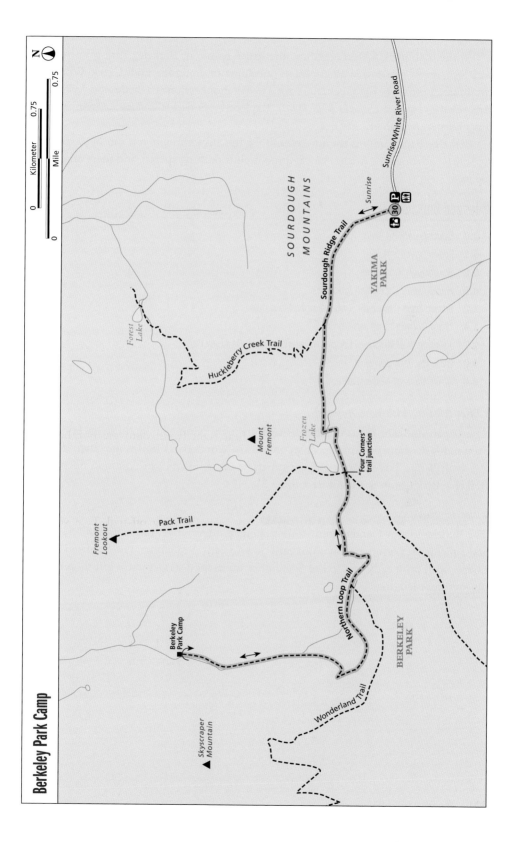

As the trail quickly loses elevation, the sparse nature of Berkeley Park gives way to a lush, green meadow with copses of Subalpine fir alongside Lodi Creek. Where the route approaches the creek, look for Lewis's monkeyflower (*Erythranthe lewisii*), Arrowleaf groundsel (*Senecio triangularis*), Explorer's gentian (*Gentiana calycosa*), and Sitka burnet (*Sanguisorba sitchensis*).

Berkeley Park Camp is the turnaround for this hike, though you can head back to Sunrise anytime you wish. The campsite itself is nothing special, and there are no views.

Miles and Directions

0.0 Sunrise parking area.

0.1 Leave pavement.

0.2 Sourdough Ridge Trail.

0.6 Huckleberry Creek Trail junction.

1.2 Frozen Lake (domestic water supply: keep out).

1.4 "Four Corners" trail junction.

1.7 Junction with Northern Loop / Wonderland Trail; Berkeley Park.

4.0 Berkeley Park Camp.

8.0 Arrive back at parking area.

Other Nearby Hiking Options

Also departing from Sunrise are trails to Burroughs Mountain, Sourdough Ridge, Edmonds Vista, Sunrise Rim, and a section of the Wonderland Trail connecting Sunrise with White River, among many others. Zealous hikers can continue on past Berkeley Park Camp to Grand Park (hike 31).

Hike Information

The Sunrise Visitor Center, with exhibits, guided interpretive programs, book sales, and a picnic area, is open daily from early July to early September. The Sunrise Day Lodge, open from early July to late September, offers food service and a gift shop but no overnight lodging.

31 Grand Park

Wildflower hunters who have not been sated by the glorious blooms in Berkeley Park can continue on down the trail a few miles farther to a huge alpine meadow with even more flowers—if you can believe it!

Start: Northwest end of Sunrise parking area
Distance: 12.6 miles out and back
Hiking time: About 6–8 hours
Difficulty: Moderate
Trail surface: Paved, rocky, dirt, forested path
Seasons: Spring and summer. Best wildflowers: June–August (July 25, 2015).
Other trail users: None
Canine compatibility: Dogs not permitted
Land status: Mount Rainier National Park

Nearest town: Enumclaw
Services: Gas, food, lodging
Permit: National Park Service entrance fee
Maps: Green Trails #269S Mount Rainier; USGS Sunrise; *Trails Illustrated Mount Rainier National Park*; DeLorme Page 85 E-8
Trail contact: Sunrise Visitor Center, Mount Rainier National Park
Special considerations: Potable water and flush toilets located at trailhead.

Finding the trailhead: From the Sunrise–White River turnoff on WA 410, head west for 14 miles on Sunrise Road, passing through the Mount Rainier National Park White Canyon Entrance Station. The road ends at Sunrise in a large parking area. **GPS: N46 54.881' / W121 38.545'**

Plants You Might See

Arnica latifolia, Mountain arnica, Asteraceae
Carex nigricans, Black alpine sedge, Cyperaceae
Cassiope mertensiana, White heather, Ericaceae
Dodecatheon jeffreyi, Jeffrey's shooting star, Primulaceae
Erigeron glacialis, Mountain daisy, Asteraceae
Erythronium grandiflorum, Glacier lily, Liliaceae
Erythronium montanum, Avalanche lily, Liliaceae
Ligusticum grayi, Meadow parsley, Apiaceae
Luetkea pectinata, Partridgefoot, Rosaceae
Lupinus latifolius, Broad-leaf lupine, Fabaceae
Pedicularis groenlandica, Elephant's head, Orobanchaceae
Penstemon procerus, Small-flowered penstemon, Plantaginaceae
Phlox diffusa, Spreading phlox, Polemoniaceae
Potentilla flabellifolia, Fan-leafed cinquefoil, Ranunculaceae

The Hike

The Grand Park Trail is an extension of the route to Berkeley Park Camp. Begin on a paved road at a reader board behind the Sunrise restrooms at the northwest end of the parking area. In 600 feet turn right (north) and leave the pavement behind. Begin

Campanula rotundifolia, *Common harebell.*
Dave Flotree/Ellen Hauptmann

Castilleja parviflora, *Small-flowered paintbrush (red form).*

ascending gently through Yakima Park on a very wide path, and in 0.1 mile turn left (west) onto the Sourdough Ridge Trail at a junction signed with eleven destinations, including Berkeley Park Camp. In another 0.2 mile turn left (west) at another trail junction towards Frozen Lake. In 0.3 mile continue straight (west) at another trail junction, away from the Huckleberry Creek Trail.

Cross a long talus field and in 0.6 mile come to Frozen Lake, domestic water supply for Sunrise. Heed the signs to stay away from the reservoir and continue up the trail for 0.1 mile to a spur trail that leads, eventually, to Sunrise Camp and White River Campground. A further 0.1 mile brings you to "Four Corners" trail junction. Continue straight ahead (west), following the sign to (among others) Berkeley Park Camp.

Continue another 0.3 mile to a junction with the Wonderland Trail; bear right (west) onto the Northern Loop Trail and enter Berkeley Park. The trail now begins to drop away from this alpine meadow on its way to the subalpine meadow at Berkeley Park Camp. In another 2.3 miles arrive at the camping area, along the trail, designated for the Berkeley Park area.

The trail continues dropping for 2.3 miles and then reaches Grand Park. It's a spectacular and expansive place, and words can't do it justice. The meadow is on a broad plateau filled with wildflowers. It's the kind of scene you think only exists in imagination. The hulk of Mount Rainier looms even larger than it could ever be in real life because the area around you appears so devoid of feature. Early in the season, when the snow is still melting, you can expect bugs, so come prepared for that in whatever manner pleases you.

The flower highlight for Grand Park is a member of the parsley family. In a typical year, mid-July is a good time to see Strickland's umbrellawort (*Tauschia stricklandii*).

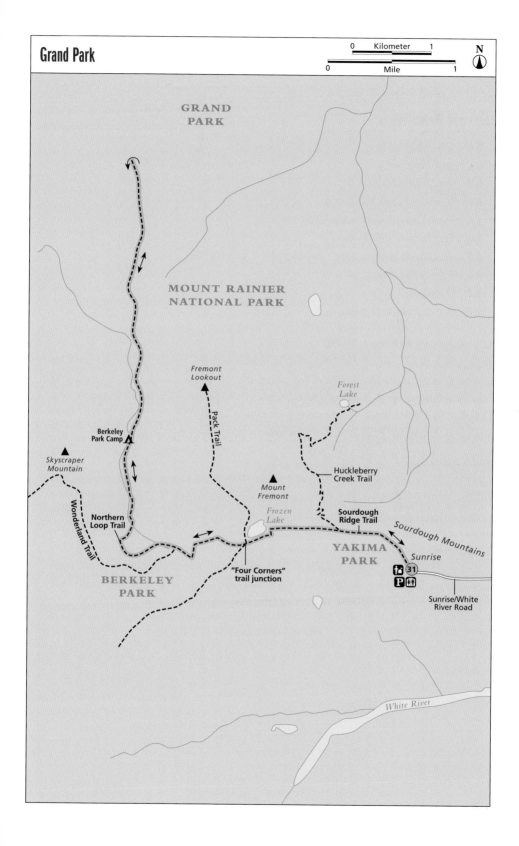

Grand Park

0   Kilometer   1
0   Mile   1

N

GRAND
PARK

MOUNT RAINIER
NATIONAL PARK

Fremont
Lookout

Forest
Lake

Pack Trail

Berkeley
Park Camp

Skyscraper
Mountain

Huckleberry
Creek Trail

Mount
Fremont

Frozen
Lake

Sourdough
Ridge Trail

Sourdough Mountains

Wonderland Trail

Northern
Loop Trail

YAKIMA
PARK

Sunrise

31

"Four Corners"
trail junction

BERKELEY
PARK

Sunrise/White
River Road

White River

This tiny plant spreads across Grand Park like a yellow carpet in the luscious green of the meadow.

Once done taking in the flowers and the view, retrace your steps back to Sunrise.

Miles and Directions

0.0 Sunrise parking area.

0.1 Leave pavement.

0.2 Sourdough Ridge Trail.

0.7 Huckleberry Creek Trail junction.

1.2 Frozen Lake (domestic water supply: keep out).

1.4 "Four Corners" trail junction.

1.7 Junction with Northern Loop / Wonderland Trail; Berkeley Park.

4.0 Berkeley Park Camp.

6.3 Grand Park.

12.6 Arrive back at parking area.

Other Nearby Hiking Options

Backpackers can extend their hike by an additional 3.5 miles to Lake Eleanor or continue on a multiday excursion following the Northern Loop Trail, returning to Sunrise. Halfway on its journey around Crescent Mountain, Sluiskin Mountain, Old Desolate, and Skyscraper Mountain, the Northern Loop Trail also meets the Wonderland Trail and Spray Park Trail. There is no camping allowed at Grand Park.

Hike Information

Sunrise was opened in 1931, designed as an alternative tourist site to relieve pressure on the Paradise area. The Civilian Conservation Corps (CCC) is responsible for constructing the many trails around Sunrise as well as the buildings housing the NPS visitor center and Sunrise Day Lodge. There were once 215 housekeeping cabins crawling up the north slope of Sunrise, but the ramshackle buildings were neither popular with tourists nor strong enough to withstand Mount Rainier's brutal winters. During World War II the cabins were sold off and moved elsewhere to provide temporary housing to defense workers in the Puget Sound region.

32 Panorama Point

There are plenty of reasons for hiking around Mount Rainier's Paradise area, but quiet and solitude are not among them. All the trails are popular all spring and summer long. On the other hand, some of the most amazing displays of wildflowers can be seen at Paradise. Of the wildflowers at Paradise, John Muir wrote in 1889, "the most luxuriant and the most extravagantly beautiful of all the alpine gardens I ever beheld in all my mountain-top wanderings."

Start: Henry M. Jackson Memorial Visitor Center
Distance: 4.2 out and back
Hiking time: About 4–6 hours
Difficulty: Strenuous
Trail surface: Forested path, rocky
Seasons: Spring, summer, and fall. Best wildflowers: July–August (August 1, 2015).
Other trail users: Climbers
Canine compatibility: Dogs not permitted
Land status: Mount Rainier National Park
Nearest town: Ashford
Services: Gas, food, lodging. Lodging also available at the adjacent Paradise Inn. Closest camping in Mount Rainier National Park located 18 miles west at Cougar Rock Campground along Longmire-Paradise Road. The Henry M. Jackson Memorial Visitor Center has a cafeteria open from 10 a.m. to 6:45 p.m.
Permit: National Park Service entrance fee
Maps: Green Trails #270S Paradise and #269S Mount Rainier Wonderland; USGS Mount Rainier East; *Trails Illustrated Mount Rainier National Park*; DeLorme Page 85 G-8
Trail contact: Mount Rainier National Park
Special considerations: Finding parking at the Henry M. Jackson Memorial Visitor Center can be challenging on most summer days. Flush toilets and potable water available at the visitor center. There is very little shade on the trail; take plenty of water and avoid becoming dehydrated. Wear a hat. Be aware of the symptoms for heat exhaustion and altitude sickness.

Finding the trailhead: From anywhere in Mount Rainier National Park, drive to the end of Stevens Canyon Road at Paradise. If you plan on staying for longer than two hours, you must park in the lower lot. People planning on a shorter stay may park in the upper lot adjacent to the Henry M. Jackson Memorial Visitor Center. **GPS: N46 47.181' / W121 44.185'**

Plants You Might See

Antennaria microphylla, Rosy pussy-toes, Asteraceae
Carex nigricans, Black alpine sedge, Cyperaceae
Cassiope mertensiana, White heather, Ericaceae
Chamerion angustifolia, Fireweed, Onagraceae
Dodecatheon jeffreyi, Jeffrey's shooting star, Primulaceae
Eriogonum pyrolifolium, Alpine buckwheat, Polygonaceae
Erythranthe lewisii, Lewis's monkeyflower, Phrymaceae
Erythronium montanum, Avalanche lily, Liliaceae
Ligusticum grayi, Meadow parsley, Apiaceae

Luetkea pectinata, Partridgefoot, Rosaceae
Pedicularis groenlandica, Elephant's head, Orobanchaceae
Pedicularis racemosa, Sickletop lousewort, Orobanchaceae
Penstemon procerus, Small-flowered penstemon, Plantaginaceae
Phlox diffusa, Spreading phlox, Polemoniaceae
Phyllodoce empetriformis, Red mountain heather, Ericaceae
Polygonum bistortoides, Bistort, Polygonaceae
Potentilla flabellifolia, Fan-leafed cinquefoil, Ranunculaceae
Vaccinium deliciosum, Cascade blueberry, Ericaceae
Valerian sitchensis, Valerian, Valerianaceae
Veratrum viride, Green false hellebore, Liliaceae
Veronica cusickii, Cusick's speedwell, Plantaginaceae

The Hike

All the trails and trail junctions in Paradise are well, and clearly, marked and there are any combination of trails departing from Paradise that will take you to Panorama Point. One of the most popular, and direct, is the Skyline Trail, but it's awfully steep and a hard row to hoe—though it is possibly more shady on sunny summer days. Views of Mount Rainier are with you the whole way up, and each step brings you closer and closer to this most incredible hunk of rock and ice.

Mount Rainier from the Panorama Point trail.

In any event, if you want to save some of your breath as well as your hamstrings, it's better to start on the Skyline Trail and then turn left (west) in 0.2 mile onto the Waterfall Trail. Climb steeply on asphalt for 0.3 mile to the Deadhorse Creek Trail. Passing the Moraine Trail, the asphalt continues almost all the way to the junction with the Skyline Trail in 0.7 mile.

A further 0.2 mile of huffing and puffing, and you'll be rewarded with

Symphyotrichum subspicata, *Douglas's aster.*

dizzying views down into the valley of the Nisqually Glacier at Glacier Vista. The trail continues to climb, sometimes on stairs constructed of rock and sometimes from 5-inch-diameter logs laid perpendicular to the trail. And sometimes the trail simply ascends.

It's plain from looking out over the meadows the trail traverses on its journey to the heavens that there were once scores of trails crisscrossing the hillside. These volunteer trails are now closed in order for the downtrodden plant life to recover.

The route up swings around; meets a junction with the Camp Muir Trail, up Pebble Creek, in 0.4 mile; and then makes a final push in 0.3 mile to Panorama Point. When you get up there, you'll instantly and fully comprehend the name. To the south can be seen Mount Adams, Mount St. Helens, and Mount Hood, with the Tatoosh Range in the foreground. The bulk of Mount Rainier hovers above you in a most formidable manner. There is a vault toilet at Panorama Point, and the line to use it is always long.

But what of the flowers you'll see? There are a lot! And what you see will

Polygonum bistortoides, *Bistort, on the Panorama Point trail.*

Erigeron glacialis, *Sub-alpine daisy.*

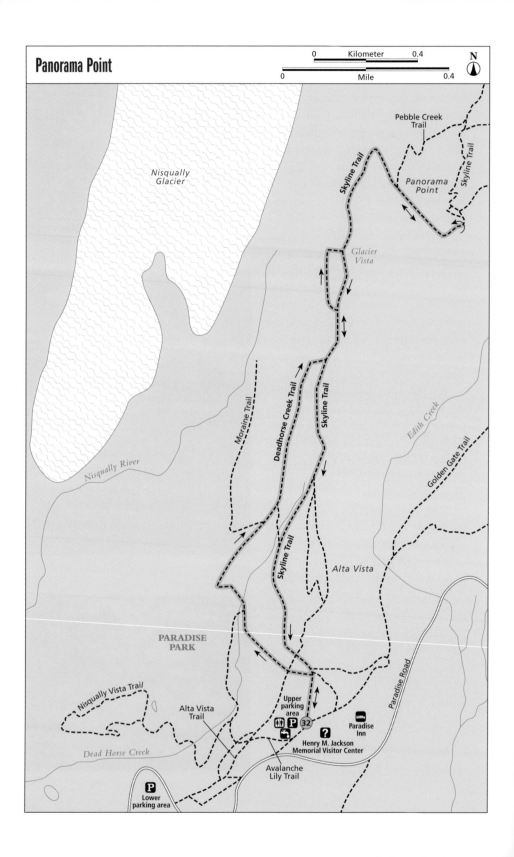

Panorama Point

0   Kilometer   0.4

0   Mile   0.4

N

Nisqually Glacier

Pebble Creek Trail

Skyline Trail

Skyline Trail

Panorama Point

Glacier Vista

Edith Creek

Moraine Trail

Deadhorse Creek Trail

Skyline Trail

Skyline Trail

Golden Gate Trail

Nisqually River

Skyline Trail

Alta Vista

PARADISE PARK

Nisqually Vista Trail

Alta Vista Trail

Paradise Road

Upper parking area

32

Paradise Inn

Henry M. Jackson Memorial Visitor Center

Dead Horse Creek

Avalanche Lily Trail

P Lower parking area

vary not only on what time of the summer you visit, but what elevation you are at. Those who come for the big single-species-whole-hillside displays will be interested in the yellow Arnica (*Arnica latifolia*) and Glacier lily (*Erythronium grandiflorus*), the blue-to-purple Mountain daisy (*Erigeron glacialis*) and its look-alike cousin Mountain aster (*Aster ledophyllus*), the blue-and-white Broad-leaf lupine (*Lupinus latifolius*), the obviously red Rosy spirea (*Spirea densiflora*), and the white Western anemone (*Anemone occidentalis*), along with so many others.

To return to Paradise, if you don't already think you are there, retrace your route back to the parking lot.

Pedicularis racemosa, *Sickletop lousewort*.

Miles and Directions

0.0   Trailhead at Henry M. Jackson Memorial Visitor Center.

0.2   Skyline / Waterfall Trail junction.

0.5   Waterfall / Deadhorse Creek Trail junction.

1.2   Deadhorse Creek / Skyline Trail junction.

1.4   Glacier Vista.

1.8   Skyline / Camp Muir Trail junction.

2.1   Panorama Point.

4.2   Arrive back at trailhead.

Other Nearby Hiking Options

Snow Lake is a 2.5-mile out-and-back hike with very little elevation gain. The High Lakes Trail makes a 2.8-mile loop around Reflection Lakes that also has minimal elevation gain. Access both trails directly from Stevens Canyon Road. Like all hikes in and about Paradise, these trails are very popular and you are guaranteed to see lots of people.

Hike Information

Mount Rainier National Park has over two million annual visitors, and on busy days it can feel as if all of them are visiting Paradise. The Henry M. Jackson Memorial Visitor Center has a lounge area, interpretive displays, and gift shop.

▶ **To make sure you are in Mount Rainier National Park when the flowers are at their best, log on to the park's "currently blooming" page at www.nps.gov/mora/ planyourvisit/wildflower -status.htm.**

33 Trail of the Shadows

Despite its cheesy title, the Trail of the Shadows is actually something really special. Whether you're staying at the National Park Inn at Longmire or passing through in anticipation of higher adventures, this short gem of a trail is well worth an hour of your botanical and historical time to explore. Let the madding crowds pass on by while you enjoy a measure of solace and quietude. It's really worth it.

Start: National Park Inn at Longmire
Distance: 0.8-mile loop
Hiking time: About 1–2 hours
Difficulty: Easy
Trail surface: Forested path
Seasons: Year-round. Best wildflowers: June–July (July 31, 2015).
Other trail users: Trail runners
Canine compatibility: Dogs not permitted
Land status: Mount Rainier National Park
Nearest town: Ashford

Services: Gas, food, lodging. Lodging also available at the National Park Inn at Longmire. Closest camping in Mount Rainier National Park located 2.2 miles east at Cougar Rock Campground along Longmire-Paradise Road.
Permit: National Park Service entrance fee
Maps: Green Trails #269S Mount Rainier Wonderland; USGS Mount Rainier West; *Trails Illustrated Mount Rainier National Park*; DeLorme Page 85 G-7
Trail contact: Mount Rainier National Park

Finding the trailhead: From the Nisqually Entrance Station for Mount Rainier National Park, drive 6.5 miles to the Longmire Historic District and park on the right (south) side of the road. Cross Longmire-Paradise Road at the crosswalk. **GPS: N46 44.982' / W121 48.810'**

Plants You Might See

Achillea millefolium, Yarrow, Asteraceae
Achlys californica, Vanilla leaf, Berberidaceae
Alnus rubra, Red alder, Betulaceae
Asarum caudatum, Wild ginger, Aristolochiaceae
Gymnocarpium dryopteris, Oak fern, Polypodiaceae
Linnaea borealis, Twinflower, Linnaeaceae
Lupinus latifolius, Broad-leaf lupine, Fabaceae
Mahonia nervosa, Oregon grape, Berberidaceae
Maianthemum dilatatum, False lily-of-the-valley, Liliaceae
Oplopanax horridus, Devil's club, Araliaceae
Oxalis oregana, Redwood sorrel, Oxalidaceae
Phleum pratense, Timothy, Poaceae
Tiarella trifoliata, Foamflower, Saxifragaceae
Viola adunca, Early blue violet, Violaceae

The Hike

Cross Longmire-Paradise Road from the National Park Inn, find the wide asphalt path, and turn right (east). The small stature of the trees in this forest of Lodgepole pine, Douglas fir, Western hemlock, and Western red cedar reflects the large degree of human disturbance this area has experienced over the years.

In 0.1 mile a short spur takes you to an interpretive display on the edge of Longmire Meadow. Read the information about Mount Rainier's eruption 375,000 years ago and marvel at the size of the glorious volcano before you. Return to the trail and immediately come to a stone encasement and seating area built in 1920 around the original hot spring developed by James Longmire in the late nineteenth century.

Symphyotrichum subspicata, *Douglas's aster.*

The trail continues for another 0.1 mile to reach the reconstructed cabin built by Elcaine Longmire in 1888. Beyond that use a broken-down bridge to cross a stone-lined spring known as "Iron Mike." The spring derives its name from the rusty-colored water that flows from it. Away from decades of human intervention, the forest around here is working its way to old-growth status.

Oplopanex horridus, *Devil's club.*

At the head of the meadow, it gets a little wetter (and buggy early in the season) and a boardwalk takes you over some of the largest Skunk cabbage (*Lysichitum americanus*) you're probably ever going to see. There is also Deer fern (*Blechnum spicant*) and Common horsetail (*Equisetum arvense*).

A travertine mound in the meadow is reached 0.4 mile after Longmire's cabin. An interpretive display explains the formation of this unusual rock/mineral type. From this point you

Asarum caudatum, *Wild ginger.*
Dave Flotree/Ellen Hauptmann

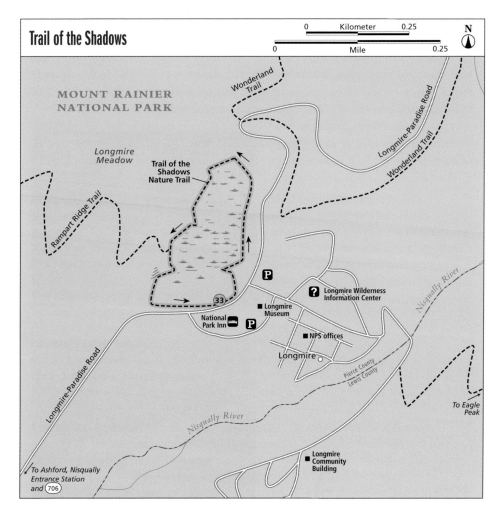

Trail of the Shadows

MOUNT RAINIER
NATIONAL PARK

Longmire
Meadow

Wonderland
Trail

Longmire-Paradise Road

Wonderland Trail

Trail of the
Shadows
Nature Trail

Rampart Ridge Trail

Nisqually River

33

P

Longmire Wilderness
Information Center

Longmire
Museum

National
Park Inn

P

NPS offices

Longmire

Pierce County
Lewis County

Nisqually River

Longmire-Paradise Road

To Eagle
Peak

To Ashford, Nisqually
Entrance Station
and 706

Longmire
Community
Building

N

▶ **James Longmire was a homesteader and developed a hotel and spa around the hot springs in Longmire Meadow.**

can also see a healthy stand of Cattail (*Typha latifolia*) growing in the meadow. The grasslike plants at your feet are primarily sedges (*Carex* sp.), rushes (*Juncus* sp.), and wood-rushes (*Luzula* sp.).

The trail continues beneath some impressive arboreal specimens, passes a junction with the Rampart Ridge Trail, crosses over the meadow's outlet stream with another patch of Skunk cabbage, and in 0.4 mile returns to the trailhead across from the National Park Inn.

Miles and Directions

0.0 Trail of the Shadows trailhead.

0.1 Longmire Spring stone encasement and seating.

Lysichiton americanum, *Skunk cabbage.* DAVE FLOTREE/ELLEN HAUPTMANN

0.2   Longmire cabin.

0.6   Travertine mound.

0.8   Arrive back at trailhead.

Other Nearby Hiking Options

The Twin Firs Trail, 2.2 miles west of Longmire, has a 0.4-mile loop through the forest that is suitable for families with young children or people needing to stretch their legs after a long drive.

34 Grove of the Patriarchs

Cross over the Ohanapecosh River using a suspension bridge on one of Mount Rainier National Park's easiest hikes. In a place where the trees all seem old, the 1,000-year-old Patriarchs are older. The grove provides an excellent introduction to a mid-elevation mixed conifer forest that is suitable for children, the curious, or the weary. It's also a great early-season excursion for visitors to Mount Rainier when all the popular high-country spots are still covered in snow.

Start: Eastside Trail in parking lot for Grove of the Patriarchs
Distance: 1.2-mile lollipop
Hiking time: About 1-2 hours
Difficulty: Easy
Trail surface: Forested path, boardwalk
Seasons: Year-round. Best wildflowers: June–July (July 31, 2015).
Other trail users: None
Canine compatibility: Dogs not permitted
Land status: Mount Rainier National Park
Nearest town: Enumclaw
Services: Gas, food, lodging. Closest camping available in Mount Rainier National Park is at

Ohanapecosh Campground. Lodging available within the park at National Park Inn or Paradise Inn.
Permit: National Park Service entrance fee
Maps: Green Trails #269S Mount Rainier Wonderland; USGS Chinook Pass; *Trails Illustrated Mount Rainier National Park*; DeLorme Page 85 G-9
Trail contact: Mount Rainier National Park
Special considerations: Flush toilets, potable water, picnic benches, and garbage cans available at trailhead.

Finding the trailhead: From the Stevens Canyon entrance to Mount Rainier National Park, drive 0.1 mile north on Stevens Canyon Road to the parking area on the east side of the road. **GPS: N46 45.489' / W121 33.441'**

Plants You Might See

Alnus rubra, Red alder, Betulaceae
Cornus unalaschkensis, Bunchberry, Cornaceae
Rubus parviflorus, Thimbleberry, Rosaceae

The Hike

You can pick up the wide, dusty trail behind the toilet building or 20 feet farther away at the actual Eastside Trail trailhead at the north end of the parking area.

The first thing to notice is how dark the forest is. That's what happens when trees have never been logged. It's one result of having national parks. These trees have had a long time to grow old, and they show it. They're tall, for sure, but their tops are often decrepit, snarled, dead. Their branches, high up in the canopy, intertwine to such a degree as to block out any influence on the earth's surface from the sun. The

The trail includes crossing over the Ohanapecosh River on a suspension bridge.

understory is slight and scattered, relegated to places where decadent trees have fallen to the ground, allowing light to infiltrate the forest floor, or where the trail has been cut through the forest.

The path heads downhill towards, and parallel to, the river. Along the way spot Bracken fern (*Pteridium aquilinum*), Vanilla root (*Achlys californica*), Deer fern (*Blechnum spicant*), Oregon grape (*Mahonia nervosa*), Red elderberry (*Sambucus racemosa*), and Devil's club (*Oplopanax horridus*). In fact, everything you would expect to find in a Douglas fir, Western hemlock, and Western red cedar forest.

In 0.3 mile the Eastside Trail continues north and the trail to the Patriarchs bears right (east). In another 0.1 mile cross the Ohanapecosh River on a suspension bridge, without a doubt the highlight of the trip for any children you have with you. Maybe even a highlight

A close pair of Pseudotsuga menziesii, *Douglas fir.*

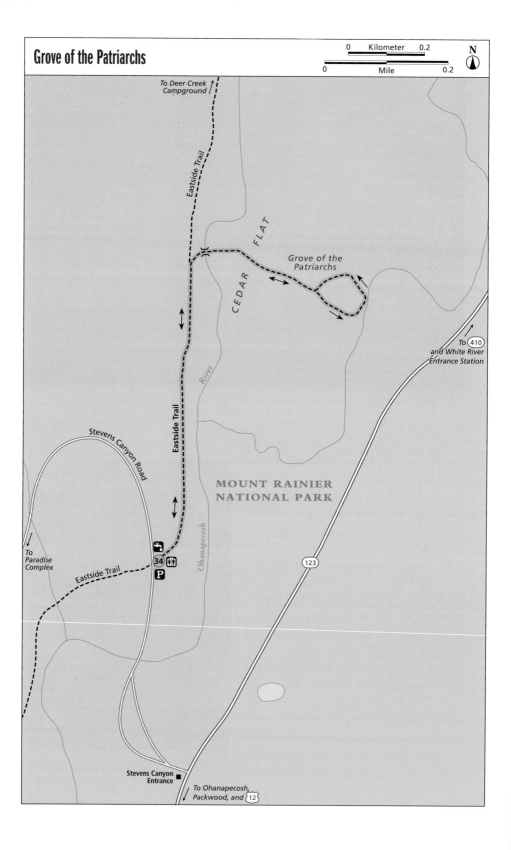

Grove of the Patriarchs

0   Kilometer   0.2

0   Mile   0.2

N

To Deer Creek
Campground

Eastside Trail

CEDAR FLAT

Grove of the
Patriarchs

Eastside Trail

River

To 410
and White River
Entrance Station

Stevens Canyon Road

Eastside Trail

MOUNT RAINIER
NATIONAL PARK

Ohanapecosh

To
Paradise
Complex

Eastside Trail

34

123

To Ohanapecosh,
Packwood, and 12

Stevens Canyon
Entrance

for the adults too! In 0.1 mile come to a boardwalk and the beginning of a loop trail around the Grove of the Patriarchs.

The big old trees here are Douglas fir and Western red cedar. Some are so tall, and the tangle of branches so thick, you cannot see the treetops. A few benches have been strategically placed before two old Douglas firs, called "The Twins." More benches are below an especially humongous nearby Western red cedar. Take some time to sit here and contemplate all the history that has occurred throughout the last 1,000 years while these beautiful monsters quietly grew.

Finish the short loop and retrace your steps back to the suspension bridge and thence the parking lot.

Miles and Directions

0.0 Eastside Trail trailhead.
0.3 Eastside Trail junction with Grove of the Patriarchs loop.
0.4 Cross Ohanapecosh River on suspension bridge.
0.5 Grove of the Patriarchs.
0.6 Complete the loop trail.
1.2 Arrive back at trailhead.

Hike Information

The Grove of the Patriarchs is a good example of the virgin forests that once covered all of western Washington. "Old-growth" is a term used to describe a forest of a certain age with trees exhibiting a mix of age classes, canopy heights, various-size tree heights and diameters, and species composition.

35 Naches Loop

This loop packs a lot of wallop within its short distance. You can immerse yourself with some of the best Mount Rainier National Park has to offer and without a lot of work! There is easy access to alpine scenery, a couple of ponds, an alpine lake, Cascade Mountain vistas, dramatic views of Mount Rainier, midsummer floral displays, and lots of fall color.

Start: Tipsoo Lake picnic area
Distance: 3.4-mile loop
Hiking time: About 2–3 hours
Difficulty: Easy
Trail surface: Forested path with one tiny stretch of highway
Seasons: Spring and summer. Best wildflowers: June–July (July 31, 2015).
Other trail users: Equestrians
Canine compatibility: Leashed dogs allowed in Okanogan-Wenatchee National Forest section. Dogs not permitted in Mount Rainier National Park section.
Land status: Mount Rainier National Park; Okanogan-Wenatchee National Forest, William O. Douglas Wilderness

Nearest town: Enumclaw
Services: Gas, food, lodging. Closest camping available in Mount Rainier National Park is at White River Campground.
Permit: National Park Service entrance fee
Maps: Green Trails #269S Mount Rainier Wonderland; USGS White River Park and Chinook Pass; *Trails Illustrated Mount Rainier National Park*; DeLorme Page 85 F-9
Trail contacts: Mount Rainier National Park; Okanogan-Wenatchee National Forest, Naches Ranger District
Special considerations: Vault toilet located at trailhead. No potable water at trailhead.

Finding the trailhead: From the junction of WA 410 and WA 123, drive east for 2.8 miles to the Tipsoo Lake picnic area and park in the large, paved parking area. **GPS: N46 52.190' / W121 31.171'**

Plants You Might See

Anaphalis margaritacea, Pearly everlasting, Asteraceae
Campanula rotundifolia, Common harebell, Campanulaceae
Castilleja parviflora, Mountain paintbrush, Orobanchaceae
Erythranthe lewisii, Lewis's monkeyflower, Phrymaceae
Eucephalus ledophyllus, Cascade aster, Asteraceae
Pedicularis groenlandica, Elephant's head, Orobanchaceae
Rhododendron albus, White rhododendron, Ericaceae
Senecio triangularis, Arrowleaf groundsel, Asteraceae
Xerophyllum tenax, Beargrass, Melanthiaceae

The Hike

The trail begins behind reader boards at the far eastern side of the large, paved parking lot. Walk east, towards Tipsoo Lake, and then head south to one of the best displays of Mountain pasqueflower (*Anemone occidentalis*) you're ever going to see. That tiny mat-forming plant at your feet with erect cream-colored blossoms and greatly pinnatifid leaves is Patridgefoot (*Luetkea pectinata*). You'll see a lot of it along this trail.

The route skirts Tipsoo Lake and then rises to cross WA 410. Remember what your mother said, "Look both ways before crossing the street." Pick up the Naches Loop trail on the other side and begin a moderate climb under a patchy forest of Subalpine fir with Sitka mountain ash (*Sorbus sitchensis*) in the understory. There are also loads of Oval-leaved blueberry (*Vaccinium ovalifolium*) alongside the trail to keep hikers more than occupied with berry picking come autumn.

As the trail ascends through a mosaic of dry meadow and forest, don't forget to look back from time to time for inspiring views of Mount Rainier's east face. In late summer the most common flower you'll see in the dry meadows is Cascade aster (*Eucephalus ledophyllus*). As everything else has begun drying out, it's nice to see hill-sides of this blue beauty, with its yellow center of disk flowers, popping through all the browning plant life.

Tipsoo Lake, Mount Rainier National Park.

Parnassia fimbriata, fringed grass-of-Parnassus.

Berries from Sorbus sitchensis, *Sitka mountain-ash.*

Subalpine forest and meadow long the Naches Loop trail.

Anaphalis margaritaceae, *Pearly everlasting.*

Erythanthe lewisii, *Lewis's monkeyflower.*

Eucephalus ledophyllus, *Cascade aster.*

Subalpine fir and Mount Rainier.

Anemone occidentalis, *Western anemone.*

The trail tops out in 1.2 miles with nice views east, to Dewey Lake, and south, to Mount Adams. Of course, you'll get another gander at Mount Rainier. Another 0.1 mile and there is a little pond, surrounded by Mountain pasqueflower, and 0.1 mile past that you leave the national park and enter the William O. Douglas Wilderness, and quickly come to a junction with the Pacific Crest Trail. Don't be surprised to see dogs leading people around or equestrians on the trail here.

Begin a long, gradual descent through a thinning forest of Subalpine fir and, mainly, Mountain hemlock, along with more dry meadows. In 0.3 mile pass another small pond—heavily impacted by splashing water-players and situated in a nice meadowy declivity

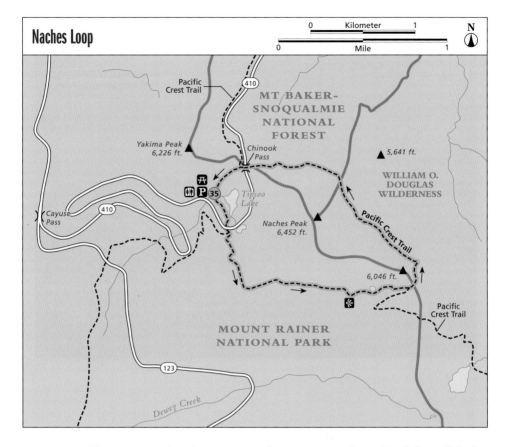

Naches Loop

crisscrossed by many social trails. At a spray of water coming down the cliff, you'll find Mountain sorrel (*Oxyria digyna*) and Fringed grass-of-Parnassus (*Parnassia fimbriata*).

In another 0.5 mile the trail leaves the wilderness area. Another 0.8 mile after that, cross over WA 410 on a pedestrian footbridge, which is also the rather beefy sign over the highway that announces entry into the park. To the right (east) is a large, paved turnout with views and vault toilets. Find the Tipsoo Lake trail on the other side and walk 0.4 mile back to your car.

Miles and Directions

0.0 Naches Peak Loop trailhead at Tipsoo Lake picnic area.

1.2 Mount Adams view.

1.4 Leave Mount Rainier National Park; enter William O. Douglas Wilderness.

2.2 Leave William O. Douglas Wilderness.

3.0 Cross over WA 410.

3.4 Arrive back at trailhead.

Mount Rainier from Naches Loop Trail.

Other Nearby Hiking Options
A short loop trail traipses around Tipsoo Lake. From its junction with the Naches Loop, a 2.4-mile round-trip hike south on the Pacific Crest Trail will take you to Dewey Lake.

Hike Information
WA 410 and WA 123 are open May to November. Some hikers elect to begin the trail outside Mount Rainier National Park at a large, paved parking area, with vault toilets, at Chinook Pass. There is no fishing, swimming, or wading allowed in Tipsoo Lake.

36 Spray Park

It feels impossible to find an unpopular or uncrowded hike in Mount Rainier National Park. The secret is to discover a trailhead that's either difficult to reach or is reachable only by an unpaved road. Access to Spray Park fits both those criteria, yet there are still plenty of people willing to try. That probably has everything to do with fantastic wildflowers and a view of "The Mountain" that is so close, you feel you could touch it.

Start: Mowich Lake walk-in campground, Mount Rainier National Park
Distance: 8.2 miles out and back
Hiking time: About 6–8 hours
Difficulty: Strenuous, with many steep sections
Trail surface: Forested path, rocky
Seasons: Summer and fall. Best wildflowers: July–August (August 4, 2015).
Other trail users: None
Canine compatibility: Dogs not permitted
Land status: Mount Rainier National Park
Nearest town: Buckley
Services: Gas, food, lodging. Limited services in Burnett (gas), Wilkinson (restaurant), and Carbonado (lodging). There is a rough walk-in campground at Mowich Lake with picnic tables, garbage cans, and food storage containers (bears in the area).
Permit: National Park Service entrance fee
Maps: Green Trails #269S Mount Rainier Wonderland; USGS Mowich Lake; *Trails Illustrated Mount Rainier National Park*; DeLorme Page 85 E-7
Trail contact: Mount Rainier National Park
Special considerations: Vault toilet at trailhead. No potable water at trailhead. Outhouse on trail at Eagle's Roost backcountry campsite.

Finding the trailhead: From Wilkeson, drive south on WA 165 (Mountain Meadows / Mowich Lake Road) for 22 miles to Mowich Lake. The final 18 miles is a wide, dusty, washboarded road not recommended for RVs or trailers. There is a self-pay entrance station and a vault toilet at the Paul Peak trailhead. **GPS: N46 55.956' / W121 51.798'**

Plants You Might See

Antennaria microphylla, Rosy pussy-toes, Asteraceae
Cassiope mertensiana, White heather, Ericaceae
Chamerion angustifolia, Fireweed, Onagraceae
Dodecatheon jeffreyi, Jeffrey's shooting star, Primulaceae
Eriogonum pyrolifolium, Alpine buckwheat, Polygonaceae
Erythranthe lewisii, Lewis's monkeyflower, Phrymaceae
Erythronium montanum, Avalanche lily, Liliaceae
Ligusticum grayi, Meadow parsley, Apiaceae
Luetkea pectinata, Partridgefoot, Rosaceae
Pedicularis groenlandica, Elephant's head, Orobanchaceae
Pedicularis racemosa, Sickletop lousewort, Orobanchaceae
Penstemon procerus, Small-flowered penstemon, Plantaginaceae

Phlox diffusa, Spreading phlox, Polemoniaceae
Phyllodoce empetriformis, Red mountain heather, Ericaceae
Polygonum bistortoides, Bistort, Polygonaceae
Potentilla flabellifolia, Fan-leafed cinquefoil, Ranunculaceae
Sedum oreganum, Oregon stonecrop, Crassulaceae
Vaccinium deliciosum, Cascade blueberry, Ericaceae
Valerian sitchensis, Valerian, Valerianaceae
Veratrum viride, Green false hellebore, Liliaceae
Veronica cusickii, Cusick's speedwell, Plantaginaceae

The Hike

Find the Spray Park trailhead in the campground beyond and to the right (west) of the reader board and vault toilet. The trail heads downhill and in 0.3 mile comes to a junction with the Wonderland Trail and turns left (south). This is an interesting forest; it's primarily a Mountain hemlock forest but you'll also see Western hemlock, Western red cedar, and even Douglas fir now and again. The shrubs are White rhododendron (*Rhododendron albiflorum*) and Black huckleberry (*Vaccinium membranaceum*). In the understory is Scouler's corydalis (*Corydalis scouleri*); its pink flowers ascending a stiff stalk look more like a troop of Phasmatodea (stick insects) than flowers. Also in the understory are the delicate white blossoms of Foamflower (*Tiarella trifoliata*), Queen's cup (*Clintonia uniflora*), Vanilla leaf (*Achlys californica*), Arrowleaf groundsel (*Senecio triangularis*), and Deer fern (*Blechnum spicant*). There are also a couple of wintergreens beside the trail: White-veined shinleaf (*Pyrola picta*), with its distinctive white leaf venation, and Pipsissewa (*Chimaphila umbellata*).

The trail crosses a creek, using a large log as a bridge, and this is a good place to see Yellow monkeyflower (*Erythranthe guttata*) and Yellow willowherb (*Epilobium luteum*). The tiny meadow beside the creek is chock-full of Fireweed (*Chamerion angustifolium*) in summer.

Gentiana algida, *Arctic gentian.*

Gentiana calycosa, *Explorer's gentian.*

Veratrum viride, *Green false-hellebore.*

Castilleja parviflora, *Small-flowered paint-brush (red form).*

Vaccinium deliciosum, *Cascade huckleberry.*   Erythanthe lewisii, *Lewis's monkeyflower.*

The Eagle Cliff viewpoint is 1.7 miles from the trailhead. It's only a diversion of 100 feet and well worth it. The view of Mount Rainier is stupendous.

Back on the Spray Park Trail, you come to a junction in another 0.3 mile. To the right (south) a spur trail leads down to the Eagle's Roost backcountry campsite and a rudimentary toilet. If you've no need for the facilities, continue 0.1 mile to another side trail well worth your time. This 0.2-mile out-and-back detour goes to a view of Spray Falls. Don't be surprised to see Pearly everlasting (*Anaphalis margaritacea*), shrubby Red alder, and the aptly named Rosy spirea (*Spirea douglasii*).

The trail now begins to climb in a serious manner and only lets up twice or thrice, now and then, to cross some pocket meadows. It's so steep in some places that stone stairs have been installed. As you leave the trees, the flowers start to come

Spray Park

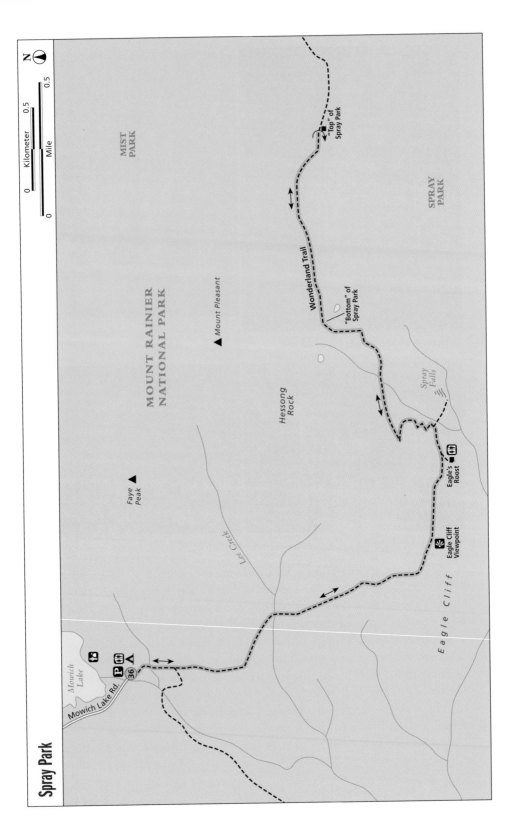

Mowich Lake

Mowich Lake Rd.

36

MOUNT RAINIER
NATIONAL PARK

▲ Faye Peak

▲ Mount Pleasant

MIST PARK

Lee Creek

Hessong Rock

Eagle Cliff Viewpoint

Eagle's Roost

Wonderland Trail

"Bottom" of Spray Park

"Top" of Spray Park

SPRAY PARK

Spray Falls

Eagle Cliff

N

Kilometer   0.5

Mile   0.5

fast and furious. Two of the best you'll see are the amazingly blue Explorer's gentian (*Gentiana calycosa*) and its look-alike white brother, Arctic gentian (*Gentiana algida*).

There is no official beginning or ending to Spray Park. Most people accept that when views of Hessong Rock are reached that they have truly entered Spray Park. The trail continues to climb steeply through fields of flowers and patches of Subalpine fir. There are plenty of volunteer trails created by curious hikers.

As you climb, it becomes rockier and rockier underfoot and the vegetation begins to thin. For purposes of this hike, we can say the trail ends at the top of a rocky acclivity, 4.1 miles from Mowich Lake. Here you'll find a broad shoulder of Mount Rainier that looks like glaciers left it only a year or so ago. Across the valley is the long ridge that comprises Mother Mountain. The way continues on to Cataract Valley, but this is a good place to turn around and head for home.

Miles and Directions

0.0 Mowich Lake campground / Spray Park trailhead.

0.3 Spray Park / Wonderland Trail junction.

1.7 Spur trail to Eagle Cliff viewpoint.

2.0 Spray Park / Eagle's Roost Trail junction.

2.1 Spray Park / Spray Falls Trail junction.

3.1 "Beginning" of Spray Park.

4.1 "End" of Spray Park.

8.2 Arrive back at trailhead.

Other Nearby Hiking Options

The northern trailhead at Mowich Lake for the Wonderland Trail, which encircles Mount Rainier, can be found 0.5 mile north of the Spray Park Trail along Mowich Lake Road. This is also access for the 6.5-mile round-trip Tolmie Peak Trail to Eunice Lake and the Tolmie Peak Lookout. The southern end of the Wonderland Trail intersects the Paul Peak Trail and meets the Spray Park Trail 0.3 mile south of Mowich Lake.

Hike Information

The road to Mowich Lake is generally open mid-July to mid-October.

Mount Baker
and the North Cascades

The jagged peaks and alpine lakes of the North Cascades gladden the hearts of all hikers and mountaineers, while the high and open alpine meadows amaze and delight the seeker of wildflowers. In summer, these green and flowery meadows and azure alpine lakes, set against a backdrop of glaciers and patchy forest, bring a cornucopia of color to the eye. It's enough to take one's breath away . . . which the elevation of the mountains will do all on its own! These rugged mountains, steep-sided valleys, and snowy peaks with their glaciers are nowhere better seen nor accessed than in the Mount Baker area.

Scenic Mount Shuksan.

37 Artist Ridge

This short trail has plenty to see. The views of Mount Baker and Mount Shuksan can only be described as "Wow!" Because the trail sees a lot of feet, the plant life suffers, but if you don't have much time to hike, or can't hike too much, and still want to see an excellent representation of the local flora, this is the trail for you.

Start: Artist Point parking lot
Distance: 1.0 mile out and back
Hiking time: About 1 hour
Difficulty: Easy
Trail surface: Gravel, rock, paved
Seasons: Summer and fall. Best wildflowers: June–September (August 7, 2015).
Other trail users: None
Canine compatibility: Leashed dogs allowed
Land status: Mount Baker–Snoqualmie National Forest
Nearest towns: Glacier and Maple Falls

Services: Food (Glacier); gas and food (Maple Falls). Camping at Silver Fir (8 miles west) and Douglas Fir (20 miles west, near Glacier) on WA 542 (Mount Baker Highway).
Permits: Northwest Forest Pass or Federal Access Pass
Maps: Green Trails #14 Mount Shuksan; USGS Mount Shuksan; DeLorme Page 43 C-8
Trail contact: Mount Baker–Snoqualmie National Forest, Glacier Public Service Center
Special considerations: Vault toilet at trailhead. No potable water at trailhead. Elevation.

Finding the trailhead: From Heather Meadows and the Mount Baker Ski Area, drive east on WA 542 (Mount Baker Highway) 2.8 miles to road's end at Artist Point. **GPS: N48 50.777' / W121 41.517'**

Plants You Might See
Anaphalis margaritacea, Pearly everlasting, Asteraceae
Carex nigricans, Black alpine sedge, Cyperaceae
Chamerion angustifolium, Fireweed, Onagraceae
Erythranthe lewisii, Lewis's monkeyflower, Phrymaceae
Sorbus sitchensis, Sitka mountain ash, Rosaceae
Vaccinium deliciosum, Cascade huckleberry, Ericaceae

The Hike

That forbidding hunk of rock and ice looming over you to the east is Mount Shuksan. Its impressive beauty is accessible by finding the Artist Ridge trail in the large parking area where WA 542 terminates. Begin walking on an asphalt trail behind the reader board at the east end of the parking lot. It quickly splits; go left and reach a viewpoint with interpretive displays. As impressive as the view of Mount Shuksan is, the view of Mount Baker to the right is even better. If the elevation of this place hasn't already done so, be prepared to have your breath taken away.

Table Mountain.

The gravel, sometimes rocky, path leads through a thin and mostly dwarfed forest of Mountain hemlock. The snow piles up here during winter, and winds on Artist Ridge can be fierce. These environmental factors account for the disfigured, twisted, and deformed trees you see, an effect known as *krummholz*, a German word meaning "twisted wood." Only where there is shelter from the storm can the trees poke their crowns very high.

The environment here is so severe that even the Red mountain heather (*Phyllodoce empetriformis*) and Alpine lady fern (*Athyrium alpestre*) look like they're having a hard time of it. Though the ground cover here is good, it is hardly substantial.

Phylodocce empetriformis, Red mountain-heather.

Look in the cracks between the rocks for a pretty little member of the rose family named Partridgefoot (*Luetkea pectinata*).

Many benches are provided alongside the trail at strategic points to facilitate enjoyment of the views. Sagely, they are placed under, or next to, tree cover to provide protection from the wind. After 0.5 mile the trail ends at Huntoon Point for more views and wind, makes a tiny loop, and heads

Artist Ridge

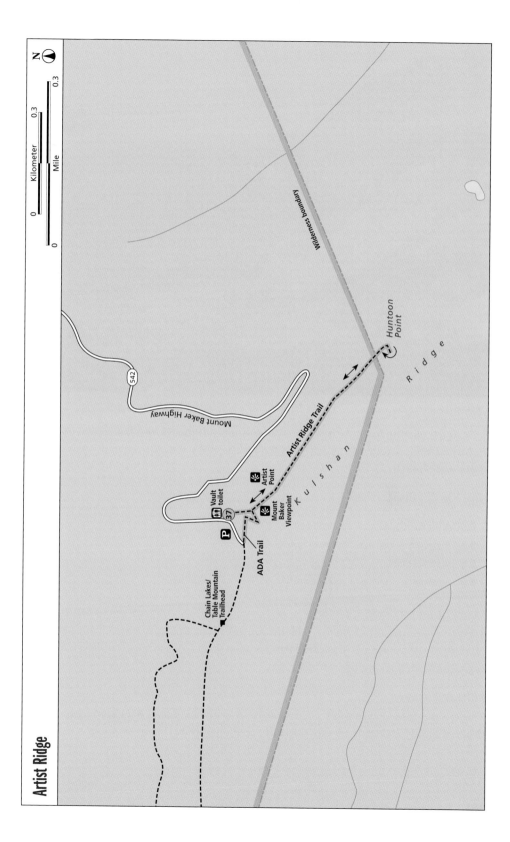

N

0   Kilometer   0.3

0   Mile   0.3

542

Mount Baker Highway

Wilderness boundary

Artist Ridge Trail

Huntoon Point

Ridge

Kulshan

Artist Point

Mount Baker Viewpoint

Vault toilet

37

P

ADA Trail

Chain Lakes/ Table Mountain Trailhead

One of the distinctive features of Mount Baker is the ability to easily drive to alpine habitat.

back to the parking lot at Artist Point. When you reach the Mount Baker viewpoint and paved trail, detour to the left (west) onto the ADA trail for different views of Baker and Shuksan.

Miles and Directions

- **0.0** Artist Point parking lot and trailhead.
- **0.1** Trail junction with ADA trail; Mount Baker viewpoint.
- **0.5** Huntoon Point.
- **1.0** Arrive back at trailhead and parking lot.

Other Nearby Hiking Options

Trails to Lake Ann (Trail #600), Table Mountain (Trail #681), Galena Chain Lakes (Trail #682), Ptarmigan Ridge (Trail #682.1), and Wild Goose Trail (Trail #684) also depart from the parking lot at Artist Point.

Hike Information

The Heather Meadows Visitor Center at the Austin Pass Picnic Area along Mount Baker Highway is open daily July through September from 10 a.m. to 4 p.m.

38 Bagley Lakes Loop

Don't be surprised if you see a lot of people on this trail during peak blooming time. After all, there are plenty of others beside wildflower hunters who appreciate the loop's subalpine meadows, lakes, and proximity to the Heather Meadows complex of trails. On the other hand, what with all the flowers to see and views to enjoy, it's entirely reasonable to assume there will be crowds—but mainly on weekends and never when it's raining!

Start: Upper parking lot for Heather Meadows and Mount Baker Ski Area
Distance: 2.5-mile loop with out-and-back
Hiking time: About 2–3 hours
Difficulty: Easy to moderate
Trail surface: Forested path, rocky
Seasons: Summer and fall. Best wildflowers: July–September (August 7, 2015).
Other trail users: None
Canine compatibility: Leashed dogs allowed
Land status: Mount Baker–Snoqualmie National Forest
Nearest towns: Glacier and Maple Falls

Services: Food (Glacier); gas and food (Maple Falls). Camping at Silver Fir (8 miles west) and Douglas Fir (20 miles west, near Glacier) on WA 542 (Mount Baker Highway).
Permits: Northwest Forest Pass or Federal Access Pass
Maps: Green Trails #14 Mount Shuksan; USGS Mount Shuksan; DeLorme Page 43 C-8
Trail contact: Mount Baker–Snoqualmie National Forest, Glacier Public Service Center
Special considerations: Vault toilet at trailhead. No potable water at trailhead. Elevation.

Finding the trailhead: From Heather Meadows and the Mount Baker Ski Area, drive south on WA 542 (Mount Baker Highway) 0.2 mile to the Mount Baker Ski Lodge upper parking lot. **GPS: N48 51.691' / W121 40.948'**

Plants You Might See

Anemone occidentalis, Mountain pasqueflower, Ranunculaceae
Arnica latifolia, Mountain arnica, Asteraceae
Aster foliaceous, Leafy aster, Asteraceae
Caltha leptosepala, Marsh marigold, Ranunculaceae
Castilleja parviflora, Mountain paintbrush, Orobanchaceae
Dicentra formosa, Bleeding heart, Papaveraceae
Erigeron glacialis, Subalpine daisy, Asteraceae
Gaultheria humifusa, Alpine wintergreen, Ericaceae
Leptarrhena pyrolifolia, Leatherleaf saxifrage, Saxifragaceae
Luetkea pectinata, Partridgefoot, Rosaceae
Parnassia fimbriata, Fringed grass-of-Parnassus, Saxifragaceae
Potentilla flabellifolia, Fan-leaf cinquefoil, Ranunculaceae
Sibbaldia procumbens, Sibbaldia, Rosaceae
Veratrum viride, Green false hellebore, Liliaceae

The Hike

Find the trailhead for Bagley Lakes and Chain Lakes at the west side of the large parking area, beside the vault toilet. The trail begins by dropping through a forest of Mountain hemlock and a well-developed understory of Sitka mountain ash (*Sorbus sitchensis*), Red mountain heather (*Phyllodoce empetriformis*), White mountain heather (*Cassiope mertensiana*), Cascade huckleberry (*Vaccinium deliciosum*), and Black mountain huckleberry (*Vaccinium membranaceum*). The Cascade huckleberry has blue berries, which hang down, and its toothed leaves end with a pointy tip. Black mountain huckleberries have erect black berries. The leaves are more finally toothed than Cascade huckleberry, and the leaves come to a point at either end.

Depending on the time of year, you will also see Pearly everlasting (*Anaphalis margaritacea*) and Fireweed (*Chamerion angustifolium*) in abundance. The willow along the trail is Sitka willow (*Salix sitchensis*). Like all willows, the undersides of the leaves are hairy. But the Sitka willow has something else: When you rock the leaves back and forth in the sun, you can see the silvery undersides shine.

Pass the junction with the Wild Goose Trail and bear right (west). It doesn't take long to reach the lake basin and the lower lake. The trail skirts along the southeast shore on a series of boardwalks. These protect the tender sidehill meadow plants but still give access to all the huckleberries you can get—if you get here early enough before the bears and other hikers.

Scenic, alpine Bagley Lakes.

Dicentra formosa, *Bleeding heart.* DAVE FLOTREE/ELLEN HAUPTMANN

In 0.8 mile you come to a lovely double stone archway bridging the creek between Upper and Lower Bagley Lake. Cross over and make a left (west) turn, then continue up the trail for 0.2 mile in order to enjoy the upper lake.

When you come to a cliff and rocky section above the lake, keep your eyes open for Butterwort (*Pinguicula vulgaris*). This inconspicuous perennial and carnivorous plant with sticky leaves has purple, penstemon-like, funnel-shaped flowers. Butterwort is found throughout North America, Europe, and Russia.

From here the trail continues up the valley to fine views of the Bagley Lakes basin and its surrounding peaks. The impressive stone building sitting atop the ridge in front of you (northwest) is the Forest Service visitor center at Austin Pass. When the trail hits a big rubble pile of talus, it's time to turn back. You could continue on to Galena Chain Lakes (hike 39), but save that for another day.

Retrace your steps to the stone archway. This time continue straight (northeast), climbing above lower Bagley Lake but descending into the basin. Keep looking back, as well as forward, as you hike through alternating trees and meadows, and appreciate the fine perspective you get of the entire drainage.

Castilleja parviflora, *Small-flowered paintbrush.*

Bagley Lakes Loop

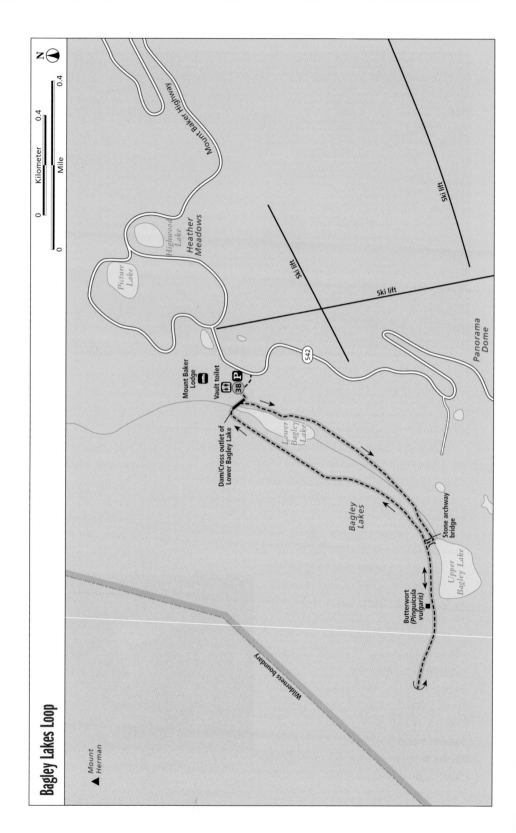

Mount Herman ▲

N

Kilometer
0   0.4

Mile
0   0.4

Mount Baker Highway

Picture Lake

Highwood Lake

Heather Meadows

Ski lift

Ski lift

Ski lift

Panorama Dome

542

Mount Baker Lodge

Vault toilet

38 P

Dam/Cross outlet of Lower Bagley Lake

Lower Bagley Lake

Bagley Lakes

Stone archway bridge

Upper Bagley Lake

Butterwort (Pinguicula vulgaris)

Wilderness boundary

Soon you come to a dam across lower Bagley Lake's outlet. This is all that remains of a hydroelectric project from the Mount Baker Lodge—a casualty to fire in 1931. The trail crosses the dam on wooden planks. Now begin to climb the final 0.2 mile to the trailhead and come to the parking area. You're back!

Miles and Directions

0.0 Trailhead at upper parking area for Heather Meadows and Mount Baker Ski Area.

0.2 Lower Bagley Lake.

1.0 Stone archway bridge.

1.2 Talus slope begins (turnaround point).

2.3 Dam/trail crosses outflow from lower Bagley Lake.

2.5 Arrive back at trailhead.

Other Nearby Hiking Options

The Wild Goose Trail (#684.2) and access to the Chain Lakes Loop Trail (#682) also depart from the upper parking lot for Heather Meadows and the Mount Baker Ski Area.

39 Galena Chain Lakes

Winding around Table Mountain, this trail meanders amidst tall and elfin subalpine forests, wet and dry meadows, and alongside lakeshores and stream banks. Throughout it all plant lovers will find the plant communities are diverse, interesting, and exciting. And, like any other hike in the Mount Baker region, the views are exquisite—as long as the sun is shining and the skies are clear, that is! You'll delight in tall cliffs, far vistas, lake basin views, and glimpses of the region's two volcanic giants. This is actually a partial loop hike and is accessible from three separate parking lots. The particular route described here requires a car shuttle, though a full loop can be made from any trailhead by utilizing the Wild Goose Trail as a connector.

Start: Artist Point parking lot

Distance: 5.6-mile partial-loop with shuttle (6.4-mile loop without shuttle)

Hiking time: About 4–6 hours

Difficulty: Moderate to strenuous, with steep sections

Trail surface: Forested path, rocky, talus

Seasons: Summer and fall. Best wildflowers: July–September (August 8, 2015).

Other trail users: None

Canine compatibility: Leashed dogs allowed

Land status: Mount Baker–Snoqualmie National Forest

Nearest towns: Glacier and Maple Falls

Services: Food (Glacier); gas and food (Maple Falls). Camping at Silver Fir (8 miles west) and Douglas Fir (20 miles west, near Glacier) on WA 542 (Mount Baker Highway).

Permits: Northwest Forest Pass or Federal Access Pass

Maps: Green Trails #14 Mount Shuksan; USGS Mount Shuksan; DeLorme Page 43 C-8

Trail contact: Mount Baker–Snoqualmie National Forest, Glacier Public Service Center

Special considerations: Vault toilet at both trailheads. Primitive toilet near Iceberg and Mazama Lakes. No potable water at Artists Point trailhead. Elevation.

Finding the trailhead: From Heather Meadows and the Mount Baker Ski Area, drive east on WA 542 (Mount Baker Highway) and in 1.6 miles turn right (west) into the large parking lot for the Austin Pass picnic area. Leave your shuttle car here. Continue another 1.2 miles in your second vehicle to where the road ends at Artist Point and park. **GPS: N48 50.800' / W121 41.605'**

Plants You Might See

Anemone occidentalis, Mountain pasqueflower, Ranunculaceae

Arnica latifolia, Mountain arnica, Asteraceae

Aster foliaceous, Leafy aster, Asteraceae

Athyrium distentifolium, Alpine lady fern, Polypodiaceae

Caltha leptosepala, Marsh marigold, Ranunculaceae

Dicentra formosa, Bleeding heart, Papaveraceae

Epilobium alpinum, Alpine willow-herb, Onagraceae

Erigeron glacialis, Subalpine daisy, Asteraceae

Gaultheria humifusa, Alpine wintergreen, Ericaceae

Leptarrhena pyrolifolia, Leatherleaf saxifrage, Saxifragaceae

Luetkea pectinata, Partridgefoot, Rosaceae

Parnassia fimbriata, Fringed grass-of-Parnassus, Saxifragaceae

Pedicularis groenlandica, Elephant's head, Orobanchaceae

Petasites frigidus, Alpine sweet coltsfoot, Hydrophyllaceae

Piperia baccata, Slender bog orchid, Orchidaceae

Sibbaldia procumbens, Sibbaldia, Rosaceae

Spirea densiflora, Rosy spirea, Rosaceae

The Hike

If Artist Point is bustling, as it can be on the popular hot and sunny days of summer, wend your way westward through the automobiles, tourists, and volcano/glacier picture-takers and find the trailhead to the side of the reader boards at the west end of the large parking lot. The Table Mountain Trail also begins here, so read the signs and make sure you lean left where the two trails diverge in less than 0.1 mile.

The forest here, as it is the entire length of the route, is a mosaic of Mountain hemlock, Silver fir, and Subalpine fir. The understory is typical for this kind of forest: Sitka mountain ash (*Sorbus sitchensis*) and the high country's most favorite berries,

Upper Bagley Lake.

Wet weather can happen at any time so it's always a good idea to carry rain gear and warm clothing.

Cascade huckleberry (*Vaccinium deliciosum*) and Black mountain huckleberry (*Vaccinium membranaceum*). In late summer–early fall, both are guaranteed to slow your hiking progress as they invite you to stop, admire, and browse.

The rocky trail leaves the forest to cross beneath Table Mountain. The herbaceous plant with the mat-forming prostrate stems and finely divided leaves with dense terminal clusters of cream-colored flowers you see around the outcropping of rocks and in the gravel alongside the trail is Partridgefoot (*Luetkea pectinata*). This little cutie is by far the most prolific ground cover on this route. Not to be undone, there is also plenty of Pearly everlasting (*Anaphalis margaritacea*), Leafy aster (*Aster foliaceus*), and Subalpine daisy (*Erigeron glacialis*).

▶ **"Galena" refers to a metallic gray or black mineral consisting of lead sulfide. It is an important source of silver.**

In 0.5 mile enter the Mount Baker Wilderness. Away from the gravelly slopes of Table Mountain, there is plenty of Red heather (*Phyllodoce empetriformis*) and White mountain heather (*Cassiope mertensiana*) to complement the Partridgefoot. If your eyes are sharp and your luck is holding, you'll even see Yellow mountain heather (*Phyllodoce glanduliflora*). In another 0.5 mile come to a junction with the Ptarmigan Ridge Trail and continue straight ahead (north). Or, if you're in the mood for seeing Ptarmigans, change your wildflower plans and turn left (south).

Begin to descend gradually and then severely to Mazama Lake. Compared to the other lakes around here, Mazama Lake is a puddle, but it's large and worthy enough for some campsites if you're in the mood for an overnight trip. There is a pretty meadow overlooking the lake that will entice flower lovers looking for orchids and other plants that like to keep their "feet" wet.

Leaving Mazama Lake, climb to a rocky point of land between Iceberg and Hayes Lakes. If you like scenery while you contemplate nature, the primitive toilet here is just for you. It's an outhouse without the house, exposed on all four sides to the awesome beauty of nature (bring your own paper).

From here start a very steep grade up to Herman Saddle. If it's a clear day, the views from the saddle to Mount Baker and Mount Shuksan are stupendous. If you're in the clouds, oh well: This *is* the Pacific Northwest! Or, North*wet*. If in the clouds, below you, somewhere, is the Bagley Lakes basin.

From Herman Saddle the steep trail crosses over rock and talus on switchbacks and long traverses, exits the Mount Baker Wilderness, and eventually reaches upper Bagley Lake. The trail stays above the lake (though there are waytrails leading down to the water) and climbs a bit more over a columnar basalt face that has been blasted out of the rock in order to

Pinguicula vulgaris, *Common butterwort is small and inconspicuous.*

Gaultheria humifusa, *Alpine-wintergreen.*

Cassiope mertensiana, *White mountain-heather.*

allow pedestrian traffic. Here you will find Butterwort (*Pinguicula vulgaris*). This little insectivorous plant is inconspicuous; look for a double-cluster of two pale green, and sticky, leaves. In a scene from some tacky horror flick, unfortunate insects who crawl across the leaves are stuck, expire, and are eventually dissolved to feed the Butterwort.

Galena Chain Lakes

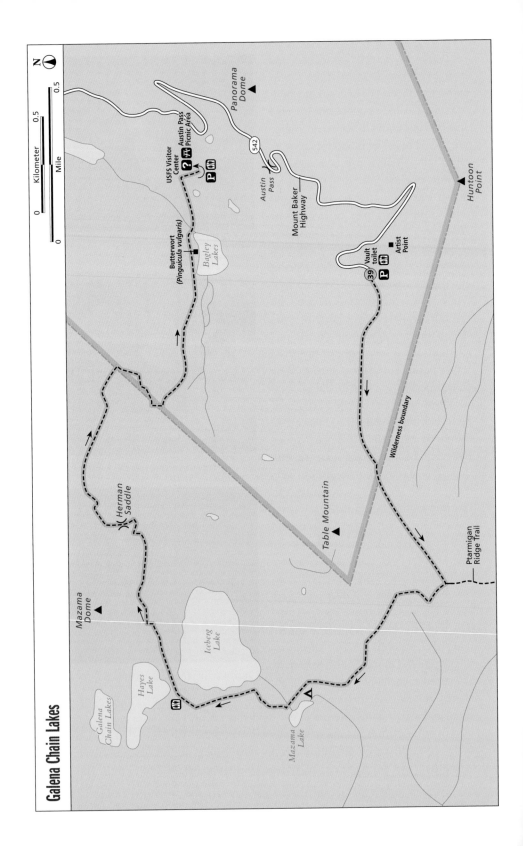

N

0   Kilometer   0.5

0   Mile   0.5

Galena Chain Lakes

Hayes Lake

Mazama Dome ▲

Iceberg Lake

Mazama Lake

Herman Saddle)(

Table Mountain ▲

Ptarmigan Ridge Trail

Wilderness boundary

Butterwort (Pinguicula vulgaris) ■

Bagley Lakes

USFS Visitor Center ❓

Austin Pass Picnic Area 🚻
P 🚻

Austin Pass

Mount Baker Highway

542

Panorama Dome ▲

Vault toilet
39 P 🚻
Artist Point ■

Huntoon Point ▲

During the spring Butterwort has pretty, blue, tubular flowers that resemble a diminutive penstemon.

Continue along the shore of upper Bagley Lake for 0.2 mile until reaching a trail junction. Bear right (southeast) and cross the outflow of the lake on a beautiful stone archway bridge. The trail splits immediately again; stay straight (east) and begin a steep 0.4 steep mile climb to the parking area and USFS visitor center and picnic area at Austin Pass. Towards the top, notice you're walking across the polished tops of columnar basalt columns. Stupendous. Stone stairs have been concreted into the face of the rock to help you climb the last 100 feet to trail's end, and some creative workers have etched six-sided grooves into the cement to emulate the original art of nature.

Lycopodium clavatum, *Running clubmoss.*

If you've been lucky enough to plan a car shuttle, you're home free. If you have only one car, and it's at Artist Point, find the Wild Goose Trail and begin 0.8 mile of climbing some 250 or more steep and exhausting and tall stairs, mostly adjacent to the highway, to end your hike. Whew!

Miles and Directions

- **0.0** Artist Point parking lot and trailhead.
- **0.8** Enter Mount Baker Wilderness.
- **1.3** Junction with Ptarmigan Ridge Trail.
- **2.0** Mazama Lake campsite.
- **2.1** Nice meadow.
- **2.4** Iceberg Lake.
- **2.5** Primitive toilet.
- **3.4** Herman Saddle.
- **4.0** Leave Mount Baker Wilderness.
- **5.0** Butterwort in the rocks.
- **5.2** Cross creek on stone archway bridge.
- **5.6** Trail ends at Austin Pass picnic area parking lot.

Other Nearby Hiking Options

Also leaving from Artist Point are trails to Lake Ann (Trail #600) and Table Mountain (Trail #681).

40 Yellow Aster Butte Fern Garden

The usual draw for Yellow Aster Butte are views of Mount Baker and Mount Shuksan and, of course, the butte's namesake flowers (actually, a species of *Erigeron*). But Yellow Aster Butte's complex of sedimentary and volcanic rock, interspersed with blocks of metamorphic and ultramafic (serpentine) rocks, contribute to an incredible diversity of fern species. In one truly remarkable area about 100 yards in diameter, called the "Fern Garden," can be found over thirty species of ferns!

Start: Yellow Aster Butte Trail (#686.1) trailhead along FR 3065

Distance: 6.4 miles out and back

Hiking time: About 3–5 hours

Difficulty: Moderate to strenuous, with steep sections

Trail surface: Forested path, rocky, with talus

Seasons: Summer and fall. Best wildflowers: July–August (August 9, 2015).

Other trail users: None

Canine compatibility: Leashed dogs allowed

Land status: Mount Baker–Snoqualmie National Forest

Nearest towns: Glacier and Maple Falls

Services: Food (Glacier); gas and food (Maple Falls). Camping at Silver Fir (8 miles west) and Douglas Fir (20 miles west, near Glacier) on WA 542 (Mount Baker Highway).

Permits: Northwest Forest Pass or Federal Access Pass

Maps: Green Trails #14 Mount Shuksan; USGS Mount Shuksan; DeLorme Page 43 C-8

Trail contact: Mount Baker–Snoqualmie National Forest, Glacier Public Service Center

Special considerations: Vault toilet at trailhead. No potable water at trailhead. Elevation.

Finding the trailhead: Thirteen miles east of the USFS Glacier Public Service Center at milepost 34, turn left (north) onto FR 3065 (Twin Lakes Road) immediately after passing the Department of Transportation Shuksan garage (not occupied during the summer; no public facilities available). Continue for 4.5 miles on a rough, potholed, dirt road to the trailhead. There is no parking lot. Find a space alongside the road, and make sure you leave room for cars to pass. **GPS: N48 56.603' / W121 39.765'**

Plants You Might See

Anemone occidentalis, Pasqueflower, Ranunculaceae

Erigeron aureus, Golden daisy, Asteraceae

Erythronium grandiflorum, Yellow glacier lily, Liliaceae

Erythronium montanum, Avalanche lily, Liliaceae

Stachys cooleyae, Cooley's hedge-nettle. Laminaceae

Veratrum viride, Green false hellebore, Liliaceae

The Hike

Find the trail at the hairpin turn in FR 3065, beside the vault toilet and behind the reader board. Ready, set, *go!* This is a trail that starts with a bang. With no preamble, the way is *up, up, and away!* And steep.

The forest here is a mix of Western and Mountain hemlock along with Silver fir and Subalpine fir. The transition from one hemlock and one fir to the other is subtle, so it's fun to keep an eye on the trees as you plod up the trail. Some of the Mountain hemlock are not only amazingly tall, but gigantic in girth. This is what they mean by "old-growth"!

As the trail climbs steadily through the forest, the understory consists of typical mid-elevation plants: Trillium (*Trillium ovatum*), False Solomon's seal (*Maianthemum racemosum*), and Queen's cup (*Clintonia uniflora*). In 0.2 mile the trail leaves the forest and gives way to an enormous avalanche chute. On sunny days this is a harsh traverse. But it ends in another 0.3 mile, and you're in the forest once more.

Mount Shuksan from Yellow Aster Butte Fern Garden.

Yellow Aster Butte and the Fern Garden.

Cooley's hedge nettle.

Red berries from Sorbus sitchensis, *Sitka mountain-ash.*

The underside of Polystichium lonchitis, *Northern holly fern, shows its spores.*

Parnassia fimbriata, *Fringed grass-of-Parnassus.*

Lycopodium clavatum, *Running clubmoss.*

Sceptridium multifidum, *Leathery grape-fern.*

Enter the Mount Baker Wilderness in a further 0.2 mile and keep climbing. Though the Fern Garden is far ahead, there is already a cornucopia of the little lovelies growing in the shady and seepy sections of trail. Watch out for Wood fern (*Dryopteris expansa*), so named for its propensity for growing on rotting logs; the delicate-looking but tough Lady fern (*Athyrium filex-femina*); and Western oak-fern (*Gymnocarpium disjunctum*), a bushy-looking fern with tender green foliage. Hikers will also recognize the ubiquitous Deer fern (*Blechnum spicant*), Bracken fern (*Pteridium aquilinum*), and Sword fern (*Polystichum munitum*). The forest is also home to Vanilla leaf (*Achlys californica*); the typical lupine of the region, Broad-leaf lupine (*Lupinus latifolius*); and Bistort (*Polygonum bistortoides*).

After 1.3 miles of slogging uphill, you reach a respite: about 100 feet of level terrain. And, it's in the shade! This makes it a good place to take a breather because the trail *really* takes off afterwards. A further 0.6 mile of huffing and puffing, along with now-and-again outstanding views of Mount Baker, brings you to a pretty meadow and another place to catch your breath. Expect typical subalpine flowers like Fringed grass-of-Parnassus (*Parnassia fimbriata*). Looking beneath the copious Red mountain heather (*Phyllodoce empetriformis*), you'll find Running clubmoss (*Lycopodium clavatum*) growing among the Patridgefoot (*Luetkea pectinata*).

Leaving this delightful meadow, the trail takes off even more steeply than before and then begins a long traverse across a carved-out bowl in the mountain. Views before you show Mount Baker, but in the foreground is the ridge that comprises Yellow Aster Butte. Situated in there is also the Fern Garden. But, carry on. There is still much to see. Forest cover from unrelenting sun (or rain) ends in 0.3 mile, and a trail junction in a further 0.1 mile signals the way up to Gold Run Pass and Tomyhoi Lake. Bear left (west) and keep traversing.

Another 0.9 mile brings you to the Fern Garden. And if you were expecting Elysian Fields, you will be disappointed. Instead, you are confronted with a large snowbank to the west, a forest of Mountain hemlock hovering overhead, and a rocky expanse of odd-colored ultramafic rock and talus before you. This is a garden? Well, yes, it is. Because before you can be found over thirty different species of fern! What is so odd is that the scene looks so completely estranged from any significant plant life.

This is a special, but totally unusual, place. Species diversity is high but, in many cases, there are only one or two individuals of each kind of fern. Several kinds of the quirky Moonworts (*Botrychium* spp.) are here, as well as many other ferns way too numerous to mention. It takes committed botanizing and a flora to see, and understand, them all, and this means it could take *years* to uncover the wonders of Yellow Aster Butte's Fern Garden.

The answer to what's going on, fern-wise, lies with geology and a little—no, a lot—of mystery yet to be figured out. Above the Fern Garden is an area with calcium-rich rocks falling down as talus meeting an area of heavy-metal ultramafic rocks that are rich in magnesium and iron. What you have are plants that prefer, or grow well in, both types of extreme substrate. This is very unusual. The species diversity of the Fern

Yellow Aster Butte Fern Garden

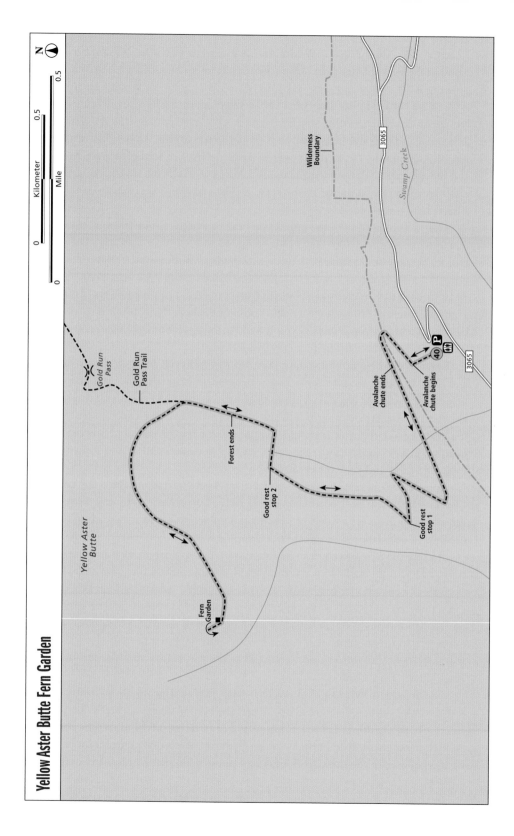

Garden is an expression of how a certain group of plants (in this case, ferns) can exploit a unique habitat created by a unique geological history. To find anything *close* to such fern diversity elsewhere, you have to go to Snohomish County. Nevertheless, the Fern Garden below Yellow Aster Butte remains more diverse than any other place in North America when it comes to the number of fern species that can be found.

If the wonders of the Fern Garden are threatening to explode your botanical mind, it's time to turn around and

Mount Baker is an active, glaciated andesitic stratovolcano with an amazing diversity of alpine wildflowers.

head back to the trailhead. Or, you can extend your hike another 1.5 miles to the alpine tarns and campsites on the other side of the steep west ridge. Further adventures await if you do so. Otherwise, be content with the adventures of science, botany, and mystery and make your return home.

Miles and Directions

0.0   Yellow Aster Butte trailhead along FR 3065.

0.2   Leave forest and enter avalanche chute.

0.5   Leave avalanche chute and reenter forest.

0.7   Enter Mount Baker Wilderness.

1.3   A good rest stop.

1.9   Another good rest stop.

2.2   Forest cover ends.

2.3   Gold Run Pass trail junction.

3.2   Fern Garden.

6.4   Arrive back at trailhead.

Other Nearby Hiking Options

FR 3065 continues northeast for another 2.4 miles to Twin Lakes and the trail (#685) to the dismantled Winchester Mountain fire lookout. From the Yellow Aster Butte Trail, a spur leads 2.1 miles over Gold Run Pass to Tomyhoi Lake.

Appendix A: Resources

Clubs, hiking forums, and access/advocacy groups, including online groups and organizations

Alpine Lakes Protection Society
www.alpinelakes.org
Give thanks to these people for their wilderness advocacy and their excellent 1:100,000 topo map that covers the Alpine Lakes Wilderness and surrounding area.

American Whitewater
PO Box 1540
Cullowhee, NC 28723
(866) BOAT-4-AW (866-262-8429)
info@amwhitewater.org
www.AmericanWhitewater.org
American Whitewater restores rivers dewatered by hydropower dams, works to eliminate water degradation, improves public land management, and protects public access to rivers for responsible recreational use by boaters, hikers, anglers, and other individuals and groups.

Burke Museum
University of Washington
17 Avenue NE and NE 45th Street
Seattle, WA 98105
(206) 543-5590
www.burkemuseum.org
Hours: Open daily from 10 a.m. to 5 p.m.
The Burke Museum of Natural History and Culture was founded in 1885 and is the oldest public museum in Washington. Affiliated with the University of Washington, the Burke Museum is research based and holds a collection with 16 million objects. The Burke serves many audiences and communities, including Washington State residents, visitors to Seattle, K–20 educators and students, Indigenous and Pacific communities, and researchers, scholars, and enthusiasts.

Green Trails Maps
PO Box 77734
Seattle, WA 98177
https://greentrailsmaps.com
Based in Seattle since its founding in 1973 as the first publisher of high-quality recreational topographical maps to Washington State, Green Trails publishes over 150 titles, covering Washington and Oregon's Cascade Mountains, Washington's Olympic

Peninsula, and other places. The maps show the most current trail, road, and access available to national forests, national parks, state and local parks, and other public lands.

Hike Metro
https://sites.google.com/site/seattlemetrobushiking
What? You don't have a car? Then take the bus! Here are some links to walks, hikes, and outdoor adventures in the Seattle area that you can reach by public transit. The best part of all is that no car is needed. Don't forget your ORCA Card!

Hiking Meetup Group (Seattle)
www.hiking.meetup.com/cities/us/wa/seattle
Sign up and meet people who share your interest in hiking.

Hiking Northwest
www.kuresman.com
A compilation of thirty-plus years of trip reports from hikes throughout our region by John Kuresman. This guy gets around!

Issaquah Alps Trails Club
PO Box 351
Issaquah, WA 98027
www.issaquahalps.org
The club serves as a voice for protection of our open spaces, trails, and quality of life. Their mission is to act as custodian of the trails and the lush, open, tree-covered mountaintops known as the Issaquah Alps.

Local Hikes (Seattle, Tacoma, Bremerton)
www.localhikes.com/MSA/MSA_7602.asp
A website providing information on local hiking opportunities contributed by volunteer reporters.

The Mountaineers, Seattle Branch
7700 Sand Point Way NE
Seattle, WA 98115
(206) 521-6000
www.mountaineers.org
The Pacific Northwest's largest recreation and conservation organization.

Mountains to Sound Greenway Trust
911 Western Ave., Ste. 203
Seattle, WA 98104
(206) 382-5565
info@mtsgreenway.org
www.mtsgreenway.org
This group is trying to reverse the trend along I-90 to become the province of strip malls, billboards, and spreading urban development. They're working to keep an accessible landscape of forests and open spaces as outdoor recreation for people and habitat for wildlife.

Northwest Hikers
www.nwhikers.net
An online forum to talk about hiking, hiker issues, and places to hike or to find a hiking companion.

Seattle Audubon Society
8050 35th Ave. NE
Seattle, WA 98115
(206) 523-4483
info@seattleaudubon.org
www.seattleaudubon.org
Seattle Audubon cultivates and leads a community that values and protects birds and the natural environment and envisions a healthy environment in balance with nature, where people enjoy, respect, and care for the natural resources that sustain the community of life.

Sierra Club, Cascade Chapter
180 Nickerson St., Ste. 202
Seattle, WA 98109
(206) 378-0114
cascade.chapter@sierraclub.org
www.sierraclub.org/washington/seattle-group
The Seattle Group focuses on Seattle local issues, including improving public transit, reducing waste, environmental justice, and endorsing and supporting green candidates.

Snoqualmie River Road Project
Federal Highway Administration–Western Federal Lands
610 E. Fifth St.
Vancouver, WA 98661
mfsnoqualmie@fhwa.dot.gov
http://flh.fhwa.dot.gov/projects/wa/snoqualmie/
No phone number
Check for construction and road closures on the Middle Fork Road.

Spring Family Trust
5015 88th Ave. SE
Mercer Island, WA 98040
A charitable trust dedicated to enhancing hiking opportunities in Washington State
with grants for trail-building and maintenance projects.

University of Washington Herbarium
Box 355325
University of Washington
Seattle, WA 98195-5325
(206) 543-1682
www.washington.edu/burkemuseum/collections/herbarium/index.php
The University of Washington Herbarium is an international resource for research
into the diversity, distribution, and ecology of Pacific Northwest vascular plants, non-
vascular plants, fungi, lichen, and algae. The herbarium is one of the largest in our
region, with over 600,000 specimens in the collections.

Washington Native Plant Society
6310 NE 74th St., Ste. 215E
Seattle, WA 98115
(206) 527-3210 or (888) 288-8022
wnps@wnps.org
www.wnps.org
The Washington Native Plant Society is a forum for individuals who share a common
interest in Washington's unique and diverse plant life. For more than thirty-five years,
WNPS has been a great source for native plant information and action.

Washington Trails Association
705 Second Ave., Ste. 300
Seattle, WA 98104
(206) 625-1367
www.wta.org
Washington Trails Association protects hiking trails and wildlands, takes thousands of
volunteers out to maintain trails, and promotes hiking as a healthy, fun way to explore
Washington.

Washington Wild
305 N. 83rd St.
Seattle, WA 98103
(206) 633-1992
www.wawild.org

Founded in 1979, Washington Wild is a nonprofit, tax-deductible organization that brings people together in the vigorous defense of our remaining wild forests, waters, and wildlife. They believe that public lands are a public issue. By educating, empowering, and mobilizing communities, Washington Wild builds powerful grassroots networks that help protect wild lands throughout the state.

Western Slope No Fee Coalition
PO Box 135
Durango, CO 81302
(970) 259-4616
http://westernslopenofee.org
Western Slope No Fee Coalition is a principal voice of the many Americans who believe in public ownership and public funding of public lands. The coalition welcomes support from people of all recreational pursuits and political persuasions.

Wild Wilderness
248 NW Wilmington Ave.
Bend, OR 97701
(541) 385-5261
ssilver@wildwilderness.org
www.wildwilderness.org
Wild Wilderness believes that America's public recreation lands are a national treasure that must be financially supported by the American people and held in public ownership as a legacy for future generations.

Wilderness Society
Pacific Northwest Office
720 Third Ave., Ste. 1800
Seattle, WA 98104
(206) 624-6430
www.wilderness.org
Their name says it all.

Appendix B: Land Management Agencies

Alpine Lakes Protection Society (ALPS)
www.alpinelakes.org

Anacortes Parks and Recreation Department
904 Sixth St.
PO Box 547
Anacortes, WA 98221
(360) 293-1918
www.cityofanacortes.org

Bureau of Land Management
San Juan Islands National Monument
Spokane District Office
1103 N. Fancher Road
Spokane, WA 99212
(509) 536-1200
BLM_OR_SP_Mail@blm.gov

Columbia Gorge National Scenic Area
Columbia River Gorge Commission
PO Box 730
1 Town & Country Sq.
57 NE Wauna Ave.
White Salmon, WA 98672
(509) 493-3323
www.gorgecommission.org/aboutus.cfm

Ebey's Landing National Historic Reserve
National Park Service
162 Cemetery Rd.
PO Box 774
Coupeville, WA 98239
(360) 678-6084

Gifford Pinchot National Forest
Forest Headquarters
10600 NE 51st Circle
Vancouver, WA 98682
(360) 891-5000
www.fs.usda.gov/main/giffordpinchot/home

Mary E. Theler Community Center
22871 NE SR 3
PO Box 1445
Belfair, WA 98528
(360) 275-4898
thelertrails@gmail.com
www.thelertrails.org

Middle Fork Snoqualmie
www.midforkrocks.org

Mount Adams Ranger District
2455 Highway 141
Trout Lake, WA 98650
(509) 395-3402

Mount Baker–Snoqualmie National Forest
Alpine Lakes Wilderness
www.fs.usda.gov/recarea/okawen/recarea/?recid=79432

Forest Headquarters
2930 Wetmore Ave., Ste. 3A
Everett, WA 98201
(425) 783-6000 or (800) 627-0062

Glacier Public Service Center
10091 Mount Baker Hwy. (WA 542)
Glacier, WA 98244
(360) 599-2714

Snoqualmie Ranger District
North Bend Office
42404 SE North Bend Way
North Bend, WA 98045
(425) 888-1421

Snoqualmie Pass Visitor Center
Snoqualmie Pass Summit
Snoqualmie Pass, WA 98000
(425) 434-6111
www.fs.fed.us/r6/mbs

Wild Sky Wilderness
www.fs.usda.gov/recarea/mbs/recarea/?recid=79424

Mount Rainier National Park
55210 238th Ave. East
Ashford, WA 98304
Park Headquarters: (360) 569-2211
Park Information: (360) 569-6575
Sunrise Visitor Center: (360) 663-2425
www.nps.gov/mora/index.htm

Nisqually National Wildlife Refuge
100 Brown Farm Rd.
Olympia, WA 98516
(360) 753-9467
www.fws.gov/nisqually

Okanogan-Wenatchee National Forest
    Cle Elum District
    803 W. Second St.
    Cle Elum, WA 98922
    (509) 852-1100
    www.fs.usda.gov/recarea/okawen/recarea/?recid=57117

    Naches Ranger District
    10237 Highway 12
    Naches, WA 98937
    (509) 653-1401
    www.fs.usda.gov/recarea/okawen/recarea/?recid=57121

Olympic National Forest
Hood Canal Ranger District
Mount Skokomish Wilderness
295142 US 101 South
Quilcene, WA 98376
(360) 765-2200

Olympic National Park
3002 Mount Angeles Rd.
Port Angeles, WA 98362
Mailing address:
600 E. Park Ave.
Port Angeles, WA 98362-6798
Visitor Information: (360) 565-3130
Road and Weather Hotline: (360) 565-3131
www.nps.gov/olym/index.htm

San Juan County Land Bank
Mailing address:
350 Court St., #6
Friday Harbor, WA 98250
Office location:
328 Caines St.
Friday Harbor, WA 98250
(360) 378-4402
Orcas Field Office:
1071 Crow Valley Rd.
Eastsound, WA 98245
(360) 376-3384
sjclandbank@rockisland.com
www.sjclandbank.org

San Juan County Parks
350 Court St., #8
Friday Harbor, WA 98250
(360) 378-8420
parks@sanjuanco.com

San Juan Island National Historical Park
San Juan Island
PO Box 429
Friday Harbor, WA 98250
(360) 378-2240
www.nps.gov/sajh

San Juan Preservation Trust
468 Argyle Ave., Ste. B
PO Box 759
Friday Harbor, WA 98250
(360) 378-2461
http://sjpt.org

Snohomish County Department of Parks and Recreation
6705 Puget Park Dr.
Snohomish, WA 98296
(425) 388-6600
http://snohomishcountywa.gov/Parks

Washington Department of Natural Resources
1111 Washington St. SE
PO Box 47000
Olympia, WA 98504-7000
(360) 902-1000
www.dnr.wa.gov

Washington State Ferry
Washington State Department of Transportation
310 Maple Park Ave. SE
PO Box 47300
Olympia, WA 98504-7300
(206) 464-6400 or (888) 808-7977
www.wsdot.wa.gov/ferries
Schedules (reservations recommended for Anacortes departures): www.wsdot.com/
ferries/schedule/Default.aspx

Washington State Parks
www.parks.wa.gov

Information Center
(360) 902-8844
infocent@parks.wa.gov
Available to answer general questions regarding state parks, Discover Pass, overnight
accommodations, recreation programs, and seasonal park closures.

Central Reservations
(888) 226-7688
reservations@parks.wa.gov
Operators available to assist with booking reservations for specific park campgrounds, group camps, and some picnic facilities / kitchen shelters, as well as cabins, yurts, and platform tents.

Beacon Rock State Park
34841 SR 14
Skamania, WA 98648
(509) 427-8265

Cape Disappointment State Park
244 Robert Gray Dr.
Ilwaco, WA 98624
(360) 642-3078

Deception Pass State Park
41020 SR 20
Oak Harbor, WA 98277
(360) 675-3767
www.deceptionpassfoundation.org

Leadbetter Point State Park
Ocean Park, WA 98640
(360) 642-3078

Appendix C: Further Reading

Wildflower and Plant Books

Biek, David. 2000. *Flora of Mount Rainier National Park*. Oregon State University Press.

Dreimiller, Joe. 1999. *A Pocket Guide to the Plants and Animals of Mount Rainier*. Elton-Wolf Publishing.

Harrington, H. D., and L. W. Durrell. 1957. *How to Identify Plants*. Swallow Press.

Hitchcock, C. Leo, and Arthur Conquest. 1978. *Flora of the Pacific Northwest, an Illustrated Manual*. University of Washington Press.

Hotchkiss, Neil. 1970. *Common Marsh Plants of the United States and Canada*. Dover.

Kozloff, Eugene N. 1976. *Plants and Animals of the Pacific Northwest*. University of Washington Press.

———. 2005. *Plants of Western Oregon, Washington, and British Columbia*. Timber Press.

Kruckeberg, Arthur R. 1991. *The Natural History of Puget Sound Country*. University of Washington Press.

Larrison, Earl J., et al. 1974. *Washington Wildflowers*. Seattle Audubon Society.

Lyons, C. P. 1999. *Washington Wildflowers*. Lone Pine.

Mapes, Lynda V., and Steve Ringman. 2013. *Elwha: A River Reborn*. Mountaineers Books.

Mathews, Daniel. 1988. *Cascade-Olympic Natural History*. Raven Editions.

Pojar, Jim, and Andy MacKinnon. 1994. *Plants of the Pacific Northwest Coast*, revised edition. Lone Pine.

———. 2013. *Alpine Plants of the Northwest, Wyoming to Alaska*. Lone Pine.

Potash, Laura L. 2015. *Sensitive Plants and Noxious Weeds of the Mount Baker–Snoqualmie National Forest*. Washington Native Plants Society and Bonneville Power Administration, September 1.

Taylor, Ronald J. 1990. *Northwest Weeds*. Mountain Press.

Whitney, Stephen R. 1983. *A Field Guide to the Cascades & Olympics*. Mountaineers Books.

———. 1989. *A Sierra Club Naturalist's Guide to the Pacific Northwest*. Sierra Club Books.

Hiking Guides

Nobody, in honesty, can write a hiking guide without giving thanks and credit to earlier authors. We may cover the same trails occasionally, but our focus and direction are never the same. In this manner we all derive benefit—readers *and* authors.

Babcock, Scott, and Bob Carson. 2000. *Hiking Washington's Geology*. Mountaineers Books.

Barnes, Nathan, and Jeremy Barnes. 2014. *Hiking through History Washington.* FalconGuides.

Copeland, Kathy, and Craig Copeland. 1996. *Don't Waste Your Time in the North Cascades.* Wilderness Press.

Gurche, Charles. 2004. *Washington's Best Wildflower Hikes.* Westcliffe Publishers.

Kruckeberg, Art, et al. 2004. *Best Wildflower Hikes Washington.* Mountaineers Books.

Lazenby, Oliver. 2014. *Hiking Washington.* FalconGuides.

McQuaide, Mike. 2005. *Mount Baker–Mount Shuksan Area.* FalconGuides.

Molvar, Erik. 2009. *Hiking the North Cascades.* FalconGuides.

———. 2015. *Hiking Olympic National Park.* FalconGuides.

Romano, Craig. 2014. *Day Hiking the San Juans and Gulf Islands.* Mountaineers Books.

Schneider, Heidi, and Mary Skjelset. 2014. *Hiking Mount Rainier National Park.* FalconGuides.

Schneider, Russ. 2014. *Hiking the Columbia River Gorge,* third edition revised by Jim Yuskavitch. FalconGuides.

Smoot, Jeff. 1991. *Adventure Guide to Mount Rainier.* Chockstone Press.

———. 2003. *Hiking Washington's Alpine Lakes Wilderness.* FalconGuides.

Stekel, Peter. 2015. *Best Hikes Near Seattle,* second edition. FalconGuides.

Wood, Robert L. 1991. *Olympic Mountains Trail Guide,* second edition. Mountaineers Books.

Hike Index